Stuart England

Angus Stroud

ANDOVER COLLEGE

ROUTLEDGE
Taylor & Francis Group

London and New York

First published 1999
by Routledge
2 Park Square, Milton Park, Abingdon, Oxon, OX14 4RN

Simultaneously published in the USA and Canada
by Routledge
270 Madison Ave, New York NY 10016

Routledge is an imprint of the Taylor & Francis Group

Transferred to Digital Printing 2006

© 1999 Angus Stroud

Typeset in Bembo by Routledge

British Library Cataloguing in Publication Data
A catalogue record for this book is available from the British Library.

Library of Congress Cataloguing in Publication Data
Stroud, Angus
Stuart England/Angus Stroud
Includes bibliographical references and index.
1. Great Britain–History–Stuarts, 1603–1714.
2. Great Britain–History–Stuarts, 1603–1714 – Examinations Study guides.
3. Great Britain–History–Stuarts, 1603–1714 – Problems, exercises, etc.
I. Title.
DA375.S82   1999
941.06–dc21   99-15137

ISBN 0–415–20652–9 (hbk)
ISBN 0–415–20653–7 (pbk)

Publisher's Note
The publisher has gone to great lengths to ensure the quality of this reprint
but points out that some imperfections in the original may be apparent
Printed and bound by CPI Antony Rowe, Eastbourne

Stuart England

England under the Stuarts has been the focus of endless historical research and controversy. When James Stuart came to the throne in 1603, he was the first monarch to inherit the crowns of England, Scotland and Ireland, and each of these kingdoms was in a state of relative prosperity and obedience. Within forty years, his son Charles I was facing rebellion in all three. *Stuart England* examines and explains this turnaround and the reasons for Charles's subsequent execution and the abolition of the monarchy.

Stuart England then describes and analyses the years of the Civil War and Republic, the motivations and significance of Cromwell's rule, the restoration of the monarchy, the reigns of Charles II and James II, and finally the events of the Glorious Revolution.

With a comprehensive selection of extracts from leading historians and sections of documents drawing on a wide range of primary sources from across the period, *Stuart England* is an essential guide for students of seventeenth-century English history.

Angus Stroud teaches history at Barton Peveril College.

Contents

Illustrations

Acknowledgements

This book has its origins in the spring term of 1998, which I spent at Corpus Christi College, Cambridge. I would like to express my thanks to the Master and Fellows for electing me to a Schoolteacher Fellowship, and for the warmth and generosity which they extended to me during my stay. I would also like to thank Barton Peveril College for allowing me to take a term's sabbatical, and those colleagues in the History department whose workload increased as a result!

The greatest debt of gratitude, however, is to those students with whom I've worked over the past six years. This book has emerged out of many hours spent with them in the classroom, and is shaped to a very great extent by their feedback and enthusiasm. I hope that it will be of some use to their successors.

Angus Stroud
Barton Peveril
June 1999

Introduction

The seventeenth century is a dramatic period of English history, and events such as the Civil War, the execution of the King, the rise of Cromwell and the Glorious Revolution have excited the comment of innumerable historians over the centuries. Despite this, it is not always easy for the first-time student to pick their way through the alternative explanations that such commentators provide. In order to do this, it is necessary to have a grasp of the main events and phenomena of the period, of how contemporaries viewed the issues and personalities of the day, and an understanding of the differing perspectives from which historians have written over time. This book aims to provide all three.

An outline of seventeenth-century England

The key features and events of this period are provided by the timeline overleaf. While it is important to have an idea of chronology, and a grasp of the period as a whole, the student should also be aware of the danger of 'reading history backwards'. That is, because you know that something particular is going to happen, there is a temptation to see everything that goes before it as leading up to and into that event. This is particularly the case with something like the Civil War, and the other focal points of the seventeenth century. We should be careful not to assume that there was anything inevitable about the execution of Charles I, the role of Cromwell, or the overthrow of James II. It is most unlikely that contemporaries in 1603 had any more notion of what was likely to happen in 1642, than we have of what the mid-twenty-first century has in store.

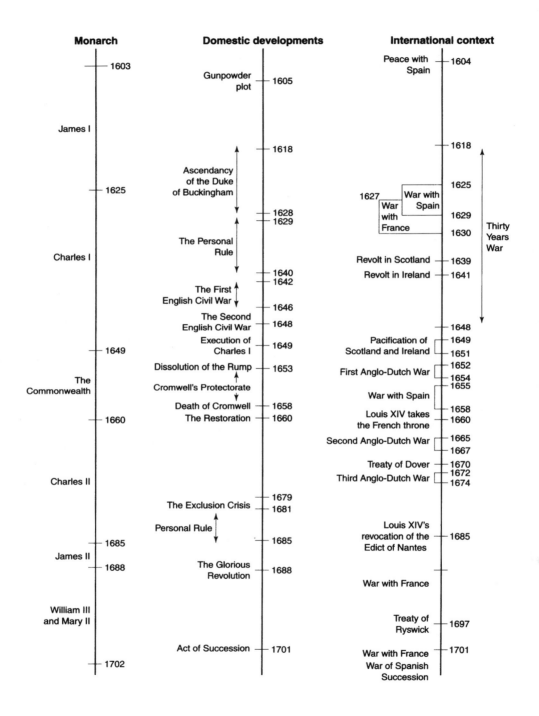

Monarch	Domestic developments	International context
— 1603		Peace with Spain — 1604
	Gunpowder plot — 1605	
James I		
	— 1618	— 1618
	Ascendancy of the Duke of Buckingham	1625
— 1625		1627 War with Spain
	— 1628	War with France 1629
	— 1629	1630
	The Personal Rule	Thirty Years War
Charles I	— 1640	Revolt in Scotland — 1639
	— 1642	Revolt in Ireland — 1641
	The First English Civil War — 1646	
	The Second English Civil War — 1648	— 1648
	Execution of Charles I — 1649	Pacification of Scotland and Ireland 1649 1651
— 1649	Dissolution of the Rump — 1653	First Anglo-Dutch War 1652 1654 1655
The Commonwealth	Cromwell's Protectorate	War with Spain
	Death of Cromwell — 1658	Louis XIV takes the French throne 1658
— 1660	The Restoration — 1660	1660
		Second Anglo-Dutch War 1665 1667
Charles II		Treaty of Dover — 1670
		Third Anglo-Dutch War 1672 1674
	— 1679	
	The Exclusion Crisis — 1681	
	Personal Rule	Louis XIV's revocation of the Edict of Nantes — 1685
— 1685	— 1685	
James II — 1688	The Glorious Revolution — 1688	
		War with France
William III and Mary II		Treaty of Ryswick — 1697
	Act of Succession — 1701	War with France — 1701
— 1702		War of Spanish Succession

Figure 0.1 Timeline of the seventeenth century

Document analysis

The documentary evidence provided here is an indication of the wealth of material that is contained in libraries and archives throughout the country. Even if students do not find an opportunity to look at such materials, they should at least be aware of the published collections of primary sources, some of which are listed in the 'Guide to further reading' section of this book. To gain an insight into any period of historical study, it is necessary to examine the attitudes and perceptions of contemporaries, to look at the records that they themselves left behind. Ultimately, it is only through the careful use of such primary evidence that historians can hope to understand and interpret events for themselves.

When analysing documents, it is important that you should not take them at face value. Try as far as possible to look behind what is written and to consider the context in which the source was produced. Although you may not always be able to come up with a definite answer, you should always bear the following questions in mind when examining documentary material:

1   *Who wrote the source?* Would the person be in a position to know what they are talking about? Would their identity be likely to colour their view of their subject?
2   *When was it written?* The longer the time gap between the event and its recording, the more opportunity there is for the author's opinion to have been influenced by events between times. There is also the possibility of events having become muddled or forgotten over time.
3   *In what circumstances was it written?* The author is bound to be influenced to some extent by their context, i.e. those things happening around them. You may find the timeline at the beginning of the book useful in helping you understand what kind of influences may have been affecting the writer.
4   *Why was it written?* What was the purpose of the author, and who was their intended audience?
5   *What use is made of language and tone?* Often a great deal can be deduced by the way in which the author writes, and the kinds of phrases and expressions that they use. Ask yourself what effect they are trying to achieve, and why they might be doing so.

In order to help you set the documents in a clearer context, there are notes on some of the main authors used towards the end of the book.

Historiography

Fundamental to any study of this period is an understanding of 'historiography', or the differing views of historians. A great deal has been written on this period, much of it contradictory, and, for the student to pick their way through this potential minefield, it helps to have some idea not only of *how* historians differ, but also *why*.

There are a range of possible reasons for why historians may put forward certain views:

1   *Evidence.* The quantity and quality of evidence available will have an effect and certainly historians studying now have access to a much greater evidence base than

they did even one hundred years ago. Equally important is the use to which such evidence is put. Historians will tend to disagree over the significance of evidence. Different degrees of importance will be attached to statistics, Government records, local studies, individual memoirs, letters, diaries, etc., according to the approach of the historian.

2   *Politics*. Many historians who have written on this subject have been influenced by their political views, and have used it as a platform to put those views across. Liberals have tended to see the period as a struggle for the forces of parliamentary democracy against monarchical absolutism. Left-wingers have tended to emphasise revolutionary aspects of the period, and to see it in terms of a class struggle. Traditionalists and right-wingers have sought to challenge this, and to present the seventeenth century more as a period of continuity and conservatism than of radicalism and conflict.

3   *Philosophy*. Historians also differ on the way that history should be approached. Some are interested in looking at economic and social forces to explain the period. They see history as an 'iceberg'; the famous names and faces that can be seen only tell one-fifth of the story. The historian should therefore seek to uncover those large impersonal forces lurking beneath the waterline, if they are to understand why the 'iceberg' has acted as it has. Alternatively, other historians tend to emphasise the role of key personalities in historical causation. Stuart England was a hierarchical society, with political power monopolised by those at the top of that hierarchy. Therefore, they feel that the historian should concentrate on these people. Other historians have tended to try and emphasise local variation, pointing out that England cannot always be seen as a unified whole; i.e. what was felt by people in Somerset was not necessarily the same as in Essex. Others have claimed that England can only be understood by looking at the big picture – by seeing it as part of a larger British, or even European, context.

4   *Context*. Historians tend to be influenced, as we all are, by the prevailing attitudes of the society in which they live. Their views on politics, religion, monarchy, revolution and much more will be affected by the attitudes of those around them. Over the last 300 years or so, those attitudes have changed enormously, and as the society in which historians live continues to develop, there is every reason to believe that their interpretations of the past will continue to change.

Schools of thought

Although it can be dangerous to try and 'pigeon-hole' historians, there are several different 'schools' or groups of thought that can be identified, into which writers with similar approaches to the subject tend to fall:

1   *Tory*: writing mainly in the years after the restoration of the monarchy (1660–88), Tory historians were fervently pro-Royalist. They saw the years of civil war and the Republic as the work of a dangerous minority in Parliament, who abused their position of privilege and tragically misled the people of England.

2   *Whig*: originating from the late seventeenth century, but becoming most influential in the nineteenth and early twentieth centuries, Whig historians tended to view English history as an inevitable progression towards parliamentary democracy and religious freedom. The seventeenth century was seen as a crucial, pivotal point in

this process; as the struggle between the absolutist tendencies of the Stuart kings and Parliament, the defender and guarantor of the rule of law, property rights and individual freedoms.

3   *Social/Economic*: dating from the early twentieth century, historians from this school have been interested in looking at the role of impersonal factors in historical causation. They have tended to see political conflicts as having their roots in larger economic and social trends and developments, and downplay the role of individuals accordingly.

The most significant school to emerge from this approach is the *Marxist* interpretation. According to Karl Marx, history was the record of conflict between social classes, and was driven by economic forces. Society necessarily goes through several distinct stages, each of which is reached via revolution. Following this model, the English Civil War was a 'bourgeois' revolution, in which an emerging 'bourgeoisie', or middle class, overthrew the old, feudal state, and opened the way to future revolution and the eventual introduction of socialism. See Figure 0.2.

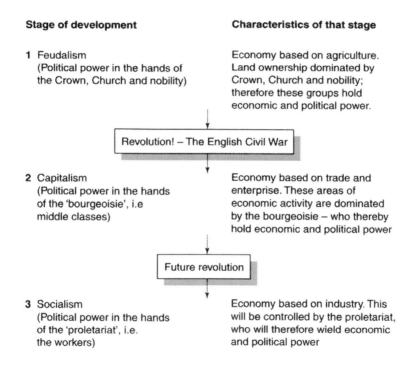

Stage of development

1 Feudalism
(Political power in the hands of the Crown, Church and nobility)

Revolution! – The English Civil War

2 Capitalism
(Political power in the hands of the 'bourgeoisie', i.e middle classes)

Future revolution

3 Socialism
(Political power in the hands of the 'proletariat', i.e. the workers)

Characteristics of that stage

Economy based on agriculture. Land ownership dominated by Crown, Church and nobility; therefore these groups hold economic and political power.

Economy based on trade and enterprise. These areas of economic activity are dominated by the bourgeoisie – who thereby hold economic and political power

Economy based on industry. This will be controlled by the proletariat, who will therefore wield economic and political power

Figure 0.2 Marxist view of history

4   *Revisionist*: emerging in the 1970s, the revisionists attacked, or 'revised', the Whig and Marxist views. Revisionism rejected their views on causation as being too simplistic and one-dimensional, and questioned the idea of 'determinism', or inevitability, that seemed to permeate their interpretations. Revisionists have tended to stress the theory that change is brought about by a complex web of different

factors, not one major cause. In addition they have tended to highlight local varia-
tions in the national picture, to further demonstrate the complexity of the situation.

Revisionism has seen events such as the Civil War and the Glorious Revolution
as the result of numerous factors. Such events were not predictable; indeed they
could be seen as almost accidental. They were less the result of ideological or class
conflict, than of the failure of the members of the ruling class to co-operate
amongst themselves, or to develop government systems that were strong enough to
cope with the demands of the seventeenth century.

5   *Post-revisionist*: post-revisionism is a term that has been used to describe the work of
those historians who, while basically revisionist in approach, have sought to challenge some of the conclusions of previous revisionist work. Some have argued that
ideological differences on constitutional and religious issues *did* play a part in
creating conflict, and that instability was the result, in part, of certain long-term
stresses. Others have maintained that in order to understand what is going on in
England during this period, we must look beyond England itself. We must set
events in a wider, British context, which will involve an awareness of the interplay
between the three British kingdoms, i.e. England, Scotland and Ireland.

There are two important points that need to be emphasised here. The first is that historians will not always fit neatly into the boxes we try to create for them. While being
aware of the different schools of thought, it is worth remembering that historians are
individuals and do not necessarily conform to the descriptions that we try to give them.
The other is that, just because certain interpretations are more recent, does not necessarily make them right. They may seem better researched, or more convincing, than
some of the other views, but that does not automatically mean that they are correct. As
long as historians (and their readers!) are subjected to the kinds of pressures listed above,
we will need to treat their conclusions with caution.

1   The Stuart inheritance

In 1603, James VI of Scotland inherited the throne of England from his cousin, Elizabeth I. Although he had enjoyed a relatively successful reign as King of Scotland, his new kingdom presented quite a different set of challenges. England was larger, wealthier and more heavily populated than Scotland, and was a far more significant player on the international stage. It also differed significantly in its religious, political and economic make-up. James was fully aware of England's relative wealth, a prospect that he apparently relished, likening himself to a 'poor man' who had finally arrived in 'the land of promise'. However, in order to provide his subjects with effective government, he would also need to develop an understanding of other aspects of England's make-up.

English society *c.* 1600

England by 1603 was a society facing considerable strain. Despite the fact that the previous century had witnessed a dramatic population rise, from around 2.8 million to over 5 million inhabitants between the 1520s and 1640s, there had been little change in the pattern of life for most people. Ninety per cent of the population still lived in rural areas and were dependent on agriculture for their means of existence. Although London was the largest city in the country, with a population of around 200,000 by 1600, there were only two other cities with more than 10,000 inhabitants, Norwich and Bristol. Five others had populations of over 5,000, namely Oxford, Salisbury, York, Newcastle and Exeter.

The sixteenth century had also been a time of rapid inflation, and although wages had risen during the period, they had failed to keep pace with prices. This, together with the increase in population, led to an inevitable rise in both poverty and vagrancy in the later sixteenth century, which caused considerable alarm to the governments of the time. Harvest failure could still led to starvation and serious disorder, which the country had experienced as recently as the 1590s.

In light of such pressures, the Government was keen to maintain the social fabric of the country, as far as possible. A hierarchical social structure was regarded as a guarantor of stability, and this hierarchy was regarded as part of God's divinely appointed plan for society. The importance of such ideas is reflected in the belief in a Great Chain of Being (see Figure 1.1). As God had arranged the universe in a certain order, the structure of society should reflect this in its own composition.

Figure 1.1 The Great Chain of Being, illustration from *Rhetorica Christiana* (1579)

'The homily of obedience', read regularly in Tudor and Stuart churches, went on to apply this principle to society as a whole:

> Almighty God hath created and appointed all things in heaven, earth, and waters, in a most excellent and perfect order ... in earth He hath assigned and appointed kings, princes, with other governors under them in necessary order ... some are in high order, some in low, some kings and princes, some inferiors and subjects, priests and laymen, masters and servants, fathers and children, husbands and wives, rich and poor: and everyone hath need of the other: so that in all things is to be lauded and praised the goodly order of God.

In particular, there was a sense of the threat posed by landless vagrants, victims of economic change, whose lifestyle meant that they were beyond the traditional control mechanisms of society. As one magistrate from Somerset warned in 1596:

> I do not see how it is possible for the poor countryman to bear the burdens duly laid on him, and the plundering of the infinite numbers of the wicked, wandering idle people of the land. ... Others there be ... which may grow dangerous, by the aid of such numbers as are [vagabonds], especially in this time of famine, who no doubt animate them to all contempt both of noblemen and gentlemen, continually whispering in their ears that rich men have gotten all into their hands and will starve the poor.

In response to this threat, a series of Poor Laws was introduced. These included a range of measures designed to alleviate poverty and to punish those who sought to escape it by moving out of their home areas. William Harrison, in 1587, described graphically how such legislation was to work:

> There is order taken throughout every parish in the realm that weekly collection shall be made for the help and sustenance of the poor, to the end that they should not scatter and, by begging here and there, annoy both town and country. ... Such as idle beggars ... the law ordaineth this manner of correction: the rogue being apprehended, committed to prison, and tried ... if he happen to be convicted for a vagabond ... he is then ... grievously whipped and burned through the gristle of the right ear with an hot iron ... if he be taken a second time, he shall then be whipped again, bored likewise through the other ear, and set to service; from whence if he depart before a year be expired and happen afterward to be [caught] again, he is condemned to suffer pains of death.

> (William Harrison, *The Description of England*, 1587)

Government

Role of monarch

As Head of State and Church, the powers and responsibilities James inherited as King of England were enormous. Government revolved around the monarch and was *its* Government. As Defender of the Faith, the monarch appointed archbishops and bishops, and directed ecclesiastical policy. Judges and magistrates were appointed by the Crown to uphold *its* laws. The monarch directed foreign and domestic policy, chose its ministers, raised and controlled armies, and decided if and when to call the people's representatives together in Parliament. Parliaments were usually summoned to provide the Crown with financial assistance, but the ultimate responsibility for finance also belonged to the monarch. Any financial difficulties would lead to a Crown debt rather than a national one, for which the monarch was responsible.

How Government worked

Lacking a standing army, an effective police force or a professional civil service in the localities, the Government was heavily dependent on persuasion to enforce its will. As we have seen, the idea of a Great Chain of Being was an important one at this time, and one that Government propaganda developed. 'The homily of obedience' emphasised the monarch's divinely appointed right to issue orders that their subjects must obey. Failure to do so would lead to anarchy: 'no man shall ride or go on the highway unrobbed; no man shall sleep in his own house or bed unkilled; no man shall keep his wife, children, and possessions'.

In addition the monarchy placed great emphasis on visual propaganda to try and secure the allegiance of its subjects. The projection of the royal image through coinage and portraiture, and of royal magnificence and wealth through architecture and Court ritual were designed to impress and inspire loyalty. The most important targets of this were 'the political nation', a relatively small group of men, whose support was vital to effective government of the country. However, this group's adherence could not be ensured by persuasion alone. The monarch had also to help meet the social and financial aspirations of such people. To do this, James would need to bear in mind the advice that Lord Burghley gave to his predecessor, that it was necessary 'that you gratify your nobility and principal persons of your realm and bind them fast to you ... whereby you shall have all the men of value in your realm to depend only upon yourself'.

In order to 'bind' such figures to it, the Crown needed to be able to offer sufficient incentives for loyalty. The distribution of such patronage was a very important aspect of government. The Crown had a vast array of rewards at its disposal: offices in Church, Court or Government; honours, such as peerages or knighthoods; leases or gifts of royal lands; the grant of monopolies on the manufacture or trade of a particular commodity; pensions and annuities; or even gifts of money. These privileges were vital to both Crown and recipient, providing loyalty and service for one, and prestige and wealth for the other. An effective patronage machine would ensure that such benefits were spread widely to ensure the maximum possible coverage of the political nation, and would avoid the over-concentration of power in one particular group or faction.

The machinery of Government

The actual machinery of Government at the disposal of the monarch was relatively limited. At a central level, the most important institution was the Privy Council, which provided the monarch with advice and implemented royal policy. Great officeholders, such as the Lord Treasurer, or Secretary of State, would usually sit on the Privy Council, and were influential figures in Court as well. The Court, although not part of the Government machine as such, was also an important source of advice to the monarch, and the main channel through which patronage was distributed. A number of central courts also sat in London, which dealt, among other things, with the enforcement of the monarch's rights and the settlement of constitutional issues. When summoned, Parliament could pass legislation and provide access to important tax revenues.

Local government was the responsibility of three main sets of office-holders: Sheriffs, Lords Lieutenant and Justices of the Peace (JPs). All were unpaid, and usually drawn from gentry backgrounds. It was these individuals upon whom the Crown had to rely, in order to keep order and to ensure that its policies were actually put into effect.

The operations of Government can be summarised in Figure 1.2.

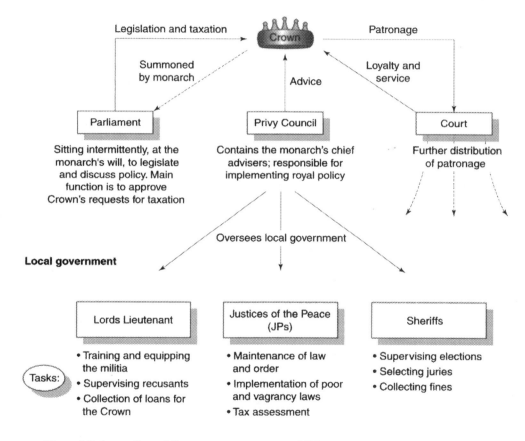

Figure 1.2 An outline of Government structure, *c.* 1600

Government by 1603

While Elizabethan government was remarkably successful given the constraints under which it was operating, there were certain issues evident by 1603. One was the importance of ensuring a wide distribution of patronage, and avoiding a monopoly over it, or Government, by any one individual or group. According to one contemporary, Elizabeth 'ruled much by faction and parties which herself both made, upheld, and weakened, as her own judgment advised'. The tensions that accompanied the rise of the

Earl of Essex, and his domination of the elderly Queen's favours towards the end of the reign, clearly illustrated the problems that could arise if this was not the case.

Another issue related to the effectiveness of local government. During Elizabeth's reign, the work-load of local government increased significantly, especially for JPs, who not only had to implement law and order as magistrates, but also oversee tasks such as the suppression of vagrancy and poor relief. In addition, many JPs were responsible for assessing levels of parliamentary taxation for their localities. During the reign, the value of subsidies fell significantly: a subsidy in 1559 brought in £140,000, but only about £80,000 by 1601. Though an important part of the Government, it was clear that there were limits to the level of co-operation that could be expected from overworked, voluntary officeholders.

Finance

Responsibility for finance also lay with the Crown, and sound finances were therefore vital to its ability to provide effective government. In theory, monarchs were expected to meet the normal costs of maintaining their Court and government through their *ordinary revenues*. These were split into four categories. Traditionally the most important source was the rents from *Crown lands*, although *customs duties* including levies such as tonnage and poundage, were also significant. These sources were supplemented from the *profits of justice*, the Crown benefiting from fines and confiscations of land, and from *feudal dues*. The latter consisted of a collection of ancient rights of the Crown, such as wardships (the Crown's right to control and profit from the estates left to heirs under twenty-one years of age) and purveyance (the Crown's right to purchase goods at a price set by itself), but were unevenly enforced.

In times of war or national emergency, the monarch would expect to have access to *extraordinary* revenues, which usually took the form of parliamentary taxation. This came in two distinct forms: fifteenths and tenths, raising around £30,000; and subsidies, raising around £80,000 each. If necessary, the Crown could attempt to cover any short-fall by borrowing, although if its financial situation were poor, finding sources of credit could present it with serious problems.

The reality of royal finance in the late sixteenth century proved somewhat different. As a result of inflation, the rents from Crown lands and the customs duties, which were charged at a fixed rate, were increasingly inadequate. Although Elizabeth took great care to minimise her spending on the Court and on patronage, the demands of the war against Spain (1585–1603), and the associated conflicts in Ireland and the Low Countries, put her under severe financial pressure. Crown lands were sold, despite the long-term implications, and large sums of parliamentary taxation sought and granted. However, these taxes were not adjusted to take account of inflation, and were assessed and collected by the local gentry, who tended to undervalue the level of their own contributions. Elizabeth did not attempt to tackle these 'structural' problems, and despite great efforts at economy, she died with a Crown debt of around £400,000 (although £300,000 in subsidies from 1601 were still to be collected, and the Crown itself was owed some substantial debts).

Documents

An indication of some of the issues that James was to face is contained in the following extracts from the Exchequer accounts of 1600:

Estimate of Her Majesty's domestic and foreign expenditure in £

The Privy Purse	2,000
Band of Pensioners	4,000
Treasurer of the Chamber	8,000
Master of the Wardrobe	4,000
Treasurer of the Household	4,000
Master of the Jewelhouse	2,000
Master of the Posts	2,840
Ambassadors etc.	4,000
Office of the Works	5,000
Treasurer of the Navy	2,000
Lieutenant of the Artillery	6,000
Master of the Armoury	400
Lieutenant of the Tower	2,000
Castles etc.	4,000
Justices	1,600
Ireland	320,000
Low Countries	25,000
Fees and annual payments	26,000
Total	422,840

Estimate of Her Majesty's yearly revenues of the Exchequer in £

Sheriffs' fines	10,000
Crown lands	60,000
Hanaper fines	4,000
Confiscations	4,000
Customs and subsidies of ports	80,000
Duty on wine etc.	24,000
Licences and fees	5,000
Recusancy fines	7,000
Church taxes	20,000
Subsidy of the clergy	20,000
Subsidy of the laity	80,000
Fifteenths and tenths	60,000
Total	374,000

1   Divide the Queen's expenditure into four categories – military, governmental, patronage and Queen's household. How much was spent on each?

2   Divide the Queen's income into four categories – taxes, customs duties, profits of justice and Crown lands. How much was received from each?

3   What conclusions might you draw from your findings? Are there any aspects of these figures that you might find particularly concerning, from the monarch's point of view?

Religion

Background

The impact of the Reformation on the religious and political map of sixteenth-century Europe was enormous. It provided a serious challenge to Roman Catholicism, as Protestant alternatives to the traditional Church emerged in a number of European countries. Although the Reformation was successful mainly in northern Europe, its impact was felt across the continent. The monopoly of the Catholic Church had been shattered, and, with it, the religious unity of Christian Europe.

The Reformation originated in Germany, and was inspired by the teachings of the monk and scholar, Martin Luther. Luther attacked both the beliefs and practices of the Catholic Church, asserting that it placed too much emphasis on tradition, superstition and ceremony, instead of following a biblical model. For Luther, this involved the rejection of much Catholic doctrine, such as the role of the Pope as head of the Church. Through the doctrine of 'The Priesthood of all Believers', he taught that all Christians could approach God, without the need for rituals, or a priest acting as intermediary. Salvation came via belief based on Scripture ('Justification by Faith'), rather than through ceremony and observing traditional Church activities, such as pilgrimages, confessions, buying indulgences or praying to saints.

Luther's teachings attracted many people, not least some secular rulers, who saw them as a way of justifying seizing control of the Church in their own countries. In England, Henry VIII used them to break away from papal control, and to establish himself as head of the Church, in 1534. Although Henry had few concerns about overthrowing papal authority, he proved more conservative elsewhere in his religious policy, and it was not until the reign of his son, Edward VI (1547–53), that the Church could really be described as Protestant. The 1552 Prayer Book established the church as Protestant, and reflected some of the teachings of the Swiss Reformer, John Calvin, who had superseded Luther as the leading figure of the European Reformation. However, with the accession of Mary I (1553–8), the situation was reversed. Catholicism, complete with papal authority, was reintroduced, and fierce persecution directed at those who maintained their Protestant beliefs.

The Elizabethan Church settlement

The Church inherited by James was one that still conformed to the settlement imposed by Elizabeth in 1559. Although the Queen was Protestant by inclination, she was less interested in doctrinal purity, than in establishing a Church that could embrace as many of her subjects as possible. Elizabeth's interest in a '*via media*' (middle way) had little to do with sentimentality, however. She was aware of the divisive potential of religion, and wanted to create something to which the vast majority of her subjects could belong. Although Elizabeth declared that she had no interest in making 'windows into men's hearts', she was determined that they should at least outwardly conform in religious matters. Hence religion could act as a means of unity and control, rather than division.

The Elizabethan Church settlement consisted of three main elements. First, the Act of Supremacy, which restored the monarch as the head of the Church. Second, the Act of Uniformity, which contained a new Prayer Book, laying out orders of service and regulations on aspects such as clerical dress and the use of ceremony, and established the principle of compulsory church attendance, via the use of recusancy fines. Third, the 39 Articles, which explained the doctrinal basis of the church. Overall, the settlement was firmly Protestant, even Calvinist, in doctrine, but in terms of its structure and style of service it had clear links to the Catholic past.

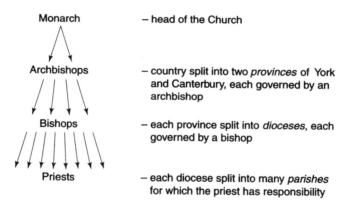

Figure 1.3 Structure of the Anglican Church

Catholics

Many Catholics did outwardly conform to the new settlement, although some 'recusants' did not attend church and became liable to recusancy fines. The position of Catholics during Elizabeth's reign and thereafter was an uneasy one. A papal bull (decree) in 1570 had deposed Elizabeth, and implied that her Catholic subjects' duty was to put that decree into effect. A series of plots between 1570 and 1586, aimed at replacing Elizabeth with the Catholic Mary, Queen of Scots, further linked Catholicism in the popular mind with treason and political violence. The war with Catholic Spain, and the Spanish Armada in 1588 in particular, associated Catholicism with foreign aggression and tyranny. Protestant propagandists played upon these images; especially important was John Foxe's *Book of Martyrs*. First published in 1563, Foxe's work was a bloody and highly romanticised history of the English nation's struggle against Catholic oppression, drawing particular attention to the persecution and burnings of Mary I's reign. As a best-seller of seventeenth-century England, second only to the Bible, its message was hugely influential throughout the Stuart era, and beyond.

Despite this popular image of Catholicism, the vast majority of English Catholics remained loyal to the Crown, and were not politically active. Although there was an upsurge in Catholic missionary activity in the 1580s and 1590s, and a corresponding increase in persecution, with around 180 Catholics being executed for treason, the Catholic minority represented little real threat to the State by 1603. They were predominantly interested in trying to practise their religion, as far as possible, free from Government interference.

Puritans

There was disquiet among some Protestants over the form of the Church settlement. Known as 'Puritans' or 'the godly', they were particularly influenced by the teachings of John Calvin, and were concerned over the continuation of Catholic practices and ceremonies in the Elizabethan Church. They wanted to see 'a further reformation' to bring the Church into line with what they considered to be the biblical model. In particular, practices such as the use of special clerical clothing, or vestments, kneeling to receive communion, and making the sign of the cross at baptism, were seen as unnecessary and unsavoury remnants of 'popish' superstition. Most Puritans were willing to work from within the Church, accepting the monarch's authority over it, for this further reformation. However, there was a minority that were not.

Presbyterians and Separatists were more radical than the more moderate Puritans, in that they rejected the structure of the Anglican Church, and the monarch's role in it. In line with Calvinist practice, Presbyterians believed that the Church should be governed not by bishops and archbishops, but by elders and overseers, appointed from within the church, rather than by the monarch. Separatists went a stage further, believing that each separate congregation should be self-governing, and rejected any kind of national, or even regional, structure.

The political implications of these views were not lost on Elizabeth. The 1590s saw a concerted persecution of the Presbyterians in particular, under the guidance of Archbishop Whitgift, who shared Elizabeth's views on the importance of conformity. The Presbyterian structure was uprooted and Presbyterianism, as an organised force, virtually destroyed. Separatists, despite their lack of numbers, were also persecuted; although ironically, it was they who were to present a more significant challenge to the established Church in the longer term.

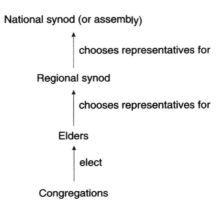

National synod (or assembly)

↑ chooses representatives for

Regional synod

↑ chooses representatives for

Elders

↑ elect

Congregations

Figure 1.4 Structure of the Presbyterian Church

By the time of James's accession, the established Church had many critics. Whilst there was a substantial body of Protestants who supported the Church settlement, there were also many moderate Puritans who did not. The events of Elizabeth's reign had done little to dampen their hostility to anything perceived as Catholic and they saw the accession of a new king as an opportunity to press again for a more 'godly' reformation.

Summary of religious differences

Table 1.1 Summary of religious differences

Beliefs	Catholic	Protestants			
		Anglicans	Mild Puritans	Presbyterians	Separatists
Church structure	Church governed by the Pope, with structure of archbishops, bishops, priests, etc.	Same as Catholics, except the Pope is replaced as head of the Church by the monarch ⟶		Calvinist structure that excludes any governing role for the Crown	Each church should be self-governing
Role of ceremony	Ceremony and ritual central to church services – the mystical nature of faith is emphasised, as is the role of the priest	Some ceremony retained and role of priest still significant ⟵		Against ceremony and 'superstition'. Priest has no special function. Emphasis on 'rational' worship, especially preaching ⟶	
Theology	Based on Church tradition – as interpreted by the Pope ⟵			Largely based on teachings of John Calvin ⟶	

Parliament

Although similar in some ways to today's institution, Parliament at the beginning of the seventeenth century differed in some important respects. Although it claimed to represent the English people, it was not a democratic institution in the sense that we would understand. It consisted of three bodies: the Crown, the House of Lords, and the House of Commons. The Lords were made up of senior churchmen, archbishops and bishops, and the hereditary aristocracy – dukes, earls, lords, etc. Although the Commons were elected, the regulations for those elections varied according to what type of constituency was being contested. In county seats, the franchise extended only to those citizens who met the minimum requirement of holding land worth at least 40 shillings a year. In boroughs, electoral rights varied widely, but again tended to restrict the franchise to relatively prosperous males. Overall, this meant that those able to vote constituted a relatively small part of the population as a whole. Those who sat in the Commons, drawn mainly from the rural gentry and urban élites, therefore tended to reflect the backgrounds and interests of their electors, rather than the 'common' people as a whole.

Parliament did not sit continuously, but rather at the monarch's convenience, being summoned to deal with specific business and then dismissed. For instance, during Elizabeth I's reign, it was called together for thirteen sessions over a forty-five-year period, and it was not unusual for there to be a gap of three or more years between Parliaments. Traditionally little more than a device for extracting taxation, its significance as an organ of government had increased during the sixteenth century, as successive monarchs had used it to reinforce their religious policies and to introduce social and economic legislation.

Elizabeth had very strong views on the place of Parliament, and the extent of its rights and privileges, which did not always coincide with its own. She identified two distinct areas of Government business: 'matters of State' and 'matters of commonwealth'. The former consisted of issues linked to royal marriage and succession, religion and foreign policy. These were part of the 'royal prerogative' (areas that were the sole preserve of the monarchy), and not to be discussed by Parliament, unless the monarch invited them to do so. The latter consisted of those areas that affected the well-being of the nation as a whole, i.e. social and economic issues.

Documents

Some historians have drawn attention to the conflicts that at times developed between Elizabeth and Parliament, seeing them as the beginnings of the struggle for control over Government, which would spill into the reigns of her successors. While most commentators now tend to question this interpretation and emphasise the degree of co-operation between Crown and Parliament during this period, there were nevertheless areas of tension and disagreement between them:

A   That the assembly of the lower House may have frank and free liberties to speak their minds without any controlment, blame, grudge, menaces or displeasure, according to the old ancient order ... that the old privilege of the House be observed, which is that they and theirs might be at liberty, frank and free, without arrest, molestation, trouble or other damage to their bodies, lands, goods or servants, with all other their liberties, during the time of the said parliament, whereby they may better attend and do their duty; all which privileges I desire may be enrolled, as at other times it hath been accustomed.

(Speaker of the House, 1562, making the customary demand for the privileges of the House of Commons; in Sir Simonds D'Ewes's *Journals*, 1682)

B   August 10, 1566: Parliament is to open at the beginning of October ... they say that the Queen's only intention in calling it is to obtain large supplies, and to defer the question of succession and her marriage. ...

September 14: It is believed for certain that Parliament will meet. ... They think that if the Queen does not marry or proclaim a successor, they will not vote her any supplies. ...

October 19: I have been informed that in the House of Commons great difference existed yesterday as to whether the question of the succession should be discussed before voting supplies, some said that the succession ... should be one of the reasons for voting supplies; others that the succession should not be discussed until supplies were voted, as they thought it was disrespectful to force the Queen in this way.

October 26: The discussion about the succession still goes on ... they had offered her [the Queen] votes of £250,000 on condition that she would agree to [their nomination], but she refused and said that she would not accept any conditions, but that the money should be given freely and graciously, as it was for the common good and defence of the Kingdom. ...

November 13: The Queen seeing that they were determined to carry on the discussion about the succession, sent them an order telling them not to do so, but ... the members thought that during sittings that they had full liberty to treat upon matters beneficial to the country: they have greatly resented the order. ...

December 2 : The grants have now been made but to a smaller amount than was proposed. The Queen asked for £300,000 English money, in three installments, and they have voted £200,000 in two. ...

January 5, 1567: The Queen went to Parliament ... and ... dissolved it altogether; as I am told that she is dissatisfied with the representatives of the people who form it.

(Letters of the Spanish Ambassador, de Silva, to Philip II, 1566–7)

C   I saw [in the last Parliament] the liberty of free speech, which is the only salve to heal all the sores of this commonwealth, so much and in so many ways infringed ... two things do very great hurt in this place of which I mean to speak. One is a rumour that runs about the house and it is 'take heed what you do, the Queen's majesty likes not such a matter; whoever prefers it, she will be much offended with him'. The other is sometimes a message brought into the House either commanding or inhibiting, very injurious to the freedom of speech and consultation. I would to God, Mr. Speaker, that these two were buried in Hell ... [the Queen refused] good and wholesome laws for her own preservation, which caused many faithful hearts for grief to burst out with sorrowful tears and moved all papists ... in their sleeves to laugh all the parliament house to scorn. ... It is a dangerous thing in a prince unkindly to treat and abuse his or her nobility and people as her Majesty did in the last parliament ... and I beseech God to endue her Majesty with His wisdom ... and to send her Majesty a melting, yielding heart unto sound counsel ... and then her Majesty will stand when her enemies are fallen, for no estate can stand where the prince will not be governed by advice.

(Peter Wentworth, 1576, in D'Ewes's *Journals*)

D   This day Mr. Treasurer ... examining the said Peter Wentworth, touching the violent and wicked words yesterday pronounced by him in this House touching the Queen's Majesty ... which words, so collected, the said Peter Wentworth did acknowledge and confess ... [and] did take all the burden thereof upon himself. And so the said Mr. Treasurer thereupon moved for his punishment and imprisonment in the Tower, as the House should think good, and consider of: whereupon, after various disputation and speeches, it was ordered ... that the said Peter Wentworth should be committed close prisoner to the Tower, for the said offence; there to remain until such time as this House should have further consideration of him.

(*The Journal of the House of Commons*, 1576)

1   What privileges does Parliament claim in source A?
2   Briefly outline the events of the parliamentary session described in source B. How would both Parliament and monarch have justified acting as they did?
3   What is the essence of Wentworth's complaints in source C?
4   From the evidence of source D, how much sympathy does there seem to have been for Wentworth's stance?

Foreign affairs

An area of particular concern by 1603 was that of foreign policy. The well-being of the nation depended in no small part on a successful foreign policy, and it was the monarch's responsibility to ensure that success. To provide national security and prestige, it was vital to develop and maintain good relations with other European powers. While alliances had their uses, the deployment of military power, although expensive, had the potential to win even greater glory both at home and abroad. An effective foreign policy would also require the securing and development of trading links overseas, and their protection from potential rivals.

Traditionally, England's main rivals had been the 'old alliance' of Scotland and France, but by the later years of Elizabeth's reign this had ceased to be the case. France had been torn apart by religious warfare, and Scotland was no longer regarded as a threat under its Protestant king, James VI, who was widely expected to be named as Elizabeth's successor. The focus of concern had instead shifted to the great Catholic power of Spain. While Elizabeth went to great lengths to avoid conflict, she did eventually find herself dragged into war with Spain in 1585, which was to continue into her successor's reign.

The Anglo–Spanish war was the result of tension arising out of a series of dynastic, religious, strategic and commercial issues. Philip II of Spain had been previously married to Elizabeth's sister, Mary I, and had briefly reigned as joint monarch of England. Elizabeth had declined his subsequent offers of marriage, made out of a desire to enhance Spain's strategic position, and to consolidate the link between the two main parts of his European empire, Spain and the Netherlands. These dynastic ambitions were further complicated by religion. As the champion of the Catholic Counter-Reformation, Philip was unhappy to see his former kingdom's descent into Protestant heresy, and was keen to see it return to the Catholic fold. Spanish hostility was fuelled by commercial conflicts over trade in the New World, which were heightened by the activities of English privateers such as Hawkins and Drake, preying on Spanish treasure ships with the tacit approval of the English Crown.

What finally forced Elizabeth into open hostilities, however, were strategic concerns that threatened the security of England itself. The prospect of the defeat of Dutch rebels struggling for independence from Spain raised the possibility of a Spanish invasion of England from the Netherlands. Elizabeth was determined not to allow this to happen, and declared war on Spain in 1585, sending an army under the command of the Earl of Leicester to aid the Dutch.

Although hugely expensive, the war against Spain was largely successful. The primary aim of securing Dutch independence was realised, and despite the considerable threat of invasion in 1588, the Spanish armada was defeated through a combination of good seamanship and bad weather. Spanish intervention in Ireland, aimed at supporting a Catholic rebellion in 1601–2, was also to end in failure. However, the Spanish war did take its toll. The 1590s were years of considerable economic and social strain, and the effects of war on trade and the constant demands for taxation placed even greater burdens on the country. While war had been necessary in terms of national security, it was clearly not something that could be afforded for much longer. The challenge that would face James would be how to bring hostilities to an end, without compromising over those issues that drove his predecessor into war in the first place.

Ireland

With Elizabeth I's death, James also inherited the crown of Ireland. Traditionally, English policy in Ireland had been to exercise the direct control over 'the Pale', an area of land around Dublin, while allowing Irish chiefs to hold a series of semi-independent lordships over the rest of the country. In the second half of the sixteenth century, this policy was to change, as the English government began to pursue a policy of 'Plantation'. This was based upon the idea that the only way truly to establish control over Ireland was to 'plant' loyal Protestant English settlers, who would hold lands confiscated from the Irish, thereby ensuring the obedience of the country to the English Crown.

This not only provoked the hostility of the Catholic Irish, but also of the 'Old English', those original English settlers of Ireland who had not converted to Protestantism and were unhappy at the prospect of direct English rule. By 1598, this discontent was serious enough to take the form of the Ulster Rebellion, under the leadership of the Earl of Tyrone. His victory at the Battle of the Yellow Ford threatened to overthrow English rule in Ireland altogether, and was followed by the intervention of Spanish troops in support of the rebels. It was only with great trouble and expense (around £2 million) that the revolt was quashed, with Tyrone eventually surrendering shortly after Elizabeth's death.

Although James was to reap the benefits of this pacification of Ireland, the problems that had provoked the revolt had still not been resolved. Religion remained an explosive issue, and the continued policy of plantations under the early Stuarts was to give fresh grievances to the native Irish population. Although the question of the authority of the English Crown over the Anglo-Irish nobility had been settled for now, the 'Old English' remained largely alienated from the 'New English' regime. The potential for future problems remained.

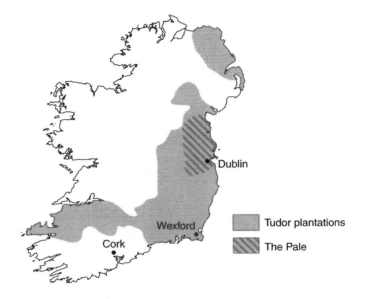

Figure 1.5 Map of the Irish plantation by 1603

England by 1603: historical perspectives

As is explained in the introductory section on historiography, historians are influenced by many different factors, and their interpretation of a whole period can often colour their view of one particular part of it. The state of England at the beginning of the seventeenth century is a case in point. Below are three interpretations, each of which takes a distinctive view of what the key issues facing the country actually were:

A [There were] features which, at the opening of the seventeenth century, differentiated England from the other countries of Europe. Owing to these characteristics, it was still possible that … we might evolve some new kind of state. … For England was a land of local government, local armaments, local feeling … where no feud existed between country and town; where ranks were ever mingling; where the gentry intermingled with the middle classes … bureaucrats and soldiers were almost unknown; the king depended for the execution of his laws on an unpaid magistracy, and for his defence on the loyalty of his subjects. The religion which most inspired the best and ablest men, did not depend, like the Protestantism of Germany or the Catholicism of France, on a State Church or a Church State, but referred the individual to his own intellect and his own conscience, and inspired him to defend his spiritual liberties. … When Elizabeth died … whether in such a land, liberty had still a chance of survival; or whether the universal tide of monarchy in Europe would not after all prove irresistible even in England … was soon to be decided.

(George Trevelyan, *England under the Stuarts*, 1904)

B [Lawrence Stone identifies four factors, or 'preconditions', that existed, which made change in the seventeenth century highly likely.] The first was the failure of the crown to acquire two key instruments of power, a standing army and a paid, reliable local bureaucracy. Second comes the decline of the aristocracy, and the corresponding rise of the gentry; a rise partly in terms of relative wealth, status, education ... and partly in terms of political self-confidence on the floor of the House of Commons as the representatives of a 'Country' ideology. Third, there was the spread through large sectors of the propertied and lower middle classes of ... Puritanism, whose most important political consequence was to create a burning sense for the need for change in the Church and eventually in the State. Last but not least was the growing crisis of confidence in the integrity ... of the holders of high office, whether courtiers or nobles or bishops or judges or even kings.

It must be stressed that none of the factors here listed made the collapse of government inevitable, much less the outbreak of civil war or the rise of a genuinely revolutionary political party. These preconditions made some redistribution of power almost inevitable, and the reform of the church very probable, but whether these changes would come about by peaceful evolution, political upheaval, or force of arms was altogether uncertain.

(Lawrence Stone, *The Causes of the English Revolution*, 1972)

C Although the years 1585–1603 did see the beginnings of 'the breakdown of the Elizabethan system', its achievements at the time of the Queen's death were still considerable. The Spanish war had ensured the preservation of the country's basic independence and security ... the Essex rebellion was hardly a serious threat; and in ecclesiastical affairs organized Presbyterianism had been crushed and Catholic divisions exploited. On the other hand, the conquest of Ireland ... contained the seeds of future tragedy; Catholicism had not been rooted out in England; moderate Puritanism was arguably stronger in the 1590s than it had ever been before ... above all, perhaps, the government's needs for war finance in these years imposed strains on its relationships with both Parliament and with the localities, which emphasized the important truth that the English governmental system was not well equipped to raise money for war. ... The tensions which it provoked ... were a warning that future governments should try very hard to keep out of armed conflicts.

(A.G.R. Smith, *The Emergence of a Nation State*, 1997)

1 How do sources A–C differ, in terms of what issues they identify as being of particular concern by 1603?
2 Why do you think that they might have such different perspectives? (You may find it helpful to refer to the introductory historiography section.)

2 James I, 1603–25

The accession of James I

On 24 March 1603, Queen Elizabeth died and her crown passed to her cousin, James VI of Scotland. That this was accomplished without incident was mainly due to the efforts of Elizabeth's Secretary of State, Robert Cecil, who had conducted secret negotiations with James and smoothed the path for his succession. The instability that many expected to follow the Queen's death did not materialise, as one contemporary noted: 'The contentment of the people is unspeakable, seeing all things proceed so quietly, whereas they expected in the interim their houses should have been spoiled and sacked.'

As James journeyed south through his new kingdom, he seems to have been largely welcomed by his subjects. There was a general sense of relief at the passing of Elizabeth, and a hope that the difficulties and strains of her later years might be a thing of the past. As a group of MPs told the King a year later:

> a general hope was raised in the minds of all your people that under your majesty's reign religion, justice, and all virtue should renew again and flourish ... and some moderate ease should be given us of those burdens and sore oppressions under which the whole land did groan.

There was also, perhaps, some apprehension at James's accession. Although he had shown himself to be an able and successful ruler in Scotland, his nationality would have been a stumbling block to many, with Scotland being a traditional enemy of England. Moreover, James did not go to the same lengths as his predecessor to project his royal image, or to cultivate public opinion. James disliked large crowds, and tried to avoid their attention whenever possible. On one occasion, when he complained about the size of the crowds surrounding his carriage, he was informed by a courtier that they merely wished to see his face. James's regal response was to exclaim: 'God's wounds! I will pull down my breeches and they shall also see my arse!'

Documents on the character of James I

So, how well-suited was James VI of Scotland to the task of also being James I of England? This question has provoked much debate among historians over the years, and this difference in opinion is one that is reflected in the observations of his contemporaries:

Figure 2.1 James I of England and VI of Scotland (1621)

A   Three qualities of the mind he possesses in perfection: he understands clearly, judges wisely, and has a retentive memory. His questions are keen and penetrating and his replies are sound. ... In short, he has a remarkable intelligence, as well as lofty and virtuous ideals and a high opinion of himself. ... He is never still in one place but walks constantly up and down, his gait [*walk*] is erratic and wandering. ... He loves the chase above all pleasures and will hunt for six hours without interruption.

   I have remarked in him three defects that may prove injurious to his estate and government: he does not estimate correctly his poverty and insignificance but is over-confident of his strength ... his love for favourites is indiscreet and wilful, and takes no account of the wishes of his people; he is too lazy and indifferent about affairs, too given to pleasure, allowing all business to be conducted by others. Such things are excusable at his age, yet I fear they may become habitual.

   (A description of the young James VI in 1584. Written by a representative of his mother, Mary, Queen of Scots, at his court and sent to her while she was in captivity in England)

B   He is tall, of a noble presence, his physical constitution robust, and he is at pains to preserve it by taking much exercise at the chase, which he passionately loves, and uses not only as a recreation, but as a medicine. For this he throws off all business, which he leaves to his Council and to his ministers. And so one may truly say that he is more Sovereign in name and appearance than in substance and effect. This is the result of a deliberate choice, for he is capable of governing, being a prince of intelligence and culture above the common. ...

   He is a Protestant ... in doctrine he is Calvinistic, but not so in politics. ... The king is a bitter enemy of our religion (i.e. Catholicism). ... He has no inclination to war, nay is opposed to it, a fact that little pleases them. ... He does not caress the people nor make them that good cheer the late Queen did, whereby she won their loves.

   (A report from Nicolo Molin, Venetian ambassador in London, 1607)

C   He was of a middle stature ... his clothes ever being made large and easy, the doublets quilted for stiletto proof ... he was naturally of a timorous disposition, which was the reason of his quilted doublets: ... his beard was very thin: his tongue too large for his mouth, and made him drink very uncomely, as if eating his drink, which came out into the cup of each side of his mouth ... his legs were very weak, that weakness made him ever leaning on other men's shoulders, his walk was ever circular, his fingers ever in that walk fiddling with that codpiece ... it is true that he drank very often, which was rather out of a custom than any delight, and his drinks were of that kind for strength, as ... High Country wine, Tent Wine, and Scottish Ale. ...

   He was very liberal, of what he had not in his own grip ... he spent much, and had much use of his subjects' purses, which bred some clashings with them in Parliament, yet would always come off with a sweet and plausible close. ... He was so crafty and cunning in petty things, as ... the change of a favourite, etc., insomuch as a very wise man was wont to say, he believed him the wisest fool in Christendom, meaning him to be wise in small things, but a fool in weighty affairs.

... He was infinitely inclined to peace, but more out of fear than conscience, and this was the greatest blemish this king had through all his reign, otherwise he might have been ranked with the very best of our Kings.

(Sir Anthony Weldon, *The Court and Character of James I*, 1651. Weldon had been a courtier of James I, but had been dismissed for writing a satirical pamphlet attacking the Scots)

D   King James ... was a prince of more learning and knowledge than any other of that age, and really delighted more in books and in the conversation of learned men, yet, of all wise men living, he was the most delighted with handsome persons and with fine clothes.

After whose [i.e. James's] death, many scandalous and libellous discourses were raised, without the least colour or ground ... in a time of license, when nobody was afraid of offending majesty, and when prosecuting the highest reproaches ... against the royal family was held very meritorious.

(Edward Hyde, Earl of Clarendon, *History of the Rebellion*, written in the 1670s. Clarendon was a minister of both Charles I and Charles II)

1   How far do sources A and B contradict source C?
2   How useful do you consider sources A–C to be in assessing James's qualities and defects as King of England?
3   How far might Clarendon's observations in source D explain Weldon's account in source C?
4   From your analysis of sources A–D, how would you assess James I's suitability as King of England?

Parliament

James I's accession was viewed with some apprehension by some parliamentarians, on account of the views that he expressed in a book published in 1598, entitled *The True Law of Free Monarchies*. James's support for the theory of 'The Divine Right of Kings' was justified on the following grounds:

A   The kings therefore in Scotland were ... before any Parliaments were holden, or laws made; and by them was the land distributed, which at the first was whole theirs ... and forms of government devised and established. And so it follows of necessity, that the kings were the authors and makers of the laws, and not the laws of the kings. ... To dispute what God may do is blasphemy ... so it is sedition [*treason*] in subjects to dispute what a king may do. ... The king is above the law, as both author and giver of strength thereto, yet a good king will not only delight to rule his subjects by the law, but even conform his own actions thereunto. ... Yet is he not bound thereto but of his good will, and for good example giving to his subjects.

(James VI, *The True Law of Free Monarchies*, 1598)

This was a theme that he returned to many times during his reign:

B The state of monarchy is the supremest thing upon earth; for kings are not only God's lieutenants upon earth, and sit upon God's throne, but even by God himself they are called gods. ... Kings are justly called gods for that they exercise a manner ... of divine power upon earth. For if you will consider the attributes of God, you shall see how they agree in the person of a king. God hath power to create or destroy, make or unmake at his pleasure, to give life or send death, to judge all and to be judged nor accountable to none. ... And the like powers have the king ... accountable to none but God only.

(James I's speech to Parliament, March 1610)

James's views were not always shared by his Parliaments:

C

1 That that which is the subjects' cannot be taken away from them without their consent, but by due course of law.
2 That laws cannot be made without the consent of the three estates [i.e. monarch, Lords, and Commons]
3 That the Parliament ... was the ... storehouse wherein these things were safely reposed and preserved, as well as the laws of the land as the rights ... of the subjects to their lands and goods. And the special privilege of Parliament is to debate freely of all things ... without any restraint or inhibition ... [and] that in all ages the King's Prerogative ... hath been examined and debated in Parliament, being the highest court of justice in the land.

(Notes from an MP's speech in a Commons committee, May 1610)

D That the liberties ... privileges and jurisdictions of Parliament are the ancient and undoubted birthright and inheritance of the subjects of England; and that ... affairs concerning the King, state and defence of the realm, and of the Church of England ... are proper subjects and matters of counsel and debate in Parliament; and that in the handling and proceeding of those businesses every Member of the House of Commons hath ... freedom of speech. ... And that every Member of the said House hath like freedom from all ... imprisonment and molestation (other than by censure of the House itself) for or concerning any speaking, reasoning or declaring of any matter.

(Commons Protestation, December 1621)

1 In sources A and B, what does the King have to say about the nature of monarchical power, and how does he support his arguments?
2 How far can sources C and D be seen to contradict James's claims, and on what grounds?

There was little new in James's claim that kings were appointed by God and ruled in his name. It was something that English monarchs, particularly since the Reformation, had taken for granted. What was more controversial was James's apparent claim that the monarch was above the Law, and that his subjects' liberties and privileges only existed by his goodwill, not by right. In practice, James did nothing to try and put these theories into effect, beyond dissolving Parliament if he felt it was encroaching on his royal prerogative, such as in 1614 and 1621. In this he was merely following the example of Elizabeth I. The main effect of his divine-right theories was probably to cause unnecessary tension with his Parliaments. James's fondness for lecturing his subjects at length in rambling speeches on constitutional theory was not something they shared, and it often provoked them to deliver indignant replies.

James's relationship with Parliament was further hampered by a lack of careful management. Elizabeth had taken great care to direct Parliament, especially the Commons, through influencing the choice of the Speaker and ensuring the presence of a number of her Privy Councillors in the House. These could then be relied on to steer business in the direction she wanted and minimise the potential for conflict. James did not appreciate the need to manage proceedings in the same way, simply expecting Parliament to respond to the royal will. The lack of councillors in the Commons to initiate debate on Crown business and steer it away from controversial areas, such as the prerogative, was probably a more significant factor in James's problems with Parliament than any fundamental clash of ideology.

Sessions of Parliament, 1604–24

The first session of Parliament in 1604 was not a productive one. A disputed election for one of the Members for Buckinghamshire, over which James claimed jurisdiction, led to a general dispute over MPs' privileges. A compromise was reached on the issue, with James reaffirming Parliament's right to judge election returns to the Commons, and of MPs' freedom from arrest, but the episode highlights the sensitivity of Parliament over its status and rights. Far more important from James's point of view was his projected Union of England and Scotland. This fell victim to the prejudice of his English subjects, who were hostile to the idea of an equal union of the two countries, under the name of 'Great Britain'. Although James revived the proposal in the session of 1607, parliamentary opposition remained strong. In addition to anti-Scottish prejudice, some MPs identified economic reasons for avoiding union; as Nicholas Fuller observed:

> one man is owner of two pastures, with one hedge to divide them; the one pasture bare, the other fertile and good. A wise owner will not pull down the hedge … if he does, the cattle will rush in multitudes, and much against their will return.

Others cited unwelcome legal and political consequences from any such move; according to Sir Edwin Sandys: 'The King cannot serve the fundamental laws by uniting, no more than a goldsmith two crowns. … We shall alter all laws, customs, privileges, by uniting.'

The second session of Parliament in 1606 witnessed far more harmonious relations. In the aftermath of the Gunpowder Plot, harsher penal laws against Catholics were passed, and Parliament signalled its support and loyalty to its King by voting subsidies totalling almost £400,000. This model of King and Parliament working effectively towards common goals was short lived, however. Following opposition to the Union in the session of 1607, both the Parliaments of 1610 and 1614 were characterised by poor management and disputes over finance and the royal prerogative. The failure of the Great Contract, and criticism of royal extravagance and impositions, in 1610 led to Parliament's dissolution. James's decision to call another Parliament in 1614 was even less productive. Although attempts were made to try and ensure the return of members more favourable to the King, they were to back-fire and produce an even more critical Commons than in 1610. Known as the 'Addled', or sterile, Parliament, its refusal to consider voting the King any taxes until it had attacked impositions and his Scottish favourites led to its dissolution within two months.

As the focus of later Parliaments was drawn away from issues of finance, so they became more productive. After an absence of seven years, Parliament was summoned in 1621, in the wake of the Palatinate's invasion. It immediately indicated its support of the monarch by voting £145,000, and moved on to launch an attack against the abuse of monopolies. James signalled his support by cancelling a number of monopoly patents, such as for the licensing of inns, and for gold and silver thread. Although the King and Parliament did come into conflict over foreign policy, and free speech, which led to Parliament's dissolution, it was evident that 1614 had not signalled the end of the possibility of co-operation between them.

This was highlighted by the Parliament of 1624. Called to vote supplies for war against Spain, it responded with great enthusiasm. The King and political nation were united in their approach to foreign policy and in their declaration of Protestant unity, and £300,000 was duly granted for the waging of a naval war. In turn, James chose not to protect his Lord Treasurer, Lionel Cranfield, from parliamentary impeachment proceedings, and gave further concessions to Parliament over the issue of monopolies. Yet this renewal of harmony between King and Parliament had come at a cost. James had accepted conditions on how the funds voted by Parliament should be spent, potentially threatening his prerogative right to direct foreign policy. Moreover, the willingness of the King to allow the revival of the medieval practice of impeaching ministers was to prove a dangerous precedent for the future.

Table 2.1 Summary: James I and Parliament

Date	Main issues	Outcomes
1604	MPs' privileges	Privileges confirmed
	Union between England and Scotland	Union blocked
1606	Catholic threat	Penal laws toughened
	Taxation	£400,000 voted
1607	Union between England and Scotland	Blocked
1610	Finance: Great Contract impositions	Deadlock/dissolution
1614	Finance: taxation; impositions; royal extravagance	Deadlock/dissolution
1621	Taxation	£145,000 voted
	Monopolies	Limited action
	Foreign policy	Conflict/dissolution
	Free speech	
1624	Taxation	£300,000 voted
	Foreign policy	Agreement on naval war vs Spain
	Monopolies	Withdrawn
	Cranfield's impeachment	Agreed

1 Judging from the above, how far would you agree with the judgement that James I's parliamentary relations were essentially unproductive?

Finance

As we have seen, the financial legacy that Elizabeth left to her successor was mixed. The Queen had avoided making any fundamental reforms in royal finance, yet by extreme economy in her ordinary expenditure, she had emerged from a period of prolonged warfare with a net Crown debt of only around £100,000, and even this debt was covered by other monies owed to the Crown. The most pressing need was for an end to the Spanish war, but this was not the issue that faced James. Even had he stuck to Elizabeth's economies, the King would have needed around £80,000 p.a. more than his unmarried predecessor, as he had three households to support: his own, the Queen's, and that of the Prince of Wales. It was also unrealistic to expect such limitations on royal expenditure to continue. There were already signs by the end of Elizabeth's reign of the difficulties caused by the lack of royal patronage. The loyalty and co-operation of the political nation depended in no small part on the rewards available to them from royal service. This was an issue that James, as a new King and foreigner amongst a largely anti-Scottish people, would have to address.

1603–12

The Treaty of London in 1604 brought an honourable peace with Spain and an opportunity to re-evaluate royal finances. However, it seems that reform was not high on James's list of priorities. Relative to the poverty of Scotland, the King saw England as a land of milk and honey, and combined with his generous and extravagant nature, James saw little reason for financial restraint. Although this may have been necessary to an extent, as we have already seen, by 1608 royal expenditure was running at over £500,000 p.a. The increase was mainly due to patronage given to the King's favourites, many of them Scots, the most prominent of whom initially was Robert Carr, Earl of Somerset. This development can be seen in the royal accounts, with items such as 'diverse rewards' climbing from £11,000 (1603) to £35,000 (1605), and 'Fees and Annuities' rising from £27,000 (1603) to £48,000 (1605).

Despite parliamentary grants of almost £400,000 in 1606, when Robert Cecil, Earl of Salisbury, took over as Lord Treasurer in 1608, he discovered a Crown debt of £597,000 and an annual deficit running at £178,000. It was under Salisbury that the first attempts at reform were made. He carried out a review of royal lands, selling the least profitable ones for £445,000, despite the long-term loss of future revenues that this would incur. He also produced a new Book of Rates, which revised customs duties in line with inflation, and introduced 'impositions' on 1,400 items, which were to bring in over £60,000 p.a. These impositions were a form of additional customs duty on selected goods, which the Crown claimed the right to 'impose' as part of its royal prerogative, without any need for parliamentary consent.

The centrepiece of Salisbury's reforms, however, was the 'Great Contract'. Realising the need to do more than tinker with Crown lands and customs, in 1610, he proposed to Parliament that they should provide an annual sum of £200,000 in return for the

King surrendering his feudal rights to wardships and purveyance. Initially the Commons was sympathetic and before the summer recess of 1610 gave agreement to the idea in principle. However, when Parliament reconvened, both sides had reconsidered their positions. Many MPs had discovered a great deal of hostility in their constituencies to the idea of permanent parliamentary taxation and were worried about how such sums could be raised. Others thought that impositions should also be surrendered by the Crown as part of any deal. On the Crown's side, it had become apparent that any gain from the Contract would be offset by a loss of feudal revenues amounting to around £115,000. Those courtiers who benefited financially from the administration of wardships and purveyance were keen to point out to James that a gain of £85,000 would hardly compensate him for the indignity of bargaining away the ancient rights of the Crown to Parliament. In the light of these developments, negotiations quickly collapsed and the Contract was abandoned.

When Salisbury died in 1612, the Crown debt stood at around £500,000 and the annual deficit at £160,000. Despite his efforts at reform, at best he had only succeeded in marginally improving the Crown's financial position. His failure to achieve any more was due to two factors. One was the King's lack of interest in reform and his inability to restrain his expenditure. Despite assurances to the contrary, James seems to have been incapable of restricting his spending, or of denying lavish patronage to his favourites. The other was the refusal of many elements within the Court, Government and Parliament to grapple seriously with the need for change, when it might cut against their vested interests. Reform may have been necessary, but it was also unpalatable for those in a position to implement it.

1612–21

The period 1612–18 saw a further decline in the health of the royal finances. The dominance of the Howard faction at court led to the appointment of the Earl of Suffolk as Lord Treasurer, who made no attempt to limit the King's expenditure. Reform was shelved, and the main financial initiative was to raise money through the sale of honours. James created a new order of baronets, with baronetcies retailing at £1,095 each. By 1614, this device had brought in almost £91,000, although as more of them were sold, so they became increasingly devalued and by 1622 one could be bought for only £220. In 1615, the focus shifted to selling peerages, with earldoms, for instance, selling for £10,000. Although the sale of honours generated much needed income, it also created its own problems. It could only be a short-term solution, because after a while the market for honours would be saturated and would dry up. It also offended the existing aristocracy, who felt that their positions were being undermined.

Attempts to supplement royal income by parliamentary grants during this period were a failure. Parliament was called in 1614 to provide the King with financial aid, but MPs seemed more interested in discussing impositions. The King consequently dissolved Parliament without gaining any subsidies, and did not call them again until 1621. With Suffolk's removal as Lord Treasurer in 1618 for corruption, control of the treasury was placed into the hands of a group of commissioners. Despite concerted efforts at cutting royal expenditure and increasing the income from impositions and feudal dues, the royal debt still stood at around £900,000 by 1620.

1621–5

Between 1621 and 1624 there was one final attempt at dealing with the problems of royal finance, under the direction of the new Lord Treasurer, Lionel Cranfield. Cranfield had already established his credentials in a number of areas. As one of the commissioners appointed in 1618, he helped identify savings of around £18,000 in the Household, uncovered waste and corruption in the navy office, and cut the spending of the Royal Wardrobe by half. He also increased revenues from wardships by around a quarter. However, this and other economies were limited in their impact; they helped to alleviate but did not solve James's underlying shortage of money. They were also brought about by cutting against the vested interests of those in and around the court, which in turn provoked a great deal of hostility towards Cranfield. As James himself noted: 'he cannot, you know, but have many enemies, for a Treasurer must have hatred if he loves his master's profits'.

Cranfield's career illustrates several important points about finance and Government during this period. No matter how much energy was directed into economies, significant progress could only be made with the support of the King; and James's support in practice was minimal. Cranfield's impeachment by Parliament and consequent fall from office in 1624 shows how exposed he was to the revenge of those people whose interests he had damaged. His opposition of Buckingham over war with Spain may have provoked his impeachment, but the King's favourite found no shortage of support in Parliament for proceedings against the Lord Treasurer. Finally, it demonstrates that even those who were apparently committed to reform were, to some extent, creatures of the system. During his impeachment, it was revealed that Cranfield was himself guilty of corruption, and had amassed a small fortune by pocketing a significant portion of those savings he had made in various Government departments.

By the end of the reign, the crown debt had risen to over £1,000,000 and had every probability of climbing further as Buckingham and Charles committed the country to war. The financial issues that James faced on his accession had never really been dealt with, and finance remained a major problem area throughout the reign. It was one that did little to smooth his relationship with Parliament.

Table 2.2 Summary: James I and finance

1603	Inherits a small surplus of cash (*c.* £90,000) – debts covered by parliamentary taxation and outstanding loans ↓
	Dramatic rise in expenditure/extravagance ↓
1608	Debt of £597,000 accumulated
	Cecil appointed as Lord Treasurer, attempts at reform meet with only limited success
1612	Debt reduced to £500,000
	Suffolk appointed as Treasurer ↓
	Stagnation/corruption/continued extravagance ↓
1618	Debt approaching £1 million
	Commissioners appointed – embark on series of cost-cutting measures
1621	Cranfield appointed as Treasurer (economies continue)
1624	Cranfield impeached. War with Spain
1625	Debt over £1 million

The favourites of James I

James's approach to patronage in general, and to his favourites in particular, was in marked contrast to that of his predecessor. Whereas Elizabeth, under the pressures of war, had cut patronage to the bone, James adopted no such policy of restraint and extravagance at court was to be one of the hallmarks of his reign. The focus of this generosity was his favourites, individual courtiers who could expect to receive enormous rewards through royal service. James's weakness for favourites was already evident before he came to the English throne, with figures such as Esme Stuart, the Earl of Lennox, enjoying dramatic and profitable rises in the Scottish court.

In England, two favourites were of particular significance: Robert Carr, the Earl of Somerset and George Villiers, Duke of Buckingham.

Table 2.3 The fortunes of two royal favourites

Robert Carr	George Villiers
1603: Arrives in England with James as a page, but fails to advance further at court. Departs for France	1615: Arrives at court, introduced by the anti-Howard faction led by Archbishop Abbot and the Earl of Pembroke
1607: Returns from France, and almost immediately gains royal favour. Knighted and made a Gentleman of the Bed-Chamber	1616: Knighted and made a Gentleman of the Bed-Chamber. Also made Master of the Horse
1611: Created Viscount Rochester, becomes closely associated with the Howard faction at court	1617: Created Earl of Buckingham
1614: Created Earl of Somerset	1618: Created Marquis of Buckingham
1615: Falls from royal favour, after being implicated in the murder of Sir Thomas Overbury. At least to some extent, the victim of the hostility of the anti-Howard faction at court	1623: Created Duke of Buckingham
	(1625: Retains his position as favourite with the new king, Charles I, until his death in 1628)

Documents

Royal favourites were of great significance during James's reign, and not only as the focus of the King's attentions. Their standing with the monarch made them the potential source of favour and patronage in their own right, and as such they became the object of much political manoeuvring and faction, and, at times, hostility. Something of this is reflected in the following sources:

A   Favourites in the Court of James I

His favourites ... were daily interposed between him and the subject, multiplying the heat of general oppressions. ... No other reason appeared in the favour of their choice but handsomness, so the love the king showed was as amorously conveyed, as if he had mistaken their sex and thought them ladies; which I have seen

Buckingham and Somerset labour to resemble, in the effeminateness of their dress-
ings; though in whoreson looks and wanton gestures they exceeded any part of
woman kind. ... The setting up of these golden calves [*idols*] cost England more
than Queen Elizabeth had spent in all her wars.

(Francis Osborne, *Traditional Memoirs*)

B   *Robert Carr, later Earl of Somerset, in 1607*

Robert Carr, who had his breeding in France and was newly returned from travel,
[was] a gentleman very handsome and well bred. ... The Scots so wrought it that
they got him into a groom's place of the Bed-Chamber. ... Observers of those
times could discern the drawing of the king's affection; until upon a coronation day
... his horse fell with him, and broke his leg ... the king went instantly to visit him,
and after, by his daily visiting and mourning over him, taking all care for his speedy
recovery. ... Lord! how the great men flocked then to see him, and to offer to his
shrine in such abundance, that the king was forced to lay a restraint, lest it might
retard his recovery. ... Then the English lords, who formerly coveted an English
favourite (and to that end the Countess of Suffolk did look out choice young men,
who she daily curled and perfumed their breaths), left all hope and she her curling
and perfuming, all adoring this rising sun, every man striving to invest himself into
this man's favour.

(Sir Anthony Weldon, *The Court and Character of James I*, 1651)

C   *Fall of Somerset and rise of Buckingham*

The true fall of Somerset was this – that love and affection, though they are the
strongest passions of the instant, yet they are not of the longest continuance, for
they are not grounded in judgement, but are rather fancies which follow the eye;
and as beauty itself does decay, so love and affection abate. ... Truly I think the
King was weary of an old favourite.

Now Sir George Villiers had kept much company with the gentlemen waiters,
who sometimes after supper did leap and exercise their bodies. But Buckingham of
all the others was most active; he had a very lovely complexion; he was the hand-
somest bodied man of England; his limbs were so well compacted, and his
conversation so pleasing, and of so sweet a disposition. And truly his intellectuals
were very great; he had sound judgement and was of a quick apprehension.

(Bishop Godfrey Goodman, *The Court of James I*)

D   *Rise of Buckingham*

King James, for many insolencies, grew weary of Somerset; and the Kingdom
groaning ... was glad to be rid of him. ... It was now observed, that the King began

to cast his eye upon George Villiers, who was then Cup-bearer, and seemed a modest and courteous youth. But King James would never admit any to nearness about himself but such an one as the Queen should commend unto him ... that if the Queen afterwards, being ill-treated, should complain of this dear one, he might make his answer, 'You were the party that commended him unto me'.

That noble Queen knew her husband well; and having been bitten with Favourites both in England and Scotland, was very shy to adventure upon this request. ... Notwithstanding this, we were still insistent, telling her majesty, that the change would be for the better. For George was of a good nature, which the other was not; and if he should degenerate, yet it would be a long time before he were able to attain to that height of evil, which the other had. In the end ... Queen Anne condescended, and so pressed it with the King, that he assented.

(Archbishop Abbot, *Narrative*, 1627)

1   What criticisms does Osborne have to make about James's dealings with his favourites?
2   What do we learn from source B about the workings of James's court?
3   According to source C, why was Buckingham able to displace Somerset in James's affections?
4   How far does Abbot's account in source D challenge Goodman's analysis?

During their ascendancies, Somerset and Buckingham were able to corner the market in royal favours and wield huge influence as a result. Elizabeth had 'ruled by factions', by spreading her patronage in an attempt to prevent any one figure or group from becoming too powerful. James, conversely, seemed less sensitive to the need to use royal favour as a political balancing tool.

James's favourites were not simply passive receivers of the Crown's generosity, and could themselves have considerable degree of influence on policy. Somerset, associated with the Howard faction, was influential within Government, particularly in moving James towards a pro-Spanish foreign policy. However, it was the rise of George Villiers to royal favour that was of particular significance, politically. It was both rapid and dramatic and, according to the Earl of Clarendon, at first was 'purely from the hand-someness of his person'. The exact nature of his relationship with the King is unclear, but even if it was not actively homosexual, the following extract from a letter from James to Buckingham reveals the strength of the monarch's feeling for his favourite:

for God so love me, as I desire only to live in this world for your sake, and that I had rather live banished in any part of the earth with you than live a sorrowful widow's life without you. And so God bless you, my sweet child and wife, and grant that you may ever be a comfort to your dear dad and husband.

Buckingham's ascendancy was to witness a drift towards a monopoly of Court *and* Government by one single figure. With a stranglehold over the King's favour and patronage, Buckingham became extremely wealthy and influential. Initially promoting the rise of Lionel Cranfield, he engineered his impeachment when the Lord Treasurer opposed his plans for war. His insistence saw the promotion of the Arminian William Laud as Bishop of St David's, much against the will of the King, who objected, with some foresight, on the grounds that 'he hath a restless spirit and cannot see when things are well'. Towards the end of the reign as James began to decline, he became increasingly involved in foreign policy, pressing for a war with Spain and negotiating Charles's marriage with the French princess, Henrietta-Maria. By James's death, Buckingham had made himself as indispensable to Charles as he had been to his father. While there is little suggestion of any sexual element in their relationship, Charles was, if anything, to rely even more heavily on Buckingham than his father had done.

Foreign policy

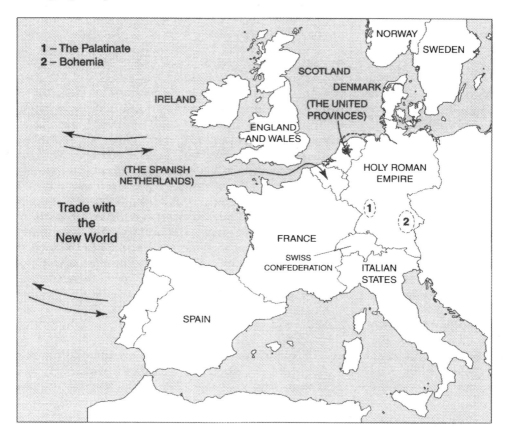

Figure 2.2 Political map of seventeenth-century Europe

1603–18

In the realm of foreign affairs, James was keen to continue the policy he had developed in Scotland, which was to pursue his goals by peaceful means, and by the promotion of international co-operation and friendship. However, he inherited a difficult situation. Although Elizabeth I had tried to avoid war as far as possible, she had found herself dragged into a long and very costly war with Spain. The need to protect England's strategic position by preventing the Spanish conquest of the Netherlands, and to a lesser extent the conflict over trade, had led to war, and were still key issues at the time of James's accession.

In 1604, James concluded peace with Spain, under the terms of the Treaty of London. In it, James was successful in bringing an end to a war of almost twenty years' duration, and in safeguarding areas of key national interest. The Dutch were still able to raise troops and money in England with which to fight the Spanish, English claims to settlement and trade in the Americas were not surrendered, and English merchants regained previous trading rights in Spain.

James's ambitions went further than a simple peace policy. He wanted to play the role of a mediator within Europe, to promote a general peace and win international prestige. He was successful to some extent in this aspiration, helping to secure a truce between the Dutch and the Spanish in 1609, and in negotiating a settlement to a dispute that threatened war between France, Spain and the Holy Roman Empire over the duchies of Julich, Cleves and Berg, in 1614. James also wanted to enhance his position through a series of marriage alliances. In 1613, he married his daughter Elizabeth to Frederick, the Elector Palatine, one of the leading Protestant princes in Germany. In order to balance his diplomatic links, he sought Catholic matches for his two sons, Henry and Charles. With Henry's death in 1612, James's attempts to secure a Spanish marriage for his heir, Charles, came increasingly to dominate his foreign policy. While such a course was perfectly logical, in that James needed allies across the religious spectrum and Spain was the most powerful Catholic nation in Europe, it caused a great deal of disquiet in England, as was expressed forcefully in the parliaments of 1621 and 1624.

It could be argued that up till 1618, James's foreign policy was highly successful. He had kept England out of wars that it could not really afford, and promoted his own and the nation's prestige through diplomacy and negotiation. However, with the outbreak of the Thirty Years War, James's attempts to maintain a position as a European arbiter, with feet in both Protestant and Catholic camps, became increasingly difficult to maintain.

1618–25

The Thirty Years War was sparked by a dispute over the kingdom of Bohemia (for more information see Chapter 8). Frederick, the Elector Palatine, was offered the throne in 1618, but his acceptance threatened the fragile power balance within the Holy Roman Empire, between Protestants and Catholics. The Holy Roman Emperor, Ferdinand, who was a Catholic, invaded Bohemia in 1620 and defeated Frederick at the battle of the White Mountain. He then went on to occupy the Palatinate. Despite calls in England for military intervention to aid his son-in-law and daughter, James's response was to redouble his efforts to negotiate a Spanish marriage, and to try to use Spain to put pressure on their Habsburg cousins to pull out of the Palatinate.

The political cost of this was seen in the 1621 Parliament, which after voting the King £145,000 in subsidies, requested that 'our most noble Prince may be timely and happily married to one of our own religion', and to know exactly 'who is our enemy?' MPs were perplexed that when their King should be rallying to the Protestant cause in Europe, he seemed to be doing very little. As one MP exclaimed:

We can hardly keep our words within these walls, but our acts must pass out. For religion is martyred in Bohemia, wounded in France, scattered in Germany, we sit in peace. The King's children in danger to be dispossessed. Their enemies, the Duke of Bavaria, Spain, the Emperor. ... Would not this blemish us and our religion, and 'twill grieve me that we should do nothing at this time.

James on the other hand saw their outspokenness as an infringement of his prerogative and dissolved Parliament accordingly.

In 1623, the situation changed as a result of an unorthodox foreign-policy initiative. Frustrated at the impasse in marriage negotiations, Buckingham and Charles decided that a personal approach to the daughter of the King of Spain might yield better results. In a bizarre escapade, they crossed the Channel and travelled overland to Spain in disguise, where Charles presented himself to the startled princess by scaling the garden wall of the royal palace in Madrid. Apart from exposing the heir of the throne to all sorts of risks to his person, the trip achieved nothing. Charles found himself effectively a prisoner at the Spanish court, and the conditions outlined by the Spanish for any possible marriage agreement, such as the restoration of public worship for English Catholics, were clearly unacceptable. Their terms for the restoration of the Palatinate were equally unpalatable, involving the restoration of Frederick's son, after his conversion to Catholicism and a marriage to a Habsburg princess.

Although a marriage treaty was agreed in principle, once Charles and Buckingham had managed to leave Spain, it became apparent that they had no intention of honouring it under such conditions. They felt humiliated by their treatment in Madrid and were determined to exact revenge. The outburst of public rejoicing that greeted them on their safe return further encouraged such thoughts, and despite James's continued reluctance to consider war with Spain, the ageing King was unable to resist the combined pressure of his son and favourite. Parliament was called in 1624 and here the move to an aggressive foreign policy found a more receptive audience. Parliament supported the request for taxation and voted £300,000. However, the conditions that they made illustrated the difficulties that would face any such course. The money was to be spent on a naval war with Spain, which it was optimistically assumed would be self-financing, through the seizure of Spanish goods, vessels and trade routes. Their insistence that the money should not be spent on a land war was an acknowledgement that England did not have the strength or resources to try to recapture the Palatinate, but it did not explain how a naval war against Spain would help to further this aim.

By 1625, foreign policy was in disarray. The naval war had not materialised, and much to Parliament's anger, the money it had granted had been spent on a failed land expedition to seize the Palatinate, under the German mercenary, Count Mansfeld. Buckingham had managed to negotiate a match between Charles and the Catholic, French princess, Henrietta-Maria, but the marriage, and terms such as those allowing the future Queen to establish her own private Catholic chapel, outraged Protestant opinion within England. Moreover, the expectations of French aid in recapturing the Palatinate, which were raised by the marriage, were never fulfilled. James had abandoned his dreams of a Spanish match and his policies of conciliation, but to little effect. The prospects of the restoration of the Palatinate to his son-in-law remained as remote as ever.

Historians' verdicts on foreign policy

The failure of James's foreign policy by 1625 was, at least in part, the result of Buckingham and Charles forcing their will on him. However, some historians have questioned the King's whole approach to his foreign affairs. Were his policies of pacifism and negotiation ever realistic, and did they actually bring the Crown or nation any benefit? Read the extracts below:

A   James disliked 'men of war' whether by land or sea. Until in his declining years he let the initiative pass to the volatile and ambitious Buckingham, he was the most thoroughgoing pacifist who ever bore rule in England. ... And not only was James most unwarlike ... but he had no conception of the importance of sea power. He ... utterly neglected the Navy. ... James' peaceful policy was put to a cruel test by the outbreak of the Thirty Years War. At that crisis his neglect of the fighting fleet foredoomed his well-meant pacific diplomacy to failure, for why should Spain or Austria, France or Holland, listen to the man who had let England's national weapon rust?

(George Trevelyan, *The History of England*, 1926)

B   He saw more clearly than his subjects that a war based merely on religious animosity or national prejudices was not likely to prosper. ... Similarly a case can be made out for the view that England should maintain her Elizabethan role of the Protestant champion. ... Unhappily James followed neither policy consistently. His statecraft prevented his joining wholeheartedly in the 30 Years War on the Protestant side, and he may have served England well by his abstinence. Nevertheless he abandoned his own policy when his son in law was expelled from his hereditary lands, the Palatinate. ... There is no evidence at all that he ever considered whether the true interests of England or Protestantism demanded that a war be waged to recover the Palatinate.

(Godfrey Davies, *The Early Stuarts, 1603–1660*, 1959)

C   By remaining at peace from 1604 to 1625, James achieved one of his major foreign policy objectives. ... The policy was, of course, highly unpopular and did drive an unfortunate wedge between James and his subjects, particularly in the last years of his reign. The king and his closest advisers knew, however, that colossal sums of money would be needed if England were to involve itself in a land war on the continent. ... Many of those who deplored James' commitment to peace had become insulated from the realities of conflict and took the considerable benefits of peace for granted. ... The successive military disasters and domestic tensions which followed Charles' entry into the maelstrom of the Thirty Years War had by the end of the 1620s provided eloquent testimony to the fact that it had been James and not his critics who had exhibited the more realistic and hard-headed approach to international affairs.

(Christopher Durston, *James I*, 1993)

D James' desire to act as a European conciliator was a tribute to his genuine humanity and love of peace as well as a reflection of his vanity, but it could hardly survive the outbreak of the 30 Years War in 1618. The most serious criticism of his foreign policy is, indeed, his failure to appreciate the significance of the changed international situation after that date. The Spanish invasion of the Palatinate ... should have indicated to him that he now had to choose between a Spanish match for Charles and support of the Protestant cause. England was the major Protestant power in Europe, and that choice should have been as clear to him as it was to most of his subjects, but James could not abandon the policies of a lifetime.

(Alan Smith, *The Emergence of a Nation State*, 1997)

1 What criticisms are made in sources A and B of James's foreign policy?
2 On what grounds do sources C and D disagree over the success of James's approach to foreign policy?
3 How convincing do you find these analyses of James I's foreign policy? Explain your answer fully.

Religion

Puritans

One area in which many people had high expectations of James was religion. Puritans in particular were encouraged by the fact that James was Calvinist in his theology, even if he did not share Calvin's views on Church government. On his journey south from Scotland, James was presented with the Millenary Petition, so called because it bore the signatures of over a thousand Church ministers. Outlining Puritan grievances, it was essentially a moderate document that wanted to see an improvement in clerical standards, and changes in the style of worship. The issues were familiar ones from the previous reign: the sign of cross in baptism, the use of clerical vestments, the lack of sermons and preaching, bowing at the name of Jesus, the existence of 'popish opinion' within the church, and so on. The petitioners were at pains to emphasise that they were not radicals, but simply: 'ministers of the gospel, that desire not a disorderly innovation, but a due and godly reformation'.

Never lacking confidence in his own judgement, particularly in religious matters, James responded to the petition by announcing that he would chair a conference at Hampton Court to discuss Puritan criticisms of the Church.

The Hampton Court Conference was held in January 1604. On the issue of reforming certain aspects of Church worship, James remained unmoved and the Elizabethan 'status quo' was confirmed by the Church canons of July 1604. However, Puritan aspirations were met in the area of clerical standards, where a series of measures were agreed to ensure a well-paid, educated clergy, and greater missionary activity in Ireland, Wales and 'the dark corners of the land'. Yet, even these reforms came to nothing, undermined by hostile bishops, landowners whose holdings of former Church lands ('impropriated tithes') would have funded any such improvements, and perhaps most importantly by the King's own laziness. Although he enjoyed the intellectual challenge and prestige of chairing such a conference, it seems that James in this, like many other areas, lacked the drive and self-discipline to ensure that policy initiatives were implemented. The one exception to this was the agreement to produce a new translation of the Bible, known as the King James or Authorized Version, which was completed in 1611, and remained standard issue in the Church into the twentieth century.

Puritan reaction to the conference was fairly muted. Only around ninety clergy refused to conform to the canons of July 1604, and were deprived of their livings by Archbishop Bancroft in the following year. James's choice of Bancroft as Archbishop of Canterbury seems at odds with his general approach to Church affairs. Bancroft was a firm believer in the need for conformity, and unsympathetic to any calls for reform. On the other hand, most of the bishops appointed by James were traditional Calvinists, who were more interested in the pastoral rather than the disciplinary aspect of their role. Bancroft's replacement in 1611, George Abbot, typified this approach, and allowed a certain degree of toleration for moderate Puritans.

James's later years were characterised by a lack of religious conflict. Abbot's period in office was unmarked by the kind of disputes that Bancroft had provoked in Parliament during the first decade of the reign. The King and his Church were seen by most of his subjects as theologically sound, an impression that James confirmed in his opposition of the Dutch theologian, Jacob Arminius, who rejected the Calvinist doctrine of predestination. However, this stance was softened to an extent towards the end of James's reign, with the elevation of two prominent Arminians, Richard Neile and Lancelot Andrewes, to the bishoprics of Durham and Winchester respectively. James also appointed another Arminian, William Laud, as Bishop of St David's in 1621, although he did so reluctantly and only under pressure from his favourite, the Duke of Buckingham. Although such appointments may have caused little concern at the time, disturbingly, they were to sign-post the religious developments of Charles I's reign.

Catholics

James's inclination towards toleration for Catholics was not one shared by the vast majority of his Protestant subjects. Claims that Rome was 'our mother church, although defiled with some infirmities and corruptions', and the fact that his wife, Anne of Denmark, had converted to Catholicism, suggested a certain level of respect and sympathy for the Catholic Church. Moreover, the King was keen to make a distinction between those Catholics who were 'quiet and well-minded men, peaceable subjects' and those who were 'stirrers of sedition and perturbers of the commonwealth', declaring that he would be reluctant, in the case of the former, 'to punish their bodies for the errors of their minds'. However, James was forced to temper his views in practice, as they posed a threat to his relations with Parliament. In 1604, initial suggestions of tolerance for Catholics had to be shelved due to parliamentary opposition, and contrary to James's hopes, the recusancy laws of Elizabeth's reign were confirmed and fines ordered to be collected.

After the Gunpowder Plot in 1605, James's attitude hardened, at least for a period. The plot was designed to blow up the Houses of Parliament, together with the royal family and the Lords and Commons, thus at a stroke eliminating the political élite of the nation. It was the work of a small, unrepresentative group of Catholics, who were probably disillusioned by James's failure to deliver toleration and who, with the peace treaty with Spain in 1604, were now deprived of the hope of any outside assistance. Yet, it was sufficiently serious to provoke new penal laws in 1606, and to unite the King and Parliament in a harsher, anti-Catholic stance. Despite this, it seems that these laws were not rigorously enforced once the initial concern had died down

As James began to explore the possibility of a Spanish marriage for his son, Charles, so his policy towards Catholics at home softened. After 1618, there were no executions of Catholics and recusancy fines were only sporadically collected. Although the King's interest in the Spanish match and the perception of a pro-Catholic foreign policy towards the end of the reign did cause some tension with Parliament, on the whole James's approach appears to have been relatively successful. The Catholic minority were generally left in peace, and while their numbers did increase slightly, any attempts at large-scale missionary activity were stamped down on. There were no more gunpowder plots and after 1605 there was no significant Catholic political activity. Perhaps most importantly, while James might have been seen as occasionally being too lenient towards Catholicism, unlike some of his successors, there was no doubt of his own Protestant convictions.

Scotland and Ireland

James's religious policy was complicated by the fact that the three kingdoms over which he ruled had very different religious make-ups. In Ireland, although the political élite mainly belonged to the established Protestant Church of Ireland, the bulk of the population were still Catholic. James continued the plantation policy of his Tudor predecessors, confiscating lands from the Catholic Irish and giving them to Scottish and English settlers. This policy led to the growth of a third religious element in Ireland, Scottish Presbyterianism. The existence of such religious diversity was a cause of potential concern, but James showed no signs of trying to grapple with the problem, and he did not try to impose any measure of religious uniformity. Given the explosive potential of any such course of action, it would seem that James's inaction was well-advised.

In Scotland, James's approach was rather more ambitious. The Scottish Church was based on the Calvinist, Presbyterian model, which meant that it was governed by a national assembly, or Kirk, independent of royal control. James wanted to introduce bishops into the Church government, which would give the Crown a measure of authority over it. With the support of the Scottish nobility, James was able to impose bishops in 1618, although the basic Presbyterian structure of the Church remained in place. Further attempts at reform were made, with the introduction of the 'Articles of Perth', aimed at creating uniformity between the English and Scottish churches. They required the introduction of ceremonial practices such as kneeling to receive communion, but were so unpopular that they were not fully enforced. Plans to introduce a new Prayer Book, drawn up in 1619, were quietly shelved. As with his dealings with the Puritans in England, although James was prepared to arouse opposition over key policies, it was not in his nature to let that opposition develop into open conflict. Above all in religious matters, he was aware of the dangers of pushing any drive for uniformity too far.

Verdicts on the reign of James I

James's record as King of England has drawn a range of comment from historians over the years:

A   He came to the throne at a critical moment. The time was fast approaching when either the King must become absolute, or the Parliament must control the whole executive administration. ... At the very moment at which a republican spirit began to manifest itself strongly in the Parliament and in the country, the claims of the monarch took a monstrous form. ... James was always boasting of his skill in what he called kingcraft; and yet ... he enraged and alarmed his Parliament by constantly telling them that they held their privileges merely at his pleasure, and that they had no more business to inquire what he might lawfully do than what the Deity might lawfully do. ... By his fondness for worthless minions he kept discontent constantly alive ... it was no light thing that on the eve of the decisive struggle between our kings and their Parliaments, royalty should be exhibited to the world stammering, slobbering, shedding unmanly tears, trembling at a drawn sword, and talking in the style alternately of a buffoon [*idiot*] and a pedagogue [*teacher of children*].

(Thomas Macaulay, *The History of England*, 1848)

B   As a hated Scot, James was suspect to the English from the beginning, and his ungainly presence, mumbling speech and dirty ways did not inspire respect. Reports of his blatantly homosexual attachments and his alcoholic excesses were diligently spread back to a horrified countryside. Correspondents from the Court regaled their friends with detailed accounts of drunken orgies in which men and women were staggering and spewing around the King; it was reported that when hunting the King did not dismount in order to relieve himself, and so habitually ended the day in a filthy and stinking condition. In the light of these stories it was clear that the sanctity of monarchy itself would soon be called into question.

(Lawrence Stone, *Causes of the English Revolution*, 1972)

C   He certainly enjoyed a calm period ... in Anglo–Irish relations ... from 1603–1625. In Anglo–Scottish relations it runs from about 1587 to 1625. In both cases it coincides with James' period of power. The correlation is too close for it to be likely that it is purely coincidental, and suggests that in this field, as in so many others, what James deserves to be praised for is what did not happen during his life-time ... largely because he lacked his son's energy, he seems to have avoided ... a three cornered British problem of the sort which caused his son so much trouble. The Church was James' priority area ... and the one where he was most successful. In the British field, the success resulted from his ability to give security to Protestants, without thereby threatening Catholics with extinction. It also resulted from his ... ability to let sleeping dogs lie.

(Conrad Russell, *The Causes of the English Civil War*, 1990)

D   There can be no doubt that James possessed some major shortcomings as a ruler, the most damaging of which were his over-reliance on favourites, his complete neglect of his public image, and his inability to live within his financial means. ... It would, however, be a mistake to suggest that James' statecraft was completely without redeeming features. ... He was emphatically not, however, the total disaster that is found in the pages of the Whig histories, and there is no reason to suppose that England was plunging headlong towards civil war in 1625. ... James I may have been an unattractive man, but he was also a shrewd, capable and moderately successful ruler.

(Christopher Durston, *James I*, 1993)

E   The new king had a long and successful record of kingship behind him in 1603. Recent research confirms what historians of Scotland long suspected: that James VI was the most competent king Scotland ever had. In great contrast to his Scottish reputation James has been one of the most maligned rulers of England. Without doubt some of the criticisms that have been levelled against him are unfair. Contemporary accounts of the deterioration in his physical appearance and habits as an old and sick man in the last five or six years have been used, wrongly out of chronological context. ... Perhaps also historians in the second half of the twentieth century can be more tolerant than some of their predecessors of James' undoubted homosexual tendencies. ... James was far from being an ideal king, but he was equally far from being the 'wisest fool in christendom'. ... Elizabeth's legacy to the new king in 1603 was not a good one. ... James' record in dealing with the problems was much better than he was often given credit for.

(Barry Coward, *The Stuart Age*, 1994)

1   What criticisms are levelled at James by sources A and B?
2   Why do you think the authors of A and B have written as they have?
3   How far are sources A and B contradicted by sources C and D?
4   How far would you accept the verdict put forward by source E?
5   Bearing sources A–E in mind, and the other material that you have looked at, how able and successful a ruler of England would you judge James I to have been?

3   Charles I, 1625–9

The accession of Charles I

The accession of Charles I marked a clear departure from his father's reign in several ways, the most obvious of which initially was his character. Short of stature and physically unimposing, Charles avoided public speaking whenever possible. This was in part due to shyness, and also to the fact that he was troubled with a serious stammer. In 1626, he excused his lack of oration to Parliament on the grounds that 'I mean to show what I should speak in actions', but such an approach meant that communication between the King and his subjects was often lacking. During times of stress and difficulty his critics were to find it all too easy to attribute sinister motives to the King or to his advisers. Charles lacked the approachability and flexibility of his father, qualities that had helped James to assure his subjects of his good intentions, even when they had questioned the wisdom of his policies. Charles's aloofness and inflexibility were to prove serious handicaps for the new King.

Buckingham's dominance at Court and his monopoly of the distribution of patronage during the early part of Charles's reign was not new, but his emergence as the main target of the Government's critics was. Disliked by the traditional nobility as a newcomer, resented by those whose access to patronage or advancement in royal service was blocked, Buckingham was also associated with the introduction of unpopular and unsuccessful policies. The responsibility for a series of expensive foreign failures, and innovation in the religious sphere, with the introduction of Arminianism, was laid squarely at Buckingham's feet. The possibility that the King and his minister might share responsibility for the Government's policies was one that the majority of his subjects either could not or would not contemplate.

Foreign policy, 1625–9

In the early years of Charles's reign, foreign policy shifted from the pacific approach of his father's reign to a far more aggressive one. Charles and Buckingham had already been instrumental in pressuring James into war with Spain in the final year of his reign, and it was this approach that continued to dominate foreign affairs.

Following the failure of Mansfeld to recover the Palatinate, Buckingham began to work towards strengthening England's position by forming an anti-Habsburg league. An alliance was negotiated with the Dutch in the Treaty of Southampton in September 1625, and with Denmark in the Treaty of the Hague in December. The latter included a promise to provide the Danes with £30,000 a month, to support their involvement in

Figure 3.1 Charles I (1631)

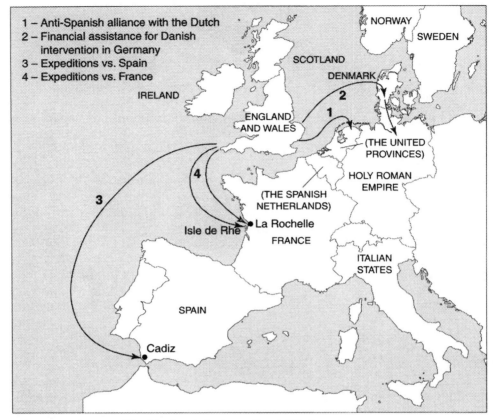

1 – Anti-Spanish alliance with the Dutch
2 – Financial assistance for Danish
     intervention in Germany
3 – Expeditions vs. Spain
4 – Expeditions vs. France

NORWAY
SWEDEN
SCOTLAND
DENMARK
IRELAND
ENGLAND AND WALES
(THE UNITED PROVINCES)
HOLY ROMAN EMPIRE
(THE SPANISH NETHERLANDS)
Isle de Rhe
La Rochelle
FRANCE
ITALIAN STATES
SPAIN
Cadiz

Figure 3.2 Map of Buckingham's foreign policy, 1625–9

the Thirty Years War. In addition to such diplomatic activity, Buckingham was also keen to take direct action against Spain and to this end some £500,000 was spent on an expedition against the Spanish naval base of Cadiz in the autumn of 1625. Despite its enormous cost, the attack was an abject failure due to poor preparation and ill discipline. A further expedition against Spain the following year was again the victim of a lack of planning and bad weather, and the fleet had to return home without even reaching the Spanish coast.

Despite fierce domestic criticism, Buckingham remained convinced that an aggressive foreign policy could pay dividends if France could be persuaded to join the anti-Habsburg league. Despite the marriage alliance in 1625, relations between the two countries were not particularly good; a reflection, at least in part, of the uneasy relationship between Charles and Henrietta-Maria themselves. Furthermore, Buckingham was outraged when the French King's chief minister, Richelieu, actually engineered a peace settlement with Spain in February 1626, without any reference to their English allies. He now began to work towards putting pressure on the French King, to ensure the removal of Richelieu and the renewal of an anti-Habsburg policy. As Buckingham noted: 'All must conspire for one end. If France, which is a vital part of this body, fails us, it will be proper to harass her, so if she refuses to do good she may be prevented from doing harm.'

This 'harassment' of France was to take the form of a war, in alliance with the French Protestants, or Huguenots, aimed at bringing about the downfall of Richelieu. Expeditions were prepared and launched against the Isle of Rhe in 1627 and to lift the siege of the Huguenot stronghold of La Rochelle in 1628. Both were failures and gave yet more ammunition to Buckingham's opponents in Parliament. Under his direction, England had taken part in a series of hugely expensive and failed military initiatives, and had nothing to show for it. She had found herself at war with the two most powerful nations in Europe, and while the Duke had manoeuvred and planned, the Protestant cause in Europe had been allowed to deteriorate. The recovery of the Palatinate looked to be an increasingly forlorn hope, and the Danish armies of Christian IV (which had received little of the financial support promised to them) had been driven out of Germany by victorious Habsburg forces, and were on the verge of surrender. England's attempt to push itself to the forefront of European affairs had been a humiliating and financially ruinous failure, and it was Buckingham that most people held responsible. He was murdered in August 1628, about to depart on another expedition to relieve La Rochelle, by a disillusioned ex-soldier from the Cadiz force, Nicholas Felton. Although Felton was acting alone, his actions seem to have had widespread popular approval, as was demonstrated by the spontaneous outbursts of public rejoicing that greeted the news of the Duke's death.

Parliamentary relations, 1625–9

1625

Indications of the difficulties ahead were evident in the first Parliament of Charles's reign, which met in June 1625. Summoned to provide money for the war with Spain, it began by voting a double subsidy worth around £140,000 and confirming the King's right to collect tonnage and poundage, the main source of customs duties, for one year only. From Charles's point of view, this response to the Crown's needs was inadequate, the sum needed to fulfil his foreign-policy obligations being closer to £1 million. Parliament's lack of generosity was due in part to a lack of realism over the cost of war, and also to a lack of trust over the way that foreign policy was being handled. The failure of Mansfeld's expedition to recover the Palatinate had caused a lot of bad feeling, especially as it was funded by subsidies provided by Parliament, specifically for a naval war.

These concerns were compounded by other issues. The limitation of tonnage and poundage seems to have been an attempt to force the issue of impositions back on to the political agenda, with the accession of a new monarch. Tensions were further heightened by controversy over the writings of an Arminian theologian, Richard Montague. Montague had published a tract in 1624, the 'New gag', which attacked the Calvinist doctrine of predestination and in the process outraged supporters of the Church's traditional doctrines. Attacks on him in Parliament were met by Charles, who signalled his own position by appointing Montague as royal chaplain. Parliament was dissolved by Charles, in response to attacks on Buckingham, without any further business being carried out.

1626–7

When Parliament was summoned again in February 1626, its mood towards Buckingham had become even more hostile. Following the failure of the Cadiz expedition in the autumn of the previous year, the Commons turned on the Duke. According to Sir John Eliot: 'Our honour is ruined, our ships are sunk, our men perished, not by the sword, not by an enemy, not by chance, but … by those we trust.' The House agreed to provide four subsidies, but delayed passing the bill up to the Lords until it had drawn up articles of impeachment against Buckingham. In them he was accused of dishonestly amassing royal offices, corruption and impoverishing the Crown. Charles's response was to dissolve Parliament, thereby saving his favourite. However, in doing so he put himself in an almost impossible position, committed to heavy expenditure, but without the access to the subsidies or the extension of the grant of tonnage and poundage that he needed.

Charles's response to this situation was realistic, and the only one available to him. With a heavy Crown debt, he lacked the credit necessary to borrow the sums he needed privately, and even the City of London, usually a regular provider for the Crown, would only lend him £20,000. In these circumstances, Charles's only option was to continue collecting customs duties without parliamentary consent, and to order a forced loan to the equivalent of five subsidies.

Within ten months £240,000 of the loan had been collected, but only in the face of significant opposition. Even though those responsible for local government collected the loan, in many cases MPs from the recently dissolved Parliament, the judges refused to endorse its legality, and Archbishop Abbot refused to license a sermon emphasising the King's right to collect it. Several MPs, including Thomas Wentworth, were imprisoned for non-payment. Their attempt to question the legality of their detention in the 'Five Knights Case' was a failure, however, the judges upholding the King's prerogative right to imprison without trial.

These tensions were heightened by other pressures brought about by the war. Coastal counties were also required to pay Ship Money, to provide for their defence by the fleet, but in Yorkshire the commissioners refused to try and collect it, on the grounds that it was something that 'we dare not presume to do'. In some counties, the authorities were obstructive over levying increased militia payments, and the billeting of troops in the southern counties, often without compensation, was also greatly resented.

1628

In the light of these problems, Charles had little choice but to recall Parliament in 1628, in order to seek its approval for further taxation. This course of action was made even more necessary by the fact that the French alliance had broken down, and Buckingham had committed England to supporting the Huguenot rising in France. England now found herself at war with both France and Spain. In the aftermath of another failed expedition by Buckingham, this time against the Isle of Rhe, the prospects for co-operation with Parliament might have seemed distant, but the session proved to be more productive than might have been expected.

It seems that MPs agreed to restrain their attacks against Charles's favourite, in order to concentrate on other matters. While responding positively to the King's request for supply by agreeing to provide five subsidies, they made any such grant on condition that he dealt with their grievances. These were put forward in 'the Petition of Right', in which they requested the King to recognise the illegality of extra-parliamentary taxation, billeting, martial law and imprisonment without trial. Charles assented and the subsidies were duly granted.

1629

When Parliament was recalled for a further session in January 1629, any expectations of continued co-operation between it and the Crown proved ill-founded. Although the removal of the Duke of Buckingham the previous year might have been expected to ease future relations, Charles was horrified by the public rejoicing that accompanied the news of his death, and may have privately held some members of the Commons responsible for his murder. In addition, Charles's decision to continue to collect tonnage and poundage without parliamentary assent had angered some MPs. The King's own view was that he was not bound by the Petition of Right, and the right to disregard such agreements was part of his royal prerogative. He was justified in collecting taxation without parliamentary agreement when it was necessary for the nation's well-being. However, for others, such actions were a clear breech of his undertaking in the previous session of Parliament. Their trust for the King was lessened, as was their willingness to co-operate with him over his requests for finance.

Also significant was the disquiet felt by many MPs over the continued promotion of Arminian clergy and opinions within the Church. By 1629, William Laud had become Bishop of London, and other key bishoprics, such as York, Winchester, Norwich and Chichester were filled by Arminians, the last of which was awarded to Montague. Arminian rejections of predestinarianism and their fondness for ritual and ceremony were seen by some MPs as being uncomfortably close to Catholicism. As Francis Rous declared:

> I desire that we may look into the very belly and bowels of this Trojan Horse, to see if there be not men in it, ready to open the gates to Romish tyranny and Spanish monarchy; for an Arminian is the spawn of a Papist.

For some in the Commons the twin-headed spectre of absolutism and Catholicism was very real. Although they took care not to attack Charles personally, citing rather sinister forces in the Court, these critics were determined to defend the country from what they saw as a serious threat to their constitutional and religious liberties. In the light of strenuous attacks on Arminianism and the collection of tonnage and poundage, in March 1629, Charles decided to dissolve Parliament. Although the Lords were compliant, the reaction in the Commons was much stronger. Two MPs, Denzil Holles and Benjamin Valentine, held the Speaker of the House in his chair, thus preventing him from closing proceedings, while the Commons, under the direction of Sir John Eliot, passed resolutions attacking extra-parliamentary taxation and Arminianism.

Charles's reaction was to arrest Holles, Valentine and Eliot, who were tried and imprisoned, and to dispense with Parliament's services for the foreseeable future. Charles was convinced that the difficulties he had encountered with Parliament were due to a small group of troublemakers, who had misled their fellow MPs. He claimed that the objective of these men was 'that all things may be overwhelmed with anarchy and confusion', a view that was shared by some more conservative observers. Charles's decision to dispense with Parliament was based less on ideological than practical grounds. He was not against Parliament *per se*; but if it could not help him to provide good government, then he would provide it without them.

How far was the breakdown of relations between the Crown and Parliament due to the actions of the Duke of Buckingham?

The period 1625–9 was one of significant political conflict and tension. Against a background of expensive, failed wars and changes in religious policy, relations between Crown and Parliament proved difficult and ultimately broke down. In the view of many people at the time, and some later historians, the problems of this period, particularly up to 1628, had their origins in the actions of one man: George Villiers, Duke of Buckingham.

Views of contemporaries

A   Nevertheless we go on with a remonstrance ... to his Majesty containing the general grievance of the realm ... namely: fear of innovation of religion; fear of innovation of government; the ill successes of our late foreign enterprises; the ill state and decay of our forts and castles ... the decay of trade, the great loss and decay of the shipping of the realm; the ill guarding of the Narrow Seas. And concluded in these very terms: that the excessive power of the Duke of Buckingham and the abuse of that power is the chief cause of these evils and dangers to the king and the kingdom.

(A letter from an MP, Sir Nathaniel Bacon, to his wife, 1626)

B   And now, just God! I humbly pray
That thou wilt take that slime away
That keeps my sovereign's eyes from viewing
The things that will be our undoing.

(Anonymous poem, 1628)

C   Awake sad Britain and advance at last
Thy drooping head: let all thy sorrows past
Be drowned and sunk with all their own tears; and now
O'erlook thy foes with a triumphant brow.
Thy foe, Spain's agent, Holland's bane, Rome's friend,
By one victorious hand received his end,
Live ever Felton; thou hast turned to dust
Treason, ambition, murder, pride and lust.

(Anonymous poem, 1628)

D   The Duke was indeed a very extraordinary person; and never any man ... rose, in so short a time, to so much greatness of honour, fame, and fortune, upon no other recommendation than of the beauty and gracefulness and becomingness of his person. ... [He distributed] all the honours and all the offices of the three kingdoms, without a rival; in dispensing whereof, he was guided more by the rule of appetite than of judgement; and so exalted almost all of his own numerous family and dependants, who had no virtue or merit than their alliance to him, which equally offended the ancient nobility, and the people of all conditions ... whilst the lands and revenue (of the Crown) was sacrificed to the enriching of a private family. ... He was of an excellent nature, and of a capacity very capable of advice and counsel. He was in his nature just and candid, liberal and generous, and bountiful.

(Clarendon, *The History of the Rebellion*, 1670s)

E I remember I was in England when the Duke of Buckingham fell, whom many men thought the only cause of all the evils; but those that were of that opinion did not find it so afterwards.

(Sir Philip Percival, 1641)

1   According to sources A–C, what criticisms were levelled against the Duke of Buckingham?
2   How far do sources D and E contradict the view of Buckingham put forward by sources A–C?
3   How would you account for the differences between these sources?

Historians' verdicts

A   The influence of Buckingham on events is in some respects contradictory. He was not afraid of Parliaments; he desired to use them and had full confidence in his power to do so; he was more willing than James or Charles to explain his policies to them and to adapt himself to their moods. ... But there his services to the monarchy end ... his foreign policy ... had disastrous effects on Charles' position at home and abroad. First, he was responsible for the French marriage ... secondly (he) engaged England in war with the two strongest European powers at once. ... While English pride was outraged and her independence endangered, domestic grievances multiplied apace – forced loans, illegal tonnage and poundage, the hardships of pressing and billeting. ... Under this provocation, Parliament broke away from its temporary alliance with the Crown and renewed the general attack upon its policy and ministers. ... Buckingham could not save Charles from the humiliations and restrictions of the Petition of Right ... (which) lay down fundamental principles of government by which sovereignty must pass, sooner or later, from the King and his Courts to the Parliament and their Courts.

(J. Deane Jones, *The English Revolution, 1603–1714*, 1931)

B   Buckingham ... was not the cause of all the evils from which England suffered in the 1620s. As long as he lived there was always an element of flexibility in the King's reaction to events – a flexibility which was lacking after he was no longer there to advise Charles. ... The Commons ... distrusted everything he seemed to represent. It may be that they also hated him because he had called England to a greatness which they longed for but were incapable of achieving. It was much easier to blame Buckingham for everything that had gone wrong than to consider the possibility that the causes went far deeper than personalities and might have to be located in fundamental weaknesses in the system of government and in the structure of society that they had inherited.

(Roger Lockyer, *Buckingham*, 1981)

C   In James' reign, Buckingham never achieved total power because the old king retained some influence over his actions ... after James' death, Charles increasingly left the direction of business to Buckingham, although he retained control over the direction of overall policy. ... The Commons identified Buckingham as the source of all its concern ... [but his] death did not solve any problems. Harmony was not restored between King and Commons, and finance and religion continued to drive them apart.

(Katherine Brice, *The Early Stuarts, 1603–1642*, 1993)

D   It is important to distinguish in any general assessment of Buckingham's ascendancy between the last years of James' reign and the early years of Charles'. The period 1618–24, despite its difficulties, appears in retrospect as a relatively happy time for both England and Scotland. These were years of peace abroad and basic religious calm at home compared with the foreign disasters and Arminian experiments of 1625–9. The parliamentary history of the 1620s, so generally treated as a unity by historians, can now be depicted more realistically as a mirror of the different political and religious moods which prevailed before and after 1625. ... The wars of 1625 to 1630 were Charles' and Buckingham's wars and they were responsible for the tensions that these conflicts imposed on English society, just as they were responsible for the introduction of Arminianism as the official doctrine of the church.

(Alan Smith, *The Emergence of a Nation State*, 1997)

1   How far do sources A and B disagree over the role of Buckingham in causing conflict between Crown and Parliament? How would you account for their difference of opinion?

2   According to sources C and D, how great a role was played by Buckingham in causing domestic conflict during the 1620s?

3   Bearing in mind the views of historians and commentators above, how convincing a case can be made that the Duke of Buckingham was so detested by his contemporaries because 'he had called England to a greatness which they longed for but were incapable of achieving'?

4 The Personal Rule of Charles I, 1629–40

The years of 1629–40, where Charles ruled without the aid of Parliament, are most commonly known as the 'Personal Rule', although some Whig authors have preferred to refer to it as 'the Eleven Years Tyranny'. Although such a label might be appropriate if such an event were to occur in modern-day Britain, it's worth remembering that, in Kevin Sharp's words: 'In 1629, Parliament was still an event; it was not an institution.' Contemporaries would not necessarily have found it strange that Parliament should not meet. It was traditionally called to provide the King with supply, and if such supply was not needed it was not called. Parliament had not met at all between 1614 and 1621, and if one considers that the Addled Parliament lasted only two months and passed no legislation at all, it could be argued that James's reign *effectively* witnessed a similar gap of eleven years between Parliaments.

Although the situation in 1629 shared some features of earlier conflicts between James and his parliaments, it was in many senses quite different. A deep rift between the King and the representatives of his people in Parliament had developed over issues of religion, finance, foreign policy and royal ministers to the point where there was a very public breakdown of trust between the two sides. Charles was quite clear in his own mind who was to blame, and stated that he would only consider recalling Parliament:

> When our people shall see more clearly into our intentions and actions, when such as have bred this interruption shall have received their … punishment, and those who are misled by them and by such ill reports as are raised upon this occasion shall come to a better understanding of us and themselves.

From Charles's point of view, the main advantage of dispensing with Parliament's services was that these troublemakers would be denied an opportunity to stir up controversy and mislead others. He could govern the country without having to put up with an unnecessary and undignified background of criticism, from those who should be helping to provide him with the means to govern. The main disadvantage would obviously be a lack of access to parliamentary revenues, a problem that Charles's ministers were to put a great deal of effort and ingenuity into trying to overcome. Another problem was that although Charles did not necessarily wish to hear criticisms of royal policy, Parliaments could act as a useful safety valve. When Parliament was recalled in 1640, at least part of its frustration with the King was due to its members not having had a chance to voice their views and concerns over the previous decade.

The Court

In the absence of Parliament, the Court became the political focus of the nation's life. Although some of Charles's former opponents, such as Thomas Wentworth, did manage to get into royal service, the base of the court remained fairly narrow. It is important to remember that not all the opposition that Charles faced between 1625 and 1629 was due to political and religious principle. Many attacked royal policies, at least in part, because they had been denied the hope of political advancement by the monopoly over royal patronage by the Duke of Buckingham. Although that stranglehold loosened after his death, the remoteness of the court of Charles I continued to be a significant issue during the years of Personal Rule.

The Court was in many ways a reflection of the King himself. Its complexion changed dramatically with the death of James I; as a contemporary, Lucy Hutchinson noted:

> The face of the court was much changed in the King, for King Charles was temperate, chaste and serious, so that the fools and bawds, mimics and catamites [*homosexuals*] of the former court grew out of fashion.

The familiarity of James's Court was replaced by strict etiquette, which reinforced ideas of order and respect. Whilst being both formal and highly cultured, Charles's Court was also very introverted and removed from the tastes and understanding of much of the political nation. Thus, while the Court of Charles I was more dignified than his father's and less likely to scandalise contemporaries by its morals, its style and manners made him far less accessible to his subjects than James had been.

As a connoisseur, Charles spent a great deal of time and money in collecting art, and employed men of international standing such as Van Dyke, Rubens and Bernini as Court artists. He is estimated to have built up a royal collection of around 1,700 paintings and sculptures, gathered from all over Europe. However, the fact that artists like these were Catholic made them and the Court suspect in the eyes of some critics. According to one Puritan critic, William Prynne, Bernini's activities were part of a Catholic plot 'to seduce the king with pictures, antiquities, images and other vanities bought from Rome'. Charles's love of masques, elaborate symbolic plays, and the participation of the Queen and himself in them as semi-divine figures, again seemed to hint at foreign and Catholic influences; as did the setting for these masques, the continental, 'Palladian' styled Banqueting House, built by Inigo Jones, and lavishly decorated with ceiling paintings by Rubens.

The concern over the cultural flavour of the Court would have been lessened, were it not for the fact that it contained a significant number of Catholics and crypto-Catholics. Figures such as the Earl of Arundel, Weston and Lord Francis Cottington were all Catholic sympathisers and Weston, at least, declared his Catholicism on his deathbed in 1635. This concern was compounded by the fact that some of these figures were not only leading courtiers, but also important Government ministers: Weston, for instance, was Lord Treasurer, and Cottington, the Chancellor of the Exchequer and Master of the Court of Wards. The presence of a Catholic Queen, with her own Catholic chapel, was also deeply alarming in the view of many contemporaries; as was the fact that Charles invited the Pope to send a resident envoy, George Con, to the court in 1636. Although Charles enforced recusancy fines with considerably more vigour than his father had, the image projected by the Court was that the King was inclined towards Catholicism. The fact that Archbishop Laud consistently urged the King to take a tougher line on Catholics and opposed the influence of the Catholic faction at Court was not widely known. For most observers, Arminianism was seen as equally suspicious and simply part of a broader Catholic plot, aimed at undermining the Protestant religion.

Government

Government during the Personal Rule was centred on the Privy Council. Meeting twice a week, it was concerned more with implementing policy than creating it, which was the province of the King and a small number of his trusted advisers. It dealt with a range of administrative matters either collectively, or in sub-committees that dealt with particular areas such as Ireland, Scotland and trade. It was also responsible for supervising local government, with which it seems to have had a reasonable working relationship for most of this period.

An example of this was the issue in January 1631 of the *Book of Orders*. Published in response to the terrible harvest of 1630, the *Book of Orders* was designed to help curb the threat of social disorder that might accompany such an event. It reminded JPs of their duties to prevent vagrancy, punish offenders, supervise poor relief, keep roads in a state of repair and so on; and put in place a system of procedures to ensure their implementation. JPs were ordered to supervise local officials such as constables once a month and to make quarterly reports out for their sheriff. The sheriff would in turn pass them on to the assize judges who would deliver them to the Privy Council. While this mechanism seems to have worked well initially, the Privy Council seems to have relaxed its demands once the danger of a crisis had died away. Either that, or the majority of JPs tired of the extra administrative burden placed on them by such reports, and stopped co-operating when they perceived that the situation no longer warranted such action. It is unlikely that the book was a concerted attempt to impose order on the localities, as Charles did in his Court and Laud did in the Church, and perhaps shows a genuine, if over-ambitious, concern for the effectiveness of local government during a period of difficulty.

Finance

The most pressing issue that faced Charles on his dissolution of Parliament in March 1629 was that of finance. Without parliamentary support, an aggressive foreign policy was simply not feasible, and recognition of this was signalled by peace treaties with France in 1629 and Spain in 1630. However, ending hostilities was not sufficient in itself to solve Charles's financial problems. With a Crown debt of over £1 million, and insufficient funds to meet his day-to-day expenditure, Charles needed to find other solutions.

One obvious solution was to try and cut expenditure. Richard Weston, who was Lord Treasurer for the first half of the Personal Rule, took up where Cranfield had left off, and launched investigations into the navy and ordinance departments, as well as the royal household. The household alone accounted for around 40 per cent of the King's revenues, and potential for savings was identified in spending on food, drink and entertainments. However, such cuts were only a short-term solution, and although Weston was successful initially in achieving savings, he soon came up against familiar obstacles. To reduce royal expenditure permanently, reductions needed to be made in the number of people in the royal household, and the number of those receiving patronage through pensions, offices, annuities, etc. To do this would cut against the interests of too many people, not least the Crown, who needed to distribute such patronage to ensure the political goodwill of its dependants.

Another option was to try and increase income. One area that produced a great deal of revenue, largely of its own accord, was customs. With the ending of hostilities, trade was given a chance to flourish again, and English merchants were able to take advantage of the fact that much of the rest of Europe was at war to expand their trade routes. Tonnage and poundage continued to be collected, and by 1638 was bringing in over £170,000. The growth of trade also saw an increase in the revenues received from impositions, which were increased in number during the 1630s, and by the end of the decade were bringing in around £200,000. However, this growth in customs revenue was insufficient in itself to meet the Crown's needs, and Weston was forced to look at new means of raising revenue, which he did by exploiting the King's prerogative rights.

Prerogative taxation

Prerogative taxation was based on traditional rights of the Crown that dated back to the Middle Ages, many of which had fallen into disuse. The first of these that was identified and exploited was 'Distraint of Knighthood'. In theory, all men with incomes in excess of £40 a year were supposed to present themselves at the coronation of a new monarch to be knighted. However, as a result of the rapid inflation over the last century, many now found themselves in that bracket who would not previously have been considered to have been of a high enough social standing to be knights. This practice had fallen out of use, and Elizabeth and James had not enforced it, although technically those who had failed to fulfil this obligation could be liable to a fine. Charles appointed commissioners who identified and collected fines from more than 9,000 individuals, which in total brought in around £170,000. Although effective in raising revenue and undeniably legal, Distraint of Knighthood incurred a heavy political cost, targeting those whose support the King needed most. As Clarendon observed, 'it had a foundation in right, yet, in the circumstances of proceedings, was very grievous and no less unjust'.

Another source of income came from Forest Fines. The boundaries of the royal forests were declared to be those of the twelfth century, dating from the reign of Henry II, and those living and working within them were held to be doing so illegally. Most people who were technically guilty of this were unaware of any infringement on the royal forest, with many of their families having lived there for several generations. Various individuals were fined for enclosing land, engaging in agriculture, exploiting the forests' natural resources, and so on. But the breaches in the forest law were not reversed and enclosures, farms and mines remained. As with the Distraint of Knighthood, the aim of enforcing forest laws was not to remedy a wrong but to raise money for the Crown. And again the cost to the Crown was in terms of the goodwill of those who were penalised, and of those who were expected to extract these fines from their neighbours. It is also worth pointing out that although such measures were profitable, they were essentially 'one-off' devices which were not a long-term solution to the Crown's needs. In the words of the Venetian Ambassador: 'All these may be called false mines for obtaining money, because they are good for once only and states are not maintained by such devices.'

Other sources of prerogative revenue that were still in use by 1629 were systematised and more fully exploited. The court of wards was reformed by Cottington and by 1638–40 income from wardships had reached a maximum of £83,000, a significant increase from the 1617–22 maximum of £35,000. The income from recusancy fines rose from an average of £5,300 a year in the later 1620s to nearly £7,000 in 1634. Certain monopolies were revived by Charles, who claimed that the limitations placed on them by the 1624 Act applied only to individuals and not companies. The most profitable one was the so-called 'popish soap' monopoly, where the sole right of manufacture of soap was given to a company that included a number of Catholics. This brought the treasury £29,000 a year by 1636. However, the financial advantage that such monopolies brought to the Crown has to be set alongside the far larger profits made by the holders of such grants, and the public indignation that they produced. Monopolies had been a bone of contention since the reign of Elizabeth, and any overall benefit they brought to Charles is debatable. Clarendon's assessment was again critical: 'Projects of many kinds, many ridiculous, many scandalous, all very grievous, were set on foot; the envy and reproach of which came to the king, the profit to other men.'

Ship Money

The best known and most profitable source of additional revenue was Ship Money. It was a traditional levy that was made on coastal counties in times of national danger to provide for their safety by equipping the navy, and had been made use of by Charles in 1626–7. In 1634, writs for payment went out to coastal counties to provide against the attacks of pirates from North Africa. In 1635, the writs for Ship Money were extended to cover inland counties as well, a practice that continued until 1640. Despite some inevitable complaints, Ship Money was extremely successful, with a payment rate of around 97 per cent in its first three years, bringing in nearly £200,000 a year. The money was paid accordingly into the Treasury of the Navy, and Charles seemed to have been successful in finding a regular alternative to parliamentary taxation.

However, serious opposition emerged in the aftermath of the John Hampden case, in 1637. Hampden was taken to court for refusing to pay Ship Money, on the grounds that it was an extra-parliamentary form of tax, and therefore illegal. Of the twelve judges who heard the case seven found for the King and five for Hampden. In the light of the fact that the judges were royal appointees, many felt that such a narrow margin of defeat was in fact a moral victory for Hampden. In the aftermath of the case, payment of Ship Money fell to 80 per cent in 1638 and the following year, together with Charles's demands for Coat and Cloth Money to fight the Scots, payment collapsed to only 20 per cent. The ultimate failure of Ship Money was based less on constitutional principle, and more on financial realities. People would or could not pay twice over, putting those responsible for collecting these sums in a very difficult position. The Privy Council gave sheriffs the task of levying the sums allocated to their counties, and also made them liable for any short-fall. Yet, in order to carry out the wishes of central government, the sheriffs found themselves undermining their standing and prestige within their own localities. In the end, it would seem that most put their loyalty to their locality first.

Documents

The imposition of Ship Money and popular reaction to it have been the subject of considerable historical interest and speculation. Below are sources relating to Hampden's case and the rather different reactions of two contemporaries towards the imposition of the new rate:

A   No pretence of prerogative, royal power, necessity or danger, doth or can make it good. ... The common law in England sets a freedom in the subjects in respects of their persons, and gives them a true property in their goods and estates, so that without their consent – that is to say their private, actual consent, or in parliament – it cannot be taken from them.

> (From the judgement of Justice Sir George Croke for Hampden, 1638)

B   Where Mr Holborne (one of Hampden's lawyers) supposed a fundamental policy ... that in case the monarch of England should be inclined to extract from his subjects at his pleasure, he should be restrained, for that he could have nothing from them, but upon a common consent in Parliament. He is utterly mistaken herein ... the law knows no such king-yoking policy. The law is of itself an old and trusty of the King's; it is his instrument or means which he useth to govern his people by ... the King of mere right ought to have, and the people of mere duty are bound to yield unto the King, supply for the defence of the kingdom. And when the Parliament itself doth grant supply in that case, it is not merely a benevolence of the people, but therein they do an act of justice and duty to the King.

> (From the judgement of Justice Sir Robert Berkeley against Hampden, 1638)

C   All things are at this instant here in that calmness that there is very little matter of novelty to write, for there appears no change or alteration in either court or affairs. ... And although payments here are great (considering the people have not hereto fore been accustomed to them) yet they only privately breathe out a little discontented humour and lay down their purses, for I think that great tax of ship money is so well digested. ... I suppose it will become perpetual; for indeed if men would consider the great levies of monies in foreign parts for the services of the state, these impositions would appear but little burdens, but time can season and form minds to comply with public necessities.

> (A letter from John Burghe, a Cambridge academic, to Charles I's ambassador in Paris, October 1637)

D   [I] humbly beseecheth your Lordships that your said petitioner ... is no ways ... guilty of not collecting the said money. That he hath gone as far and further than the former Sheriffs ... have done when they gathered in a like sum of money as is now required. Therefore if the true grounds and reasons of the slow payment do not proceed from your said petitioner's neglect or contempt there are other sources thereof; deadness of trading, low prices of all commodities raised from the plough and pail, scarcity and want of money, great military charges of the last passed summer etc. with innumerable groans and sighs.

(A letter from Sir Simonds D'Ewes, Sheriff of Suffolk, to the Privy Council, explaining his problems in collecting Ship Money, June 1640)

1   How do Berkeley and Croke differ in their view of the legality of Ship Money, in sources A and B?
2   How do sources C and D differ in their analysis of public reaction to Ship Money?
3   How would you account for the differences between what Burghe and D'Ewes have to say in sources C and D?

Conclusions

In strictly economic terms, the Crown's financial policies were very successful. By the later 1630s income had risen to around £900,000 and more or less matched expenditure. However, against this was the fact that the debt still remained significant – £315,000 by 1637 – and that some future sources of income had already been pledged as security for loans. Despite this, the Crown was in a healthier financial position than it had been since the accession of James I. Yet while the expedients of the 1630s were sufficient for the King's ordinary needs, it was apparent that in order to conduct a war Charles still needed access to parliamentary taxation. The taxpayers' strike of 1639 demonstrated clearly that there were limits to which prerogative taxation could be pushed, and to which local government could be expected to work against its own interests. It was this realisation that was to lead Charles to summon Parliament again in 1640.

Wentworth and Ireland

The authority of a king is the keystone which closeth up the arch of order and government, which contains each part in due relation to the whole; and which, once shaken ... all the frame falls together in a confused heap of foundation and battlement, of strength and beauty.

(A letter from Sir Thomas Wentworth to Laud)

One of the most successful areas of Charles's administration, at least in the short term, was in Ireland. Sir Thomas Wentworth was sent there as Lord Deputy in 1633 and immediately set about imposing a policy of 'Thorough'. A term coined together with his friend and ally, William Laud, Thorough was a style of government that aimed at increasing the authority and powers of the Crown, and increasing the efficiency of the Government.

Ireland had traditionally been a drain on the English treasury and Wentworth set out to reverse the trend. He forced three subsidies through the Irish Parliament in 1634 and then refused to deal with its grievances, as he had previously promised. The 'Graces', or rights to hold property that the Catholic Irish and older English settlers had wanted confirmed, were not provided and instead Wentworth embarked on a new programme of plantations. Old families lost titles and lands to new Protestant settlers, who provided a new élite whose interests were closely tied to the Government. The powers of prerogative courts were expanded, fines imposed on those who infringed on the Crown's rights, and large areas were claimed as royal lands. In the Church, Laudians were appointed and a programme put into effect to try and reclaim ecclesiastical lands.

Through ruthlessness, energy and adept political manoeuvring, Wentworth achieved a great deal by the time he was recalled to England by Charles in 1639 to help deal with the Scots. Royal authority seemed established and Ireland brought into obedience. However, his policies alienated virtually every interest group in Ireland, except that of the new settlers, and within two years of his departure, his achievements had been swept away in the backlash of rebellion. His actions and approach to Government also alarmed many in England, who feared that his recall heralded the implementation of similar policies there, for which Ireland had only been a dry run.

Arminianism

With Archbishop Abbot's death in 1633, Laud was promoted to Canterbury and with the archbishopric of York already in the hands of his ally, Richard Neile, Arminian control over the Church hierarchy was almost complete. Although there were still a few traditional figures in senior positions, such as John Williams, Bishop of Lincoln, who were Calvinists theologically, the majority of the bishops' bench were Arminians. It was this group that clearly had the support of the King, who was content to leave the direction of Church affairs largely under the control of Laud.

The 1630s saw a determined and wide-reaching attempt at reform in the Church. Yet despite his distinctive theological views, Laud did not make any attempt to alter the 39 Articles or to make any new declarations of church doctrine. Instead he was more concerned to bring order and uniformity to the Church, by raising the quality and status of the clergy, and through his programme of 'Beauty of Holiness' to improve the state of Church buildings and increase the use of ceremony.

Beauty of Holiness

> This I have observed farther, that no one thing hath ... drawn aside from the sincerity of religion professed by the church of England, than the want of uniform and decent order in too many churches of the kingdom.

> (A letter from William Laud to Charles I)

For Laud, decency and order in church were central to his ideas of reform. Local rates were imposed, to provide for repairs to the fabric of churches, decoration and to supply items such as church organs. Although such works were undoubtedly needed, the levying of church taxes to pay for them was predictably unpopular. Laud was also determined to impose uniformity in church practice. Unlicensed preaching was suppressed, and the importance of the sacraments, particularly communion, emphasised: the Body of the Lord was to have greater importance than His Word. The use of ceremonies laid

Figure 4.1 Frontispiece from Thomas Fuller's *The Holy State* (1642)

down in the Prayer Book of 1559, but never consistently enforced, and not enforced at all since Archbishop Bancroft, was revived. The use of the sign of the cross, bowing at the name of Jesus, and the use of clerical vestments, were all now required, and clergy were brought before the Church courts if they refused to conform. Most controversially, Laud also made orders for the relocation of the altar to the east end of the church, where it should be railed in; as opposed to the previous practice, whereby a communion table was placed in the centre of the church.

Documents

Laud's reforms sparked a great deal of debate. Puritan pamphleteers suspected his motives and attacked the Archbishop for introducing popery into the church, and even Bishop Williams went into print, criticising the order to relocate the communion table, describing it as 'a needless controversy'. Laud himself stoutly defended his actions, insisting that they were necessary for the benefit of the Church. Some indication of the nature of the debate is given in the sources below:

A   Unity cannot long continue in the Church when uniformity is shut out at the church door. ... No external action in the world can be uniform without some ceremonies; and these in religion, the ancienter they be the better, so they may fit the time and place. Too many overburden the service of God, and too few leave it naked. And scarce anything hath hurt religion more in these broken times than an opinion in many men, that because Rome had thrust some unnecessary and many superstitious ceremonies upon the Church, therefore the Reformation must have none at all; not considering that ceremonies are the hedge that fence the substance of religion from all the indignities which profaneness and sacrilege too commonly put upon it.

(A letter from Laud to Charles, 1635)

B   There happened ... in the town of Tallow a very ill accident on Christmas Day, 1638, by reason of not having the communion table railed in, that it might be kept from profanations. For in sermon time a dog came to the table, and took the loaf of bread prepared for the holy sacrament in his mouth, and ran away with it. ... Some of the parishioners took the same from the dog, and set it again on the table. After sermon, the minister could not think fit to consecrate this bread ... so there was no communion.

(A letter from Laud to Charles, 1639)

C   John Starkys of Latton ... together with others was ringing in Latton Church after morning prayer ... did from the belfry repair to the communion table in the chancel of the church and pull down the rails from about the table with their hands ... and carry the broken rails near to the whipping post of that town and there set them on fire. ... He sayeth that the reason of his so pulling down the rails was because they gave offence to his conscience, and that the placing of them was against God's laws and the King's as appeareth by the 20th chapter of Exodus. [Note alongside: 'Skynner and Wennell removed the table and set it in the chancel, as it had formerly stood.']

(A record from proceedings against Starkys, 1640)

D

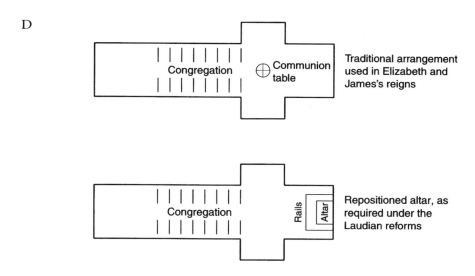

Figure 4.2 Positioning of the altar

1 According to sources A and B, what lay behind Laud's promotion of ceremony and the alterations to the altar?

2 Look at sources C and D. Why do you think Starkys and his associates acted as they did, and what would be their reaction to Laud's claims in sources A and B?

The clergy

Central to Laud's reforms was the need to have like-minded men in positions of power within the Church. Most of the key bishoprics were held by Arminians, men such as Wren at Norwich and Montague at Chichester, on whom Laud could rely to ensure uniformity within their dioceses. He wanted to elevate the status of bishops, to emphasise their divinely appointed authority and their role in promoting conformity within the Church. He was also determined that bishops should act in a manner that was worthy of their offices, and tried to discourage absenteeism and to prevent them financially exploiting their positions.

This concern for standards was reflected in the clergy as a whole. Laud insisted on the need to improve the level of education among the clergy, and seems to have met with some success, for instance by 1640 around 80 per cent of clergy within the diocese of Worcester were graduates. He was also successful in securing the appointment of many clergy as JPs, which in turn gave them greater status within their local area. Another area to which Laud turned his attention was that of the shortage of money in the Church. Many Church 'livings', that is lands designated to support the clergy of a particular parish, had been partially or wholly bought up by local landowners with the result that these parishes were drastically underfunded. Laud used Church courts, and where necessary the Privy Council, to try and force those people who held these 'impropriated tithes' to pay a percentage of the land's income to their local clergy.

The Personal Rule also saw increased activity of clergy outside their traditional, post-Reformation roles. Several bishops sat on the Privy Council and others held important Government posts, such as Bishop Juxon of London, who was Lord Treasurer. Others such as Laud became active in 'prerogative courts', such as the Star Chamber and the High Commission, and used them alongside Church courts to ensure conformity and to enforce the Church's rights.

While these reforms undoubtedly did much to raise the status and power of the Church, they were also extremely unpopular among many vested interest groups. The holders of impropriated tithes and those who had lost their positions as JPs in the localities, mainly from gentry families, did not welcome such reforms. The social origins of the Arminian bishops themselves were a cause for concern among many, who resented the powers that had been given to people such as Laud (son of a clothier) and Neile (son of a candle-maker). The activities of the Church and prerogative courts cut against the interests of some highly influential figures, and there was a great deal of public sympathy for those who fell foul of them, such as Bastwick, Burton and Prynne. In addition, there was a sense among many that the clergy were becoming too powerful, and that their emergence in secular Government and the law courts was an uncomfort- able reminder of pre-Reformation England.

The case of Bastwick, Burton and Prynne

Laud's most well-known use of prerogative courts was in pursuing a case against the Puritans, Bastwick, Burton and Prynne, in the Star Chamber. They had written pamphlets attacking Laud and his fellow bishops, and the Archbishop was adamant that they should be prosecuted accordingly:

A   Now I beseech you look upon the pride and ingratitude of (the bishops). ... Great
      and mighty are their privileges, and yet they are neither thankful to God nor the
      King ... but would have more. They have the keys of heaven to shut out who they
      will. They have the keys of Hell, to thrust in who they please. They have the keys
      also of our purses to pick them at their pleasure ... they have the keys likewise of
      all the prisons of the kingdom. ... If you should meet him (Laud) coming daily
      from the Star Chamber, and see what pomp, grandeur and magnificence he goeth
      in, having also a great number of gentlemen and other servants waiting on him;
      some of them carrying up his tail, for the better breaking and venting of his wind
      ... when he goeth in great state and in great power to Cambridge and Oxford ...
      with a rod in his hand ... to whip those naughty scholars, that will not learn well
      their lessons of conformity ... will not cringe to the altar, nor turn their faces to

the East, nor worship the communion table. ... For the Church is now as full of ceremonies, as a dog is full of fleas.

(*The Litany of John Bastwick*, 1637)

B   I have done nothing as a prelate ... but with a single heart, and with the sincere intention for the good government and honour of the Church, and the maintenance of the orthodox truth and religion of Christ ... in this Church of England. For my care of this church, the reducing of it into order ... and the settling of it to the rules of its first reformation, are the causes (and the sole causes, whatever may be pretended) of all this malicious storm. ... Our main crime is that we are bishops; were we not so, some of us might be passable as other men. And a great trouble 'tis to them that we maintain that our calling of bishops is *jure divino*, by divine right. ... No man can libel against our calling (as these men do), be it in pulpit, print or otherwise, but he libels against the King and the State, by whose laws we are established. Therefore these libels, so far forth as they are against our calling, are against the King and the Law, and can have no other purpose than to stir up sedition among the people.

(Laud's justification of proceedings against Bastwick, Burton and Prynne, 1637)

C   Dr. Bastwick spake first, and said had he a thousand lives he would give them all up for this cause. Mr. Prynne ... showed the disparity between ... the times of Queen Elizabeth, and the times then [of King Charles], and how far more dangerous it was now to write against a bishop or two than against a King or Queen ... that here they are fined £5,000 a piece, to be perpetually imprisoned in the remotest castles, where no friends must be permitted to see them, and to lose their ears without redemption ... [and] here he must be branded on both cheeks ... Mr. Burton ... spake much while in the pillory to the people. The executioner cut off his ears deep and close, in a cruel manner, with much effusion of blood, an artery being cut, as there was likewise of Dr. Bastwick. Then Mr. Prynne's cheeks were seared with an iron made exceeding hot; which done, the executioner cut off one of his ears and a piece of his cheek with it; then hacking the other ear almost off, he left it hanging and went down; but being called up again he cut it quite off.

(John Rushworth, *Historical Collections*, 1659)

1   What are the criticisms of the bishops and the church that Bastwick makes in source A?
2   What in Laud's view (source B) are the underlying reasons behind these criticisms? How does he justify the action taken against the libellers?
3   Considering the use of language and tone, what comments might be made about the reliability of source C?

An assessment of Laud

By 1640, the opposition to Laud and his policies had become increasingly public and hostile. One London pamphleteer insisted 'so odious hath he grown that we believe he stinketh in the nostrils of God', while another urged the city's apprentices to march on the Archbishop's residence, Lambeth Palace, resulting in the palace being stormed by a mob, around 500 strong. Although Laud escaped harm, he was subsequently impeached in 1641 by Parliament and imprisoned in the Tower, before he was finally executed in 1645. His opponents in Parliament had little doubt as to the nature of his crimes, as is revealed by extracts from his Impeachment Articles:

VII That he hath traitorously endeavoured to alter and subvert God's true Religion by law established in this realm; and instead thereof, to set up Popish Superstition and Idolatry; and to that end hath declared and maintained in Speeches and printed Books divers Popish Doctrines and Opinions, contrary to the Article of Religion established by law. He hath urged ... popish and superstitious ceremonies, without any warrant of law; and hath cruelly persecuted those who have opposed the same, by corporal punishment and imprisonment; and most unjustly vexed others who refused to conform thereto ... contrary to the law of the kingdom. ...

X   He hath traitorously and wickedly endeavoured to reconcile the Church of England with the Church of Rome.

1   Bearing in mind what you have read about Laud, and considering the summary table below, how far would you consider these charges to be accurate?

Table 4.1 Arminianism and the religious divide

Issue	Catholicism	Arminianism	Traditional Anglicanism	Puritanism
Ceremony	Central	Vital to maintenance of the dignity of church services	Some use of ceremony, though disregarded by many during reign of James I	Ceremony superstitious and popish
Role of priest	Central – mediates between God and humanity	Vital role in church services and performing the sacraments	Some significance	Limited role only – main function is preaching God's word
Predestination	Free will	Free will	←———— Considered to be a fundamental doctrine ————→	
Communion and the position of the altar	Transubstantiation – magic performed on the high altar at the east end of the church	Great spiritual significance – altar moved to east end of church and railed in	Remembrance only – communion table in centre of church ————————→	
Role of bishops	Answerable only to the Church and God	'Divine Right of Bishops' – though strong supporters of the King's divine right	Bishops accepted, but their role is to pastor rather than to discipline and enforce conformity	Suspicious of bishops; some wish to see the episcopacy abolished

Scotland and the First Bishops War

Contrary to his father, Charles had no real experience or understanding of Scottish politics. He had left Scotland at the age of four and was brought up in England thereafter. As King, he paid little personal attention to his northern kingdom (visiting only twice in 1633 and 1641), and his few interventions in Scottish affairs, such as his attempt to revoke grants of royal lands on his accession in 1625, had tended to the tactless and had been more successful in creating hostility than in producing their desired end. Added to this was the fact that, as in England, Charles had cut himself off from Scottish opinion to a large extent through his choice of advisers. As a result there was a danger that his policies could be both ill-considered and misunderstood by his northern subjects. This was particularly so in religion. One of James's great achievements in Scotland had been the creation of a modified form of Presbyterianism, which, while essentially Calvinist, facilitated a degree of royal control over the Church through a system of bishops. While this was acceptable to most Scots, this status quo was seriously threatened under Charles and Laud, as a result of their attempts to introduce Arminian policies into Scotland.

In October 1636, without any consultation with either the Scottish Parliament or Kirk (church assembly), Charles announced the imposition of a new Prayer Book. The Prayer Book was very similar to the English one, and included the positioning of altars at the east end of the church, kneeling for communion, confession and so forth. While in England strict adherence to these things was contentious, in Presbyterian Scotland it was simply unacceptable to the vast majority of the population. Charles's attempt to bring about religious order within his kingdoms was poorly judged. Riots ensued in churches where the new Prayer Book was used, and although his Scottish council advised its withdrawal, Charles refused to accept their advice. In February 1638, its opponents in Scotland responded by forming a 'National Covenant', which was to oppose these 'innovations and evils which have no warrant in the word of God and do tend to the re-establishing of popish religion and tyranny'. As the situation escalated, so the Scots' demands grew to include a reformation of the Church along continental lines, and in November 1638 the Kirk met and abolished the episcopacy.

Charles's response was mixed. To buy time, he announced the suspension of the Prayer Book, while making preparations to enforce obedience in his Scottish kingdom. However, his attempts to mobilise the militia and to raise money through loans and Coat and Cloth Money met with little enthusiasm south of the border. The army that he had managed to assemble by the summer of 1639 was clearly insufficient and he was forced to negotiate. He accepted a truce at Berwick in June, which disbanded both sides' armies and called for meetings of the Scottish Parliament and Kirk. However, the truce did not lead to a settlement. The Scots reiterated their demands for the removal of bishops from the Church and declared that every male in Scotland should be required to take the Covenant. Charles was equally determined not to back down. His response was to recall Wentworth from Ireland, who in turn advised him that he would need to recall Parliament if he were to raise the money he needed to pacify Scotland by force.

The Short Parliament and the Second Bishops War

Parliament met for the first time in eleven years on 13 April 1640. The King's opening remarks to the session suggest that he had learnt little in the interim of how to communicate his position effectively. He confined himself to commenting that: 'There never was a king that had more weighty cause to call his people together than myself. I will not trouble you with the particulars.' On Charles's behalf, Lord Keeper Finch laid out the Crown's priorities. First, sufficient supplies should be voted to crush the Scots. Second, tonnage and poundage should be granted 'to repair the insolence of previous parliaments'. Third, any parliamentary grievances would be listened to, if there was time; if not another session would be held later in the year to deal with them.

The reaction of the Commons was unfavourable. As the MP for Tavistock, John Pym observed: 'the last Parliament was dissolved before our grievances had been met'. Unsurprisingly, many suspected that granting supply to the Crown would again lead to such an outcome. Although the Lords were willing to provide subsidies immediately, the stance of the Commons was different: redress of grievances, *then* supply. Arminianism, the use of prerogative courts, monopolies, Ship Money, Coat and Cloth Money, and the collection of tonnage and poundage without parliamentary consent were all identified as points of concern. Indeed, some MPs sympathised with the Scots' stand against the introduction of Arminianism. They saw reconciliation rather than war with the northern kingdom as a more appropriate course of action, and began to draw up a petition to the King accordingly. Charles's reaction was one of anger and disbelief, and on 5 May he dissolved Parliament after only three weeks.

Together with Wentworth, who had recently been created the Earl of Strafford, Charles set about trying to identify alternative options. To rely on prerogative taxation was clearly not feasible, in the light of the taxpayers' strike in 1639, although a fresh batch of writs for Ship Money was sent out. Attempts to gain financial backing through a Spanish alliance and to bring native troops over from Ireland both failed, although they did succeed in further promoting the spectre of the King being under the influence of sinister Catholic forces. Some money was raised through a range of dubious means, such as the levying of a 'loan' from the City of London and the seizure of £130,000 worth of bullion deposited for safe keeping by private merchants at the Tower of London, but it was not enough for Charles's needs. In the light of these problems, it was decided to use the militia as the basis for an army. However, the idea proved to be ill-founded. Most militiamen's loyalty was to their county, and the traditional notion of the militia being a local defence force did not fit well with it being used to fight a war on the Scottish borders. The force that did finally muster in Yorkshire in July was effectively a conscript army, short of money and already significantly under strength through desertion.

When the Scots launched an offensive in August, with a well-disciplined force of 25,000 men, it was apparent that such forces as the King had at his disposal were insufficient. The King's forces were routed at the battle of Newburn and forced to abandon Newcastle and its coalfields to the Scots. Another truce was agreed in October, in which the King accepted the Scottish occupation of the border counties, and undertook to pay the Scots £850 a day, until final peace terms were arranged. Charles was in an impossible position. With winter approaching, the Scots were in control of London's coal supply and had to be appeased, and there was no hope of him being able to fulfil the financial obligations of the truce without parliamentary assistance. His only option was to summon Parliament once again, which he did in November 1640.

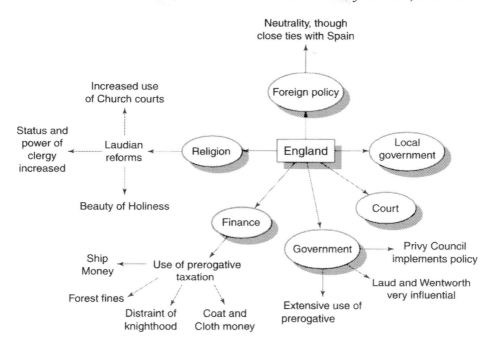

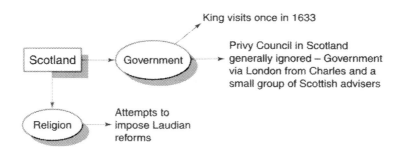

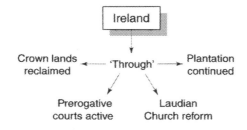

Figure 4.3 Summary of Charles I's Personal Rule in the Three Kingdoms

Analysis of the Personal Rule

The most serene, quiet and halcyon [happy] days that could possibly be imagined.

(Lord Falkland, 1641)

Looking back from the constitutional conflict and instability of 1641, Lord Falkland clearly had very fond memories of the Personal Rule; although they were not ones that were shared by all his parliamentary colleagues, or many later historians. How should we judge the 1630s? Coward's reminder that we 'ought not to rely excessively on hindsight' is particularly important when looking at the Personal Rule. There can be a tendency for us to assume that there was conflict everywhere, because we know that civil war was going to break out in 1642. As Coward points out: 'Too often historians, knowing that revolutionary events in the 1640s followed the 1630s … have been blinded to the positive aims of Charles' government and have predated the development of serious opposition to the crown.'

If this is the case, then how should we see John Hampden's opposition to Ship Money, and that of Bastwick, Burton and Prynne to Laud's reforms? Were they dramatic exceptions to the rule, or indications of the nation's mood as a whole? Was the Personal Rule essentially a period of success for Charles that was only undermined by the rebellion in Scotland, or a period of unacceptable constitutional and religious experiment, which would have collapsed of its own accord? Below are a range of interpretations.

Historians' verdicts

A   [The First Bishops War] was the first alarm England received towards any trouble, after it had enjoyed for so many years the most uninterrupted prosperity, in a full and plentiful peace, that any nation could be blessed with: and as there was no apprehension of trouble from within, so it was secured from without by a stronger fleet at sea than the nation had ever been acquainted with. … The revenue had been so well improved and so warily managed that there was money in the Exchequer proportionable for the undertaking of any enterprise: nor did this first noise of war and approach towards action seem to make any impression upon the minds of men, the Scots being in no degree either loved or feared by the people.

(Clarendon, *History of the Rebellion*, 1670s)

B   Many English Kings had occasionally committed unconstitutional acts: but none had ever systematically attempted to make himself a despot [*tyrant*], and to reduce the Parliament to a nullity [*nothingness*]. Such was the end which Charles distinctly proposed to himself. … The provisions of the Petition of Right were violated by him … a large part of the revenue was raised without any legal authority; and persons obnoxious to government languished for years in prison, without being called upon to plead before any tribunal. … The government was able to fine, imprison, pillory and mutilate without restraint. … The whole nation was alarmed and incensed. … At this crisis an act of insane bigotry suddenly changed the whole face of public affairs. Had the King been wise, he would have pursued a cautious and soothing policy towards Scotland till he was master in the South ... however, Charles and Laud determined to force on the Scots the English liturgy. ... To this step our country owes her freedom. The first performance of the foreign cere-monies produced a riot. The riot rapidly became a revolution. ... An attempt was made to put down the insurrection by the sword: but the King's military means and military talents were unequal to the task. ... No resource was left but a Parliament.

(Thomas Macaulay, *The History of England*, 1848)

C　Religion was a useful rallying cry. We must not exaggerate its importance. ... 'Religion was not the thing first contested for' said Cromwell, probably the Parliamentary leader for who religious questions meant the most; 'but God brought it to that issue at the last'. The cry of Protestantism in danger stirred deep patriotic feeling, and was pleasantly vague. ... The personal government of Charles I broke down ... because it lost the confidence of the propertied classes. There were no safe investments under the English *ancien régime*. ... In 1640 the government resorted to the desperate measures of a fraudulent bankrupt ... Sir John Davies had said, in a work dedicated to James I, 'The first and principal cause of making kings was to maintain property and contracts, and traffic and commerce among men'. James' son hardly performed this function. ... The government was brought down by a revolt of the taxpayers. In 1639, encouraged by the presence of the Scottish army, they went on strike; and the government was shown to be unable to exist without their goodwill.

(Christopher Hill, *The Century of Revolution*, 1961)

D　After the unruly scene of 1629, the early 1630s were marked by calm and quiet. ... Peace brought the expansion of trade and the benefits of neutrality in a Europe at war. The merchants soon abandoned their protests about customs duties. Some MPs imprisoned in 1629 made their apologies and were pardoned. Sir John Eliot himself faded from the public eye. His death in the Tower in 1632 attracted little attention. ... There may well have been support for government initiatives like the Book of Orders which tackled pressing problems. ... The calm and peace continued. The ordinary budget was better balanced. Ship money was generally paid despite diffi-culties. Undoubtedly, there were tensions and grievances; Charles' religious policy, framed to unite the realm in a common liturgy, divided the Church and alienated some gentry. But those tensions neither stimied [*obstructed*] government, nor threat-ened revolt. In the many volumes of correspondence, public and private, we find few demands for a parliament. Nor should that surprise us. ... After 1624 war necessitated frequent sessions; with the peace those circumstances changed.

War undoubtedly provided the opportunity for the expression of discontents. But more significantly ... it created problems and grievances not evident before. At court, the decision to fight the Scots meant the end of domestic reform, a crash from financial stability to indebtedness and the distraction of the council from the business of normal government. In the counties, that decision, like the wars of the

1620s, strained the fabric of local government and threatened the peace of local society.

(Kevin Sharpe, 'The Personal Rule of Charles I', in H. Tomlinson (ed.) *Before the English Civil War*, 1983)

E   The assassination of Buckingham and the end of the European war removed some of the most obvious causes of political friction, but the 'comparative political calm' of the 1630s was deceptive. Without parliaments there was no obvious arena where a principled challenge to the king's policies could be mounted, which is not to say that principled opposition did not exist. ... The attempts of Saye and Hampden to challenge the legality of (ship money) were untypical ... until the burdens of the Scottish war were added, most people paid ship money with little open dismay ... but alarm at the novelty of regular ship money levies is apparent in more private sources.

   ... Disquiet again affected broad social groups. Ship money sharply increased the numbers of those liable for national levies while religious and cultural divisions involved broad sections of society. Evidence is lacking for those outside the political elite, but it is probably again significant that so many of those returned as MPs in 1640 had distinguished themselves by opposition to the king's religious and political policies. The thousands who emigrated to the 'howling wilderness' of New England, along with the many more who considered the step, are testimony to the fears for true religion in England.

(Ann Hughes, *The Causes of the English Civil War*, 1991)

1   How do sources A and B disagree? What do you consider to be the most likely reasons for their different interpretations of the 1630s?

2   Why was the Personal Rule ultimately a failure, according to source C?

3   How far do sources D and E disagree over the degree of opposition to the Personal Rule?

4   Identify one source that you find most convincing, and one that you find least convincing in their analysis of the Personal Rule. Explain the grounds for your choice.

5 Political conflict, 1640–2

Table 5.1 The Long Parliament: main events, November 1640–January 1642

1640	November:	Long Parliament assembles
	December:	Votes to provide the King with limited funds to keep the Scots at bay
1641	February:	Triennial Act
	March–May	Trial and execution of Strafford
	May–June:	Prerogative taxation and courts abolished
	June:	The Ten Propositions
	August:	Charles leaves to negotiate peace with the Scots
	November:	Irish Rebellion
		Grand Remonstrance
		Charles returns from Scotland
	December:	Militia Bill
1642	January:	Attempted arrest of the Five Members
		The King leaves London

Attacking the prerogative, November 1640–September 1641

> There is a design to alter law and religion – the party that affects this are papists.
>
> (John Pym, speech to Parliament, 7 November 1640)

The first session of the Long Parliament ran from November 1640 to September 1641, and was remarkable for the degree of unity it displayed for most of that period. The vast majority of MPs were unified in their determination to undo the key features and mechanisms of the Personal Rule. Even figures like Lord Falkland and Sir Edward Hyde, who were to emerge later as the leaders of a parliamentary Royalist party, supported attempts to restrain the royal prerogative, and remove those individuals who they held responsible for having misled the King. Pym's claim above was representative of Parliament's approach: evil advisers around the King were trying to steer the nation towards absolutism and Catholicism, and it was them – not the King himself – that they opposed. They would seek to restore political harmony between the King and his people by restoring the traditional balance to a constitution that had been imbalanced by sinister elements, whose advice had led the King to misuse his prerogative.

The first concern of the parliamentary leaders, most notably the Earl of Bedford in the Lords and John Pym in the Commons, was to delay any permanent settlement with the Scots until they had secured their own position. While the Scots army remained on

English soil, Charles could not afford to dissolve Parliament and they could force him to make concessions. Parliament showed a willingness to co-operate to an extent by underwriting a Crown loan from the City of London in November, and voting two subsidies in December. However, all this enabled Charles to do was to keep the Scots paid for the time being. It came nowhere near providing him with the means to dispense with Parliament.

In order to safeguard their position, MPs were determined to ensure more regular parliaments. This was achieved under the Triennial Act, which Charles was persuaded to sign in February 1641. This required that Parliament should meet at least every three years, and for a minimum of fifty days. It was further strengthened on 10 May, by an act preventing the dissolution of Parliament without its own consent. This was a crucial measure from Parliament's point of view, which allowed them to attack the royal prerogative, without facing the threat of dissolution.

Trial of Strafford

In order to secure its own safety, the other key task identified by Parliament was the removal of the Earl of Strafford. Some ministers were impeached, such as Laud and Wren, and others, such as Windebank and Finch, had to flee to avoid a similar fate, but it was Strafford who seemed to inspire most fear and hatred among MPs. The most ruthless and able of Charles's advisers, Strafford had provoked widespread distrust through his activities in Ireland. Parliament was convinced that he wished to impose similar policies in England, and given the chance would do so using troops from Ireland. In the words of one MP, he was a 'spirit and instrument to act and execute ... wicked and bloody designs in these kingdoms'. Strafford was arrested within a week of Parliament meeting, and impeached by the Commons.

The main accusations levelled against Strafford were of alienating the King from his Parliament and urging an unnecessary war against the Scots; implementing arbitrary government in Ireland; and plotting to bring an army over from Ireland to do the same in England. Thus Strafford, according to the articles of impeachment drawn up by the Commons, was guilty of high treason. However, when his case came to trial before the Lords in March, it became apparent that despite the level of feeling against him, convicting him of treason would be difficult. Pym, acting as chief prosecutor, asserted that Strafford was guilty of treason, in that his actions had led to a breach between the King and his subjects. Yet the evidence to support this claim was patchy and inconclusive, and as the Earl himself pointed out, it was difficult to substantiate the charge of treason against a minister whose actions were taken with the support of the King. As it became apparent that it was unlikely that Strafford could be convicted on the charges against him, so the Commons changed their tactics and introduced a Bill of Attainder. Whereas guilt had to be proven according to the rules of law in an impeachment case, under a Bill of Attainder an individual could be held to be guilty of treason by a simple vote in both Houses of Parliament. The Commons voted in favour by 204 to 59 votes; and although the Lords delayed the bill initially, in the light of rumours of an army plot designed to rescue Strafford, they also voted in favour by a margin of 26 to 19. Under pressure from Parliament, and the London mob, who stormed the palace in Whitehall, Charles found himself forced to sign the Bill of Attainder, and Strafford was executed among great scenes of public rejoicing on 12 May at Tower Hill.

Destruction of prerogative government and the first signs of disunity

Strafford's death allowed Parliament to concentrate on other issues, in particular the limitation of the royal prerogative. Freed from the threat of dissolution, a series of acts were passed abolishing many of the key features of Charles's Personal Rule. The Prerogative Courts of Star Chamber and High Commission were abolished, and Ship Money and Distraint of Knighthood declared illegal. In addition, the limits of the royal forest were redefined, and the collection of tonnage and poundage without parliamentary consent outlawed.

Yet despite the fact that much of Parliament's agreed programme had been achieved by June 1641, there appeared to be little sign of political stability returning. From the point of view of Pym and his allies, the problem was how to safeguard the concessions that they had already won. They feared, with some justification, that if Charles had the opportunity, he would refuse to observe these limits on his prerogative, having only agreed to them under duress. Therefore, further restraints might be needed, in order to protect those that were already in place.

From Charles's perspective, any chance of co-operating with his opponents had been removed by the deaths of Bedford and Strafford. During April, Charles had offered positions in Government to some of his parliamentary critics, and there were possibilities that Bedford, the Earl of Essex, Lord Saye and Sele, Pym, Denzil Holles and Oliver St John would all be given offices. Bedford's death at the beginning of May removed the only one of this group for whom Charles had any measure of trust. Any remaining chance of compromise was removed by the opposition's refusal to spare Strafford, and Charles instead looked to build an alternative party within Parliament from those who had opposed Strafford's Attainder, such as Lord Digby.

Charles's hopes were strengthened by the first signs of disunity amongst Parliament. In addition to the disquiet felt by some MPs over the methods used to dispose of Strafford, the issue of religion was also causing some concern. In February 1641 the Commons had debated the Root and Branch Petition, which called for the abolition of the episcopacy. Although the Arminian bishops had done little to endear themselves to the parliamentary classes during the 1630s, many MPs feared that the removal of bishops from Church government could have dangerous implications. In a society that regarded hierarchy as a vital cornerstone, its removal in the Church might, by association, threaten that which operated in secular society. Despite heated debate over the issue in the Commons, no agreement could be reached beyond limiting the role of bishops in Government, and even this was rejected by the Lords. Petitioning by both sides continued over the summer, and certainly some MPs began to fear that Parliament might become a vehicle for dangerous religious and political radicalism.

This fear was compounded in June 1641, when Pym put forward his Ten Propositions. Although they were passed in both Houses, the Propositions contained a significant departure from the original programme that had united MPs in November 1640. They called for the King to submit his choice of ministers to Parliament for their approval, a measure that could not easily be presented as a correction of an imbalance of power that had grown up during the 1630s. The Crown's right to choose its ministers was an old and established part of the royal prerogative, and not something that Charles was likely to accept. Parliament had moved from reacting against the innovations of the Personal Rule, to suggesting innovations in its own right, something that gave great cause for concern to more conservative members. When Charles left to conclude a peace treaty with the Scots in August 1641, there were the first signs of the emergence of a royal party within Parliament, a prospect that had simply not existed nine months earlier.

Division: October 1641–January 1642

The Irish Rebellion and Grand Remonstrance

When Parliament reconvened at the end of October, Pym again raised the two matters that had created the first signs of division in the summer: parliamentary approval of ministers and the removal of bishops from the House of Lords. In order to protect the gains that had already been made, Pym seems to have identified control over the King's ministers as a key issue; while he hoped that reforming the powers of the bishops could satisfy the minimum requirements of more radical members, without alienating the more conservative ones. However, Pym's hopes of uniting Parliament behind this relatively limited programme were almost immediately undermined by the news of rebellion in Ireland.

Irish Catholics, who had suffered under Wentworth's religious and land reforms, rose up against their Protestant masters, and vivid stories of their massacre reached London by the beginning of November. The news had an enormous impact in England, fanning the flames of anti-Catholic hysteria and even raising the possibility of the King's complicity in the events in Ireland. An indication of the nature of the rebellion and its potential effects on the English political situation is given in the sources below:

Documents

A   Irish Catholics are a nation not conquered, nor ought they to live under the laws that have late been enacted: they ought to have free use of their religion, without interruption, which they now have cause to fear would be restrained, if not utterly taken away: therefore we which are constant friends to the Catholic faith, proclaim to all our loving brethren, that it is high time to stir ... and come now to assist us who are now in the field to defend the religion with our swords.

(Proclamation of the rebels, October 1641)

B   Charles, by the grace of God, king of England, Scotland, France and Ireland, defender of the faith, etc. to all Catholic subjects within the kingdom of Ireland, greeting: [the Parliament in England] hath not only presumed to take upon them the government and disposition of those princely rights and prerogatives ... but also have possessed themselves of the whole strength of the kingdom, in appointing governors, commanders and officers in all places therein, at their own will and pleasure without our consent ... [such things] are very likely to be carried out by the vehemence of the Protestant party of the kingdom of Ireland, and endanger our regal power and royal authority there also. ... Use all politic means and ways possible to possess ... all the forts, castles and places of strength and defence within the kingdom ... also to arrest and seize the goods, estates, and persons of all the English Protestants, within the said kingdom to our use.

(A royal commission, almost certainly a forgery, published in Ireland, October 1641)

C The rebels daily increase in men and munitions ... exercising all manner of cruelties, and striving who can be most barbarously exquisite in tormenting the poor Protestants, wheresoever they come, cutting off the privy members, ears, fingers and hands, plucking out their eyes, boiling the heads of little children before their mothers' faces, and then ripping out their mothers' bowels, stripping women naked ... driving men, women, and children, by hundreds together upon bridges, and from thence to cast them down into rivers, such as drowned not, they knock their brains out with poles, or shoot them with muskets, that endeavour to escape by swimming out; ravishing wives before their husbands' faces, and virgins before their parents' faces, after they have abused their bodies, making them renounce their religion, and then marry them to the basest of their fellows.

Oh that the Lord, who hath moved the kingdoms of England and Scotland, to send relief to those afflicted Protestants, would likewise stir them to effect their undertaking, with all possible expedition [*speed*], lest it be too late!

(A letter from Ireland, read out to the House of Commons, December 1641)

D

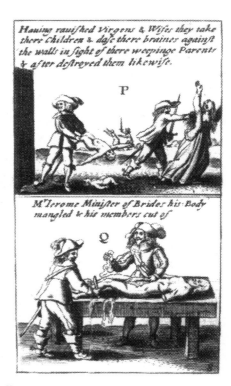

Figure 5.1 A Protestant view of the Irish Rebellion (1641)

1　Judging from source A, what were the aims of the Irish rebels?
2　According to source B, why was Charles willing to lend his support to the rebellion?
3　Despite the fact that source B is probably a forgery, how far do you think it may have been believed by the King's opponents in England?
4　What comments might be made over the reliability of sources C and D?

The effects of the Irish Rebellion on the English political scene were enormous. It was clear that action needed to be taken: added to Parliament's desire to save their co-religionists, was a widespread fear that such a rebellion would lead to an invasion of England itself. The problem that faced Pym and his supporters was who would control the army that would have to be raised to deal with the rebellion. They feared that if the army was under the King's control, once it had dealt with the Irish it might be used against Parliament. The gains of the last year would be lost, Parliament dissolved and prerogative rule restored. From Charles's point of view, to relinquish his right to lead the army was unacceptable. Not only did it strip the Crown of one of its most fundamental prerogatives, but it could also open the way for any such force to be used against him, to ensure further erosions of his power.

It was against this background that Pym suggested that the King be sent an 'Additional Instruction', which would urge him to use only 'such councillors as should be approved by Parliament', or else Parliament would be forced to 'take such a course for the securing of Ireland as might likewise secure ourselves'. Such a suggestion that Parliament might raise an army on its own authority if the King did not meet its demands was bound to create further tensions. The Instruction was only passed in the face of stiff opposition, led by Sir Edward Hyde, by 151 to 110 votes.

Pym then immediately produced a revised list of parliamentary grievances and demands in the 'Grand Remonstrance'. It dealt with a wide range of issues, but its most important clauses were those that insisted on Parliament's right to choose the King's ministers and control any army sent to Ireland. Added to this were demands for restricting the powers of bishops, and the call for a Church assembly to consider the need for further religious reform. Such calls to limit the King's powers further, along with vague references to religious change, were too much for many moderates, and the Grand Remonstrance was only passed by a margin of 159 to 148 amid stormy scenes in the Commons on 22 November. It was not only its content that alarmed many MPs, but also the violence of its language and the fact that it was designed to put Parliament's case not to the King, but before the people. As Sir Edward Dering complained: 'When I first heard of a remonstrance, I imagined like faithful councillors we should hold a glass up to his Majesty … I did not dream that we should remonstrate downwards and tell stories to the people.' Any appeal to popular opinion was seen as dangerous by conservatives, who feared that the involvement of the masses in political debate could in turn threaten their own position.

The Grand Remonstrance illustrated that by the end of November 1641, a year after its first meeting, Parliament was split down the middle. Pym's initially moderate proposals, designed to remedy the excesses of the Personal Rule, had become more extreme as he sought to protect the concessions that had already been extracted from

Charles. In Gerald Aylmer's words, Pym was forced 'to adopt radical and eventually revolutionary policies in order to secure conservative objectives'. In doing so, however, he had broken parliamentary unity and helped to create a substantial body of Royalist support. One of the preconditions of civil war – the existence of two sides – had been met.

The Five Members Incident

When Charles returned from Scotland on 25 November, he found his position had improved significantly in his absence. He had support from influential moderates such as Hyde and Falkland, and faced a divided opposition. These divisions within the Commons were further demonstrated on 7 December when a bill introduced by Arthur Haselrig proposed that control of the fleet and militia be given to an admiral and general nominated by Parliament. His Militia Bill's first reading was approved by 158 to 125 votes. Yet, such developments also demonstrated that Charles's position was still far from ideal. His opponents still had a majority in the Commons and were continuing to demand further reforms. Following elections to the council of the City of London at the end of December, in which some of his supporters were displaced by candidates with links to the opposition, he decided to take action.

As in 1629, Charles seems to have been convinced that opposition within Parliament was largely the result of the influence of a small group of troublemakers. If this group of extremists could be removed, then perhaps the more moderate voices in Parliament would be able to reassert themselves and co-operation with the Crown might again be possible. He was encouraged in this by the Queen, who was determined to see her husband take a more decisive line with his opponents. On 3 January 1642, orders were issued accordingly for the arrest on the grounds of High Treason of Lord Kimbolton and five MPs from the Commons: namely Denzil Holles, Sir Arthur Haselrig, John Pym, John Hampden and William Strode.

The following day, the King entered the Commons, accompanied by an armed guard. However, the five members had been warned of the King's actions, and had already fled and taken refuge with supporters in the city. Charles failed in his attempts to press the Speaker to reveal their whereabouts, and was forced to leave empty handed. Not only had the King failed to carry out his *coup* effectively, but he had misjudged the situation. His actions were a clear breach of parliamentary privilege and allowed his opponents to cast him as an aggressor with no respect for the constitution. Humiliated and concerned for the safety of his family in an increasingly hostile capital, Charles left London on 10 January for Hampton Court.

Documents

Below are documents relating to the incident, including two eye witness accounts of the attempted arrest of the five members:

A   The charges against the Five Members:

i)   That they have traitorously endeavoured to subvert the fundamental laws and government of the kingdom of England, to deprive the King of his regal power, and to place ... an arbitrary and tyrannical power over the lives, liberties and estates of his Majesty's ... people.

ii) That they have traitorously endeavoured, by many foul aspersions upon his Majesty and his government, to alienate the affections of his people ...

iii) That they have endeavoured to draw his Majesty's late army ... to side with them in their designs.

iv) That they have traitorously invited and encouraged a foreign power to invade his Majesty's kingdom of England.

v) That they have traitorously endeavoured to subvert the rights and very being of parliaments.

vi) And that they have traitorously conspired to levy, and actually have levied, war against the King.

B   The King came, with all his guard ... and two or three hundred soldiers and gentlemen. The King commanded the soldiers to stay in the hall, and sent us word that he was at the door ... the King then came to the door ... and commanded all that came with him, upon their lives not to come in. ... Then the King came upwards, towards the chair, with his hat off, and the speaker stepped out to meet him. Then the King stepped up in his place, and stood up on the step, but sat not down in the chair. After he had looked a great while, he told us he would not break our privileges but treason had no privilege; he came for those five gentlemen. ... Then he asked the speaker if they were here or where they were. Upon that the Speaker fell on his knees, and desired his excuse for he was a servant of the House, and had neither eyes, nor tongue, to see or say anything but what they commanded him. Then the King told him ... he did expect the House should send them to him, and if they did not he would seek them himself, for their treason was foul. ... Then he assured us that they should have a fair trial, and so went out, putting off his hat till he came to the door.

(Sir Ralph Verney, *Notes of the Proceedings of the Long Parliament*)

C   His Majesty ... came to the house, attended with a great multitude of men, armed in warlike manner with halberds, swords and pistols, who came up to the very door of the House, and placed themselves there ... to the very great terror and disturbance of the members then sitting. ... And his Majesty, having placed himself in the Speaker's chair, demanded of them the persons of the said members to be delivered unto him, which is a high breach of the rights and privileges of Parliament and inconsistent with the liberties and freedoms thereof. ... And afterwards his Majesty did issue forth several warrants ... for the apprehension of the persons of the said members; which by law he cannot do. ... Many soldiers, Papists and others, to the number of about five hundred, came with his Majesty ... armed with pistols and swords and other weapons, and divers of them pressed to the door of the said House ... some holding up their pistols ready cocked near the said door and saying 'I am a good marksman; I can hit right, I warrant you.' ... afterwards some of them being demanded what they thought the said company intended ... answered that

... if the word had been given, they should have fallen upon the House of Commons and have cut all their throats.

(*The Commons Journal*, 6 January 1642)

1 What actions of Parliament could the King have pointed to, in order to back up his accusations in source A?
2 How far would *you* accept the validity of the charges in source A?
3 How do the accounts of the attempted arrest of the Five Members differ in sources B and C?
4 What use does the author of source C make of language and tone to put his message across?
5 What concerns would you have over using this collection of documents as a basis for studying the Five Members Incident?

The drift into war

The Civil War started in August 1642, but much of the previous months were spent by both sides in waging a propaganda war and preparing for hostilities. Although the King's departure from London in January had increased the possibility of armed conflict, it was not until March that this became a probability with the issue of the Militia Ordinance. The King's refusal to accept the Militia Bill led Parliament to respond by issuing an ordinance on its own authority, which put the militia under the control of Lords Lieutenant of its own appointment. The justification of this move was to defend the nation against 'the blood counsels of papists and other ill-affected persons' and to ensure 'the safety of his Majesty's person'. Interestingly, Parliament was still portraying its actions as those of loyal subjects opposing the sinister forces around the King, at least for the sake of public consumption.

The Militia Ordinance had claimed new, emergency powers on Parliament's behalf. It prompted the withdrawal of Royalist MPs, either to their localities to rally support, or to join the King who was now at York. The Queen had already left for Holland to buy arms and munitions, and Charles himself was involved in a failed attempt to seize the northern arsenal at Hull, which contained enough weaponry to supply around 16,000 men. Despite such actions, both sides were reluctant to take any steps that might allow the other to portray them as the aggressor. As late as June, Parliament issued the Nineteen Propositions, which laid out its terms for a peaceful settlement:

1) Your Majesty's Privy Council and such great officers and ministers of state ... shall be approved by both Houses of Parliament.
2) That the great affairs of the kingdom ... may be debated, resolved and transacted only in Parliament.
4/5) They unto whom the government and education of the King's children shall be committed shall be approved of by both Houses of Parliament ... and that no marriage shall be concluded or treated for any of the King's children, with any foreign prince ... without the consent of Parliament.

8) That your Majesty would be pleased to consent that such a reformation be made of Church government and liturgy as parliament shall advise.

9/16) That your Majesty will [accept] the course that the Lords and Commons have appointed for ordering the militia ... that the ... military forces now attending your Majesty may be removed and discharged.

13) That the justice of Parliament may pass upon all delinquents.

15) That the forts and castles of this kingdom may be put under the command and custody of such persons as your Majesty will appoint with the [agreement] of your Parliament.

17) That your Majesty will be pleased to enter into a more strict alliance with the States of the United Provinces and other neighbouring princes and states of the Protestant religion.

19) That your Majesty will be graciously pleased to pass a bill restraining Peers made hereafter from sitting or voting in Parliament, unless they be admitted thereunto with the consent of both Houses of Parliament.

The King made his reply as follows:

> There be three kinds of government among men; absolute monarchy, aristocracy and democracy ... [these work] as long as the balance hangs even between the three estates ... the ill of absolute monarchy is tyranny, the ill of the aristocracy is faction and division, the ill of the democracy are tumults ... [and] violence.
>
> In this kingdom the laws are jointly made by a king, by a House of Peers, and by a House of Commons. ... The government, according to these laws, is trusted to the King. ... The prince may not make use of this high and perpetual power to the hurt of those for whose good he hath it. ... The House of Commons (an excellent convenor of liberty, but never intended for any share in government, or in the choosing of them that govern) is solely entrusted with the levy of money, and the impeaching of those who for their own ends have violated the law. ... The Lords, being trusted with judiciary power, are an excellent screen between the prince and the people, to assist each other against the encroachments of the other.
>
> Since therefore the power, legally placed in both houses, is more than sufficient to restrain the power of tyranny ... we shall not be able to discharge that trust which is the end of monarchy, since this would be a total subversion of the fundamental laws, and that excellent constitution of this kingdom ... the Church ... would in all probability follow the fate of the (monarchy) ... till at last the common people ... destroy all rights and properties, all distinctions of families and merit, and by this means this splendid and excellently distinguished form of government end in a dark, equal chaos of confusion.

1 What demands are included in the Nineteen Proposals that Parliament had not made before?

2 What areas of the royal prerogative would be left in the King's hands if he accepted these Proposals?

3 According to Charles how should the Government of England function, and why is it unnecessary for him to relinquish any of his powers?

4   According to the King, what would be the consequences of his agreeing to the Nineteen Proposals?

5   How would you account for the tone and contents of both the Nineteen Proposals and the King's reply to them?

Following his rejection of the Nineteen Proposals, in June Charles issued his own orders to his supporters in the Commissions of Array, which commanded them to start gathering troops and arms for his service. Many local gentry found themselves in an awkward position, being commanded by both sides to secure the local militia and arsenal for them. Over the summer, some localities saw violent confrontations between rival groups, but still more witnessed a reluctance to take sides. When the King finally signalled the beginning of the Civil War on 22 August by raising his standard at Nottingham, although both sides had been able to attract armed support, there seems to have been little general enthusiasm for war. As the inhabitants of Cheshire protested in their declaration of neutrality, to them the King and Parliament were like Siamese twins and 'must laugh and cry, live and die together; and both are so rooted in our loyal hearts that we cannot disjoint them'.

Table 5.2 Summary: The drift to war, 1642

January:	Attempted arrest of the Five Members
	Charles leaves London and takes up residence at Hampton Court
February:	Queen Henrietta-Maria leaves England to buy arms and munitions on the Continent
March:	Militia Ordinance
	Charles moves to York
April:	Charles attempts to seize the northern arsenal at Hull
June:	Nineteen Propositions
	Charles issues Commissions of Array
August:	The King raises his royal standard at Nottingham, signalling the beginning of hostilities

The outbreak of war: historians' views

The outbreak of the Civil War in 1642 was undoubtedly one of the pivotal moments of the seventeenth century, and as such has attracted a huge amount of attention from historians. How is the interruption of over 160 years of domestic peace to be interpreted? How far back do the roots of conflict go, and in what areas should we seek them: the economy, society, personalities, ideology, Government structures, or perhaps a mixture of these?

Traditionally, Whig historians sought to explain the Civil War in terms of the clash between liberty and absolutism, as Parliament struggled to prevent the King from undermining the traditional rights and freedoms of the English people. This interpretation was challenged, however, by Marxists who shifted the focus away from constitutional issues, emphasising instead the role of class conflict in provoking hostilities. Even so, what both 'schools' did share was a sense of inevitability about the Civil War. The nation was plunged into war by a monarchy trying to stand against the tide of history, whether it was seen in the form of an increasingly confident Parliament or a rising bourgeois class.

More recently, revisionists have challenged these ideas of determinism, but have not necessarily managed to reach a consensus over alternative explanations. While some have emphasised the role of short-term factors, such as Charles's personality and the divisive effects of his religious policies, others (sometimes termed 'post-revisionists') have seen the English Civil War as part of a larger British context, or have suggested that longer-term factors may, after all, have had an important place in provoking conflict.

This division of opinion is reflected in the sources below:

A   The English Revolution of 1640–1660 was a great social movement like the French Revolution of 1789. An old order that was essentially feudal was destroyed by violence, a new and capitalist social order created in its place. The Civil War was a class war, in which the despotism of Charles I was defended by the reactionary forces of the established Church and feudal landlords. Parliament beat the King because it could appeal to the enthusiastic support of trading and industrial classes in town and countryside, to yeomen and progressive gentry, and to wider masses of the population whenever they were able by free discussion to understand what the struggle was really about. ... The seventeenth-century English Revolution changed the organisation of society so as to make possible the full development of all the resources of that society. A transition to socialism will be necessary to win the same result in England today.

(Christopher Hill, *The English Revolution 1640*, 1940)

B   The Crown had weathered the storm induced by a century of population growth and price inflation. By the 1630s ... the economic and social outlook was rosier. The Crown doubled its real income between 1630 and 1637 and had the lowest national debt in Europe. ... Far from being a state sliding into civil war and anarchy, the early Stuart state saw ... fewer treason trials, no revolts, fewer riots. ... It can thus be argued that the civil wars grew out of the policies and out of the particular failings of a particular king, Charles I. ... Constitutional issues were the occasion of the civil war but not the main cause. ... It was the religious issue which stood out as the decisive one. ... The civil war was not a clash of social groups; it was the result of incompetent kingship which allowed religious militants to settle their disputes about the nature of the church ... by fighting it out. It was the last and greatest of Europe's Wars of Religion.

(John Morrill, 'What was the English Revolution?', *History Today*, March 1984)

C   It must be emphasised that the Civil War arose after more than a century of significant economic and social change. Between the 1520s and the 1620s, the population of England probably doubled from about 2.3 million to 4.6 million; in the same period prices rose dramatically ... population rose faster than the resources to support it; and those resources were in any case concentrated on the most prosperous section of society. ... The increasing numbers of the poor and uncertainty about the attitudes of independent middling groups were a crucial factor in the fears of Charles and his supporters at the growth of 'popularity'. The unrest of the early 1640s, particularly in London ... played a large part in attracting gentry support to the king and his emphasis on order, obedience and hierarchy. ... On the other hand ... the social alliance of the respectable in defence of true religion and English laws and liberties can be seen as an alternative response to the social tensions of the century.

In the long period of social change from the early sixteenth century, sharp divisions emerged over religion and politics and different choices on the future development of England slowly and ambiguously emerged. This is not to argue that a conflict in the form which erupted in 1642 was in any sense inevitable. However ... in these circumstances settlement was much harder to achieve.

(Richard Cust and Ann Hughes, 'Introduction; After revisionism', in *Conflict in Early Stuart England*, 1989)

D   [The Civil War] was the result of three long-term causes of instability, all of them well established before Charles came to the throne ... the problem of multiple kingdoms, the problem of religious division, and the breakdown of a financial and political system in the face of inflation and the rising cost of war ... it took the conjunction of the three of them to drive England into civil war ... both the religious and financial problem had been visible by the 1550s, and they had not created civil war in ninety years since then ... the attempt Charles made in 1637 to enforce English religion on Scotland was ... the likeliest reason for a merging of these three long-term causes of instability.

The English Civil War is the name we give to that part of the British Civil Wars which was fought by Englishmen on English soil. That part is rather a small one. It is not even the first part of the British Civil Wars; Newburn held that honour, followed by the Irish Rebellion. ... After the King was defeated ... the struggle between King and Parliament was rapidly broadening out into a struggle between England and the rest for supremacy over the British Isles ... it was the same issue which had been at stake at the very beginning of the troubles in 1637. ... If we look at the British Civil Wars as a whole it is clear that they began and ended as a struggle between England and the rest for supremacy over the British Isles. Because England began this struggle under a highly unpopular regime, the struggle divided England itself. ... The English Civil War, then, was something of a diversion; it was the fourth round in a ten round battle.

(Conrad Russell, *The Causes of the English Civil War*, 1990)

E   Charles I was ill-suited to cope with his plight, and must rank as one of the most inept of all English kings. Possessing none of the flexibility of his father, he shared to the full James' views on the divinity of kingship; he also had a total conviction in his own rectitude [*correctness*]. While it would be foolish to conclude that the Civil war occurred simply because Charles was king, it would be equally foolish to underestimate the part played by his personality ... Charles' attitude had immediate political consequences. He failed to appreciate the need to explain his action – never one of James' failings. His terse speeches from his throne to his Parliaments reveal not only his awkwardness but also his vision of rule: the proper course was conformity not argument. ... Charles can be afforded few accolades for statesmanship, and the distrust with which many of his subjects later viewed him is readily comprehensible. As disaster loomed even Laud sadly concluded that the King 'neither know how to be, nor to be made, great'.

(Derek Hirst, *Authority and Conflict: England, 1603–58*, 1986)

1   How does source A seek to explain the outbreak of civil war?
2   How does source B challenge this interpretation?
3   How does the approach of Cust and Hughes in source C try to qualify Morrill's argument?
4   How does Russell seek to explain the English Civil War in source D? How convincing do you find his arguments?
5   How far do you agree with Hirst's analysis in source E that Charles's personality was a crucial element in causing civil war?

6   Civil war, 1642–6

Side-taking

Documents

With the coming of civil war, many people were forced to consider, some for the first time, where their loyalties should lie. Below are a number of sources that give an indication of how their allegiances were decided:

A   A great part of the Lords forsook the Parliament, and so did many of the House of Commons, and came to the King; but that was, for the most of them, after the Edgehill fight. ... A very great part of the knights and gentlemen of England in the counties (who were not Parliament men) adhered to the King; except in Middlesex, Essex, Suffolk, Norfolk, Cambridgeshire etc. where the King with his army never came. And could he have got footing there, it's like that it would have been there as it was in other places. And most of the tenants of these poor gentlemen, and also most of the poorest of the people, whom the other called the rabble, did follow the gentry and were for the King.

   On the Parliament's side were the smaller part of the gentry in most of the counties, and the greatest part of the tradesmen and freeholders and middle sort of men, especially in those corporations and counties which depend on clothing and such manufactures ... the reasons which the party themselves gave was because, say they, the tradesmen have a correspondence with London, and so are grown to be a far more intelligent sort of men than the ignorant peasants that are like brutes, who will follow any that they think the strongest ... and the freeholders, say they, were not enslaved to their landlords as the tenants are. ... The other side [the King's] said, that the reason was because the gentry, who commanded their tenants, did better understand affairs of state than half-witted tradesmen and freeholders do.

   It was principally the differences about religious matter that filled up the Parliament's armies and put the valour and resolution into their soldiers. Not that the matter of bishops or no bishops was the main thing (for thousands that wished for good bishops were on the Parliament's side) ... but the generality of the people through the land (I say not all, or every one) who were then called Puritans ... that used to talk of God, and heaven, and Scripture, and holiness ... adhered to the Parliament. And on the other side, the gentry that were not so precise or strict against an oath, or gaming, or plays, or drinking, nor troubled themselves so much about the world to come ... but went to church and heard Common Prayer, and glad to hear a sermon which lashed the Puritans ... were against the Parliament.

(Richard Baxter, *Autobiography*, 1680s)

B   For my part, I do not like the quarrel, and do heartily wish that the king would yield and consent to what they [Parliament] desire; so that my conscience is only concerned in honour and in gratitude to follow my master. I have eaten his bread, and served him near thirty years, and will not do so base a thing as forsake him; and choose rather to lose my life (which I am sure I shall do) to preserve and defend those things which are against my conscience to preserve and defend; for I will deal freely with you, I have no reverence for the bishops, for whom this quarrel [exists].

(The words of Sir Edmund Verney, recorded in Clarendon, *History of the Rebellion*, 1670s)

C   Sir John Gell, a Derbyshire gentleman, who had been sheriff of the county, at that time when the illegal tax of ship money was exacted, and was so violent in the prosecution of it ... that he looked to punishment from the Parliament; to prevent it, he very early put himself into their service, and ... prevented the cavalier gentry from seizing the town of Derby, and fortified it, and raised a regiment of foot. ... No man knew for what reason he chose that side; for he had no understanding enough to judge the fairness of the cause, nor piety or holiness; being a foul adulterer all the time he served the Parliament, and so unjust, that without any remorse, he suffered his men indifferently to plunder both honest men and cavaliers.

(Lucy Hutchinson, *The Memoirs of Colonel Hutchinson*, 1660s)

D   Henry Marten ... was a great lover of pretty girls, to whom he was so liberal that he spent the greatest part of his estate. When he found a married woman that he liked ... he would contrive such or such a good bargain, twenty or thirty pounds per annum, to have her near him. He lived from his wife a long time ... King Charles had a complaint against him for his wenching [*womanising*]. It happened that Henry was in Hyde Park one time when his Majesty was there, going to see a race. The King espied him, and said aloud: 'Let that ugly rascal be gone out of the park, that whoremaster, or else I will not see the sport.' ... So Henry went away patiently, but it lay stored up deep in his heart. ... He was as far from a Puritan as light from darkness [but] shortly after he was chosen Knight of the Shire [i.e. elected as MP] ... and proved a deadly enemy to the King.

(J. Aubrey, *Brief Lives*, 1680)

E   Oh, sweetheart, I am now in a great straights [*dilemma*] what to do. Walking this other morning at Westminster, Sir John Potts ... saluted me with a commission ... to take upon me, by virtue of an Ordinance of Parliament, my company and command [in the Norfolk militia] again. I was surprised what to do, whether to take or refuse. 'Twas no place to dispute, so I took it and desired some time to advise upon it. I had not received this many hours, but I met with a Declaration point blank against it by the King ... I shall do according to my conscience; and this is the resolution of all honest men I can speak with. In the meantime, I hold it good wisdom and security to keep my company as close to me as I can in these dangerous times, and to stay out of the way of my new masters.

(A letter from the MP, Thomas Knyvett, to his wife, May 1642)

F   Every county had the civil war, more or less, within itself. Some counties were in the beginning so wholly for the Parliament, that the King's interest appeared not in them; some so wholly for the King, that the godly, for those were generally the Parliament's friends, were forced to foresake their habitations, and seek other shelters: of this sort was Nottinghamshire. All the nobility and gentry, and their dependants, were generally for the King, ... Sir Thomas Hutchinson continued with the Parliament, was firm to their cause, but infinitely desirous the difference might rather have been composed by accommodation [*agreement*], than ended by conquest ... Mr. Henry Ireton ... had an education in the strictest ways of godliness, and being a very grave and solid person ... was the chief promoter of the Parliament's interest in the county.

(Lucy Hutchinson, *Memoirs of Colonel Hutchinson*, 1660s)

1   According to Baxter, how did social and economic factors affect which side people fought for?
2   What was the role of religion in determining allegiance?
3   How far might Baxter's analysis need to be qualified in the light of sources B–F?

Baxter's analysis of side-taking highlights the social and economic differences between the two sides, and it is one that has a certain amount to recommend it (see Figure 6.1). Marxist historians have been quick to point out that the parts of the country where the King had most support were in the north, the west and in Wales, agricultural areas that were relatively backward economically and in which the old feudal bonds of tenant farmers and labourers to great landlords and traditional religion were still strong. The areas in which parliamentary support was the strongest, conversely, were the south and the east, which were more advanced economically, and more involved in trade and commerce. Other economically advanced areas elsewhere in the country, such as the West Riding of Yorkshire, a centre of cloth manufacturing, were also Parliamentarian. In the Marxist interpretation, these were the areas in which the bourgeoisie and Puritanism were emerging to threaten the old order (see Figure 6.1).

However, although social differences may have played a role in determining side-taking, it would be dangerous to over-emphasise them. Both sides were led by people of similar social backgrounds, drawn from the aristocracy or gentry. It is difficult to see the Civil War as an overt challenge of the bourgeois gentry to the feudal aristocracy, when parliamentary armies, especially early on in the war, were led by aristocrats such as the Earls of Essex and Manchester. Similarly, other key Royalist figures such as Sir Ralph Hopton, the leader of the King's western armies, were Puritans of gentry backgrounds.

Principle battle

1 Edgehill, October 1642

Royalist territory

Newcastle

York

Hull

Nottingham

1

Pembroke   Gloucester   Oxford

Bristol   London

Plymouth

Figure 6.1 Map of England divided, autumn 1642

Certainly none of the leading Parliamentarians saw the conflict in terms of social revolution, and would have been horrified at any such suggestion. Even those historians who have seen the Civil War in such terms, would accept that the opponents of the King were revolutionaries by effect, rather than by intention.

It is also important to remember that although certain areas may have declared for King or Parliament in 1642, it was often only after a struggle between rival members of the gentry over control of their locality. For instance, Hertfordshire and Kent, which were Parliamentarian during the Civil War, had Royalist supporters active in them in the early stages of the conflict. As Lucy Hutchinson remarked, 'every county … had the civil war within itself' to determine its allegiance. It is important to note that neutralism was also a powerful sentiment in the early days of the war, and that for many side-taking was an evil to be avoided for as long as possible. Thomas Knyvett's reaction (source E) to the approach of war was not unusual. In some counties and towns neutrality pacts were drawn up by the gentry to try and ensure that the war did not reach them. For example, a neutrality declaration was issued in Cheshire in August 1642 that refused to accept the validity of a war between King and Parliament, and towns such as Worcester, Lincoln and Salisbury attempted to shut their gates against both sides. Thus, although social and economic factors may have played a part in side-taking, the association is by no means as clear cut as some may have claimed.

Baxter also identifies the importance of religion in determining side-taking, and this is a judgement that finds favour with many current historians. The fear of Catholicism and Arminianism, which to many were indistinguishable anyway, drove many to side with Parliament, and not only Puritans. Although there were some who looked for a further reformation of the Church, more were simply concerned to protect it from the dangerous popish innovations imposed on it by Charles and Laud, and from the Catholic sympathisers who surrounded the King. For one Parliamentary pamphleteer, the war was being waged '*for* the King', to save him from 'the Queen, a papist' and other Catholics, who had taken away his 'strength and power'.

Others were alarmed by Parliament's assault on the bishops, and feared the social consequences of Puritan reform. As a Royalist supporter in Cheshire, Sir Thomas Aston, asserted, they, 'under the pretext of reforming the Church ... shake off the yoke of all obedience, either to ecclesiastical, civil, common, statute, or customary laws of the kingdom'. Both King and Parliament, therefore, were able to portray themselves as the protectors of Church, one from the dangers of religious radicalism, and the other from popery.

Both sides were also able to claim they were defending traditional government. Charles was keen to point out that he stood against:

> a faction of malignant, schismatical [*divisive*] and ambitious persons whose design it is and always has been to alter the frame of government, both of Church and State, and to subject both King and people to their own lawless and arbitrary power.
>
> (Charles I, *His Majesty's Answer to a Printed Book*, May 1642)

His quarrel was not 'against the Parliament, but against certain men' within that Parliament, who were abusing their positions. Their actions over the last eighteen months had been an attempt to undermine the traditional balance of King, Lords and Commons. If they continued to go unchecked, the result would be anarchy. For Parliament, the use of armed force was necessary to save the King from evil advisers, or 'delinquents', whose activities threatened to undermine the liberties and freedoms of all Englishmen, and replace them with absolutist tyranny.

In reality, then, there was a complex web of factors that motivated men to fight for a particular side. Ideology, political and or religious, could play a part, with individuals opting to support whichever side they saw as defending the State or Church. Ties of loyalty to landlords and political patrons were also significant, and for many people the issue was less one of principle, than siding with whoever seemed more likely to succeed, at least in their own locality. Perhaps the most significant sentiment, however, was the reluctance of many to take sides at all. As Baxter points out, it was not until *after* the first battle of Edgehill, until the point of no return, that many of the political nation finally declared their allegiances. War was not something that most people sought or wanted; it was something they were dragged into.

War

1642

The prospects for both sides when war finally broke out in August 1642 were mixed. Parliament had many strategic and logistical advantages. Most importantly it had London, and with it control of the largest port in the country and the customs duties paid by its merchants, the armoury at the Tower, and access to loans and funding through the city. It also held most of the other major ports, such as Plymouth, Bristol and Portsmouth, and the fleet, which enabled it to supply garrisons in hostile territory, such as Hull and Pembroke, and to restrict the flow of foreign aid to the King. Moreover, Parliament's control of the more prosperous regions of the country, in the south east and East Anglia, gave it potential access to far greater financial resources than the King. Yet, Parliament also faced the problem of a large and divided leadership, with at least two separate groups within it. The 'war party', led by radicals such as Haselrig, Sir Henry Vane and Henry Marten, favoured war as a means of defeating the King and enforcing a settlement on him. The 'peace party' led by figures such as Holles, conversely, saw armed force as a way of pressuring the King to agree to a negotiated settlement. Trying to straddle both these groups, and maintain Parliament's unity of purpose was a middling group, led by Pym and Oliver St John.

Conversely, the Royalist cause had the great advantage of the King himself. He was able to provide his supporters with a single focus of loyalty, in his own person, and the potential for undivided, focused leadership. Unfortunately, this advantage was negated to an extent by his indecisiveness, and his inability to control feuds among his generals. He also had access to large reserves of manpower and finance, through his noble supporters, with figures such as the Earl of Newcastle who raised, equipped and maintained regiments at their own expense. In addition, he had a much larger number of experienced officers than his opponents at the beginning of the war, with many of the English officers who had fought as mercenaries in the Thirty Years War joining him. The King did have certain advantages particularly early on in the conflict, but it was clearly in his interests to strike at London as early as possible, before Parliament had time to fully utilise its greater resources.

The King moved from Nottingham to Shrewsbury to collect troops from Wales, and, accompanied by his nephew, Prince Rupert, began to march towards London. He was intercepted by the main Parliamentarian army under the leadership of the Earl of Essex at Edgehill, where the first battle of the Civil War was fought on 23 October 1642. It was an indecisive and confused affair, but could be considered a victory of sorts for the King, as Essex's withdrawal from the battlefield overnight left his path open to continue the advance on London. By November, the Royalists had been halted on the outskirts of London, at Turnham Green, by Essex's forces, supplemented by the London militia, and the King retreated to Oxford, where he established his future headquarters.

The winter of 1642–3 saw a renewed attempt at negotiations between the two sides, largely as a result of the insistence of the peace party in Parliament. Dismayed at the bloodshed of the autumn, moderates were desperate to reach a peaceful settlement with the King, a sentiment heightened by the fact that London was now cut off from its coal supply in the north-east. Parliamentary commissioners spent over two months in Oxford, but any hopes for a deal foundered on the continuing differences over Church reform and control of the Crown's ministers; and on Charles's reluctance to commit himself to the terms of any treaty, while there was any hope of his military position improving.

1643

The spring and summer of 1643 was the period during which the King and his forces enjoyed their greatest success, and came the closest to being able to enforce a military solution. The King's forces enjoyed a string of victories, and seemed to threaten a three-pronged advance on London. The northern army, under the Earl of Newcastle, had captured Yorkshire by defeating the parliamentary forces under the Fairfaxes, at Adwalton Moor, and was poised to march south. The western army, under Sir Ralph Hopton, had captured most of the south-west for the King following decisive victories over William Waller at Lansdown in Somerset, and Roundway Down in Wiltshire, and by the end of the summer had advanced into Hampshire. The forces under the King's direct control had managed to keep the main parliamentary army occupied in the Thames Valley for much of this time, and the high point of Royalist fortunes came in July with Prince Rupert's capture of Bristol, the second largest port in the country. The cumulative effect of these victories hit parliamentary morale hard, and it was only with difficulty that Pym was able to defeat the peace party's proposal to offer Charles favourable terms for ending the war.

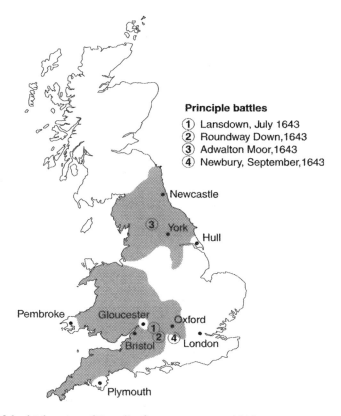

Principle battles

1. Lansdown, July 1643
2. Roundway Down, 1643
3. Adwalton Moor, 1643
4. Newbury, September, 1643

Figure 6.2 Map of the high point of Royalist fortunes, autumn 1643

Any hopes the King may have had for a co-ordinated advance on London, however, were undermined by the existence of parliamentary forces behind their lines. Two of the main Royalist armies found their lines of supply under threat, and there was an unwillingness amongst their soldiers to leave their home areas exposed to possible attacks by parliamentary forces. Thus Newcastle delayed any march south to deal with the Fairfaxes at Hull, and the King himself moved west to besiege Gloucester, to neutralise the threat to his links with his Welsh recruiting grounds. In the event, both sieges failed and the King lost much of the momentum gained by earlier victories. Parliamentary forces had the opportunity to regroup, and Essex, reinforced by the London militia, was able to march west and relieve the siege of Gloucester. Charles's subsequent advance on London was effectively halted by Essex at the Battle of Newbury, in September. Meanwhile, in East Anglia, the army of the Eastern Association, under the Earl of Manchester (previously Lord Kimbolton, the only member of the Lords to be impeached along with the Five Members), was expanded and reorganised, and won a series of victories that secured Lincolnshire for Parliament. Significantly, it was this campaign that saw the emergence of a highly talented cavalry commander within the Eastern Association, Oliver Cromwell.

By the autumn of 1643, stalemate had been reached, and both sides looked for fresh sources of support to break the deadlock. On 7 September, Parliament confirmed an alliance with the Scots, in the Solemn League and Covenant, agreeing that they would reform religion 'according to the word of God and the example of the best reformed churches'. To the Scots this meant the adoption of Presbyterianism in England, which was not necessarily an interpretation shared by all their English counterparts, some of whom were strongly opposed to the Scottish form of Church government. This was to be the source of fundamental problems in the longer term, but the immediate effect of the Solemn League and Covenant was to provide Parliament with what they needed, a well-disciplined army of 20,000 troops threatening the King's grip on the north of England.

Within a week of Parliament's alliance with the Scots, the King confirmed the Cessation Treaty with the Irish rebels. This was in effect a truce with the Irish, which would allow the King to bring over to England those troops that had been dealing with the rebellion. However, in parliamentary propaganda this rapidly became the realisation of the fears of autumn 1641, with the King employing Irish Catholics to suppress his Protestant subjects. Any military benefits that Charles managed to gain by using Irish forces were, at least in part, offset by the political costs of such action.

1644

In 1644, the tide began to turn in Parliament's favour. In January 1644, the Scots crossed the border and laid siege to Newcastle, and Sir Thomas Fairfax caught and destroyed the Irish army that had just landed at Nantwich, in Cheshire. A further blow to the King came in March 1644, with Waller's defeat of his western army at Cheriton, in Hampshire. By the summer, the situation in the north had become desperate, with Newcastle's army under siege in York, surrounded by the Scots, the army of the Eastern Association under Manchester, and the northern army under Fairfax. The King's response was to send a relief force under Rupert to Newcastle's aid. Rupert duly marched north, drew the parliamentary forces away from York, and, outmanoeuvring them, entered the city on 1 July. He then insisted on bringing his enemies to battle, and, despite being outnumbered by around 28,000 to 18,000, drew up his forces at Marston Moor, on 2 July. In the bloodiest battle of the Civil War, Rupert's forces were decisively defeated. Although Rupert himself and his cavalry managed to escape south, Newcastle's infantry were destroyed and York surrendered two weeks later.

The loss of the north, and Parliament's numerical superiority should have enabled them decisively to press home their victory at Marston Moor, but they were undermined by a lack of unity in their aims and their leadership. The Scots were unwilling to advance any further south until they had completed their siege of Newcastle, which did not fall until the end of October, effectively the end of the campaigning season. Parliament's position was further eroded by the defeat of the Earl of Essex, at Lostwithiel in September. Essex had ignored the orders of the parliamentary high command, and marched south-west, where he had been outmanoeuvred by Charles and trapped in Cornwall. Although Essex and his cavalry escaped, the defeat led to the capture of his infantry and artillery. In addition to Essex's failure, divisions were again surfacing between the war and peace parties, as was illustrated by conflict within the leadership of the army of the Eastern Association, between Manchester and Cromwell. Manchester was accused by Cromwell of not prosecuting the war vigorously enough, and of not wanting to bring about victory, and in a sense the accusations against the Earl were justified. Manchester had fought all along to bring about a negotiated peace with the King, and he was not alone among Parliamentarians in fearing that a total victory over the King might open the doors to dangerous political radicalism. In Cromwell's view, it was this reluctance to take decisive action that led to Manchester's failure to defeat the King at the second battle of Newbury, in October, which ended in an inconclusive draw.

1645–6

It was these problems of the autumn of 1644 that led Parliament to pass the Self-Denying Ordinance, in January 1645. The Ordinance excluded any members of Parliament from holding positions of military command, thus relieving Essex and Manchester of their posts, although in acknowledgement of Cromwell's military skills he was exempted from the conditions of the Ordinance. This was followed by another important military reform, the creation of one unified field army, known as the New Model Army, under the command of Sir Thomas Fairfax. Although it was to develop into a formidable fighting machine, initially the New Model Army did not differ greatly from its predecessors. It still contained the same soldiers, largely in the same regiments and under the same officers, and still faced the familiar problems of irregular pay and desertion, although perhaps to a lesser degree. However, its creation did help overcome the localism that had caused problems when regional forces had been reluctant to move out of the areas in which they had been raised. In addition, its unified command structure, under Fairfax, facilitated better planning and more decisive action.

The New Model Army had its first chance to demonstrate its abilities at the Battle of Naseby, in June 1645. Its forces were almost double those of the King's, but again Rupert came close to winning the day by routing the opposing wing of cavalry. In the event, Parliament's victory owed much, as at Marston Moor, to Cromwell's ability to rally his cavalry on the other side of the battlefield, and direct them against the Royalist infantry in the centre, while Rupert's charged off the field in pursuit of their opponents. Naseby resulted in the destruction of the King's last major field army, and with the

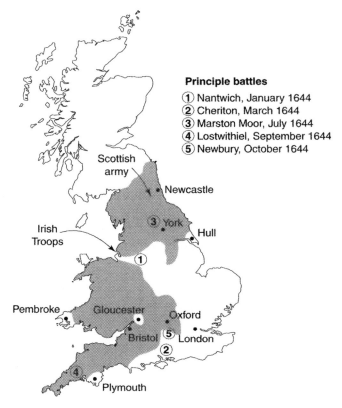

Principle battles
1. Nantwich, January 1644
2. Cheriton, March 1644
3. Marston Moor, July 1644
4. Lostwithiel, September 1644
5. Newbury, October 1644

Scottish army

Newcastle

Irish Troops

York

Hull

Pembroke

Gloucester

Oxford

Bristol

London

Plymouth

Figure 6.3 Map of the campaigns of 1644

defeat in July of Royalist troops at Langport, in Somerset, marked the beginning of the end for the King. Pockets of resistance were gradually mopped up, and eventually in the spring of 1646, the New Model Army laid siege to Oxford. Charles, however, evaded capture and escaped from Oxford in disguise, surrendering instead to the Scots at Newark, with whom he hoped he could negotiate better terms than with Parliament. The King's opponents had finally won the war; they now needed to try and find a way of winning the peace.

Battle

As it has been noted, battles in the seventeenth century were more like 'seduction than rape'. In the absence of accurate maps, watches or communications systems, it was very difficult for army commanders to co-ordinate their own forces let alone monitor their opponents' and force them to battle against their will. Despite the use of cavalry patrols and scouts, it was difficult to estimate the size of an enemy army, or to predict its exact whereabouts, and often such information was not available until opposing forces had stumbled into each other. Even then, withdrawal was often possible, and an organised pursuit by opponents difficult. Therefore, battles usually only happened when both sides were keen to force an engagement.

As a result, civil war battles tended to be set piece affairs. Armies were generally drawn up along the following lines. In the middle stood the infantry units, consisting of pikemen and musketeers, which were flanked by a body of cavalry on each wing. Heavy artillery was positioned at the rear, together with a reserve of cavalry, to be deployed as the battle unfolded. Dragoons, who were mounted soldiers who usually fought on foot, were deployed on the flanks to harass enemy cavalry. Battle usually commenced with the engagement of the opposing wings of cavalry, while the infantry manoeuvred into position. When the musketeers had exhausted their ammunition, the pikemen would then advance, in enormous formations, to engage in hand-to-hand fighting, known as 'push of pike'. However, it was often what happened on the wings of the armies that proved more important. If one side could rout the opposing cavalry, it was sometimes then possible to rally them and direct them against the enemy foot soldiers. If such a manoeuvre could be achieved, it was usually to prove decisive.

The tactics and realities of battle are best understood by looking at some of the actual encounters that took place during the Civil War. Two of its key battles, Edgehill and Marston Moor, are dealt with in greater detail below:

Edgehill

After mustering his forces from the Midlands and Wales, the King left Shrewsbury on 12 October and started to advance towards London. The Earl of Essex, who commanded the main Parliamentarian army, managed to intercept him as he marched through Warwickshire. It was in both sides' interests to give battle. A victory for the King would allow him an uninterrupted and almost certainly successful advance on London, whereas victory for Parliament would see the defeat of the King's only significant field army, and probably the end of the war.

Both armies drew up accordingly at Edgehill on 23 October, with the King's forces stationed at the top of a slope. The two sides were fairly evenly matched, with Essex's forces consisting of around 26,000 men and the King's of around 24,000, although the Royalist army did have an advantage in numbers of cavalry. They took up their battle positions in the conventional manner, with their infantry placed in the centre, and their cavalry divided into two wings, on either side.

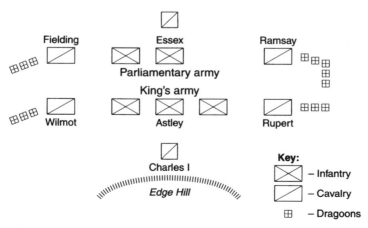

Figure 6.4 The battle of Edgehill, 23 October 1642

The battle began at about one o'clock, with an exchange of artillery fire that lasted about an hour. This was then followed by a cavalry charge by Rupert on the right wing, which broke the parliamentary cavalry. However, rather than regrouping and attacking the now exposed enemy infantry in the flank, Rupert's cavalry galloped off the field in pursuit of their opponents, and seized and looted the parliamentary baggage train. A similar pattern was followed on the other wing, with the Royalist cavalry under Henry Wilmot routing their opponents, and disappearing from the battlefield in hot pursuit. When the cavalry began to filter back to the main battle, they were tired, their horses exhausted, and their effectiveness had been largely spent.

In the centre, the tide was going against the King. Outnumbered by the parliamentary infantry, the Royalist foot was further disadvantaged by the fact that two of the enemy's cavalry regiments had avoided the rout on their right wing, and turned on them. The Royalists sustained heavy losses, and the King himself was in some danger for a time, his standard-bearer, Sir Edmund Verney, being killed and the royal standard captured. The standard was subsequently recaptured by Royalist cavalry, who had begun to return to the battlefield, and, shortly after, as night was falling, both sides drew off to regroup. They spent the night on the battlefield and in the morning were still facing each other. Yet neither side had much enthusiasm for recommencing battle. Men and horses were exhausted and hungry, and many were shocked by the harsh reality of warfare and bloodshed that they had witnessed, in the first pitched battle in England in over 150 years. Eventually it was Essex who withdrew from the field, retreating north and leaving the road to London open. The King claimed a victory, but in reality Edgehill was inconclusive. Although the King resumed his march on the capital, Essex was still able to manoeuvre his forces around him and block his advance again, this time successfully at Turnham Green in November.

An interesting contemporary account of the battle is provided by Edward Knightly, a captain in the parliamentary army, in a letter to a relative:

On Sunday 23 October about one o'clock in the afternoon the battle did begin and continued until it was very dark; the field was very great and large and the King's forces came down a great and long hill, he had the advantage of the ground and the wind, and they gave a brave charge and did fight very valiantly; they were of 15 Regiments of Foot and 60 Regiments of Horse, our Horse were under 40 Regiments and our Foot 11 Regiments: my Lord General [the Earl of Essex] did give first charge, presenting them with two pieces of ordinance which killed many of their men, and then the enemy did shoot one to us which fell twenty yards short in ploughed land and did no harm; our soldiers did many of them run away … and there did run away 600 horse … and when I was entering the field I think 200 horse came by me with all the speed they could out of the battle, saying that the King hath the victory and that every man cried God and King Charles. I entreated, prayed and persuaded them to stay and draw up in a body with our troops, for we saw them fighting and the Field was not lost, but no persuasion would serve, and then turning to our three troops, two of them were run away [and] of my troop I had not six and thirty men left … I stayed with those men I had … and divers of the enemy did run that way, both horse and foot. I took away about ten or twelve horse, swords and armour. I could have killed 40 of the enemy [but] I let them pass, disarming them and giving spoil to my troopers. … The armies were both in confusion. … The enemy ran away as well as our men.

Marston Moor

Marston Moor was fought following Prince Rupert's dramatic march north to relieve the siege of York, in the summer of 1644. Rupert insisted that he had orders from the King to not only save York, but also to bring the parliamentary forces to battle, although the Marquis of Newcastle and Lord Eythin, Newcastle's infantry commander, opposed the idea. They pointed out that the enemy army was significantly larger than that at their own disposal and favoured caution. The parliamentary forces consisted of three main elements: the Scots, led by the Earl of Leven; the Eastern Association army of the Earl of Manchester; and the Northern army under Lord and Sir Thomas Fairfax. If the Royalists could avoid being brought to battle, it was unlikely that the mixed parliamentary army would be able to maintain themselves, or their unity, in the field for much longer. Eythin was eager to remind Rupert of their last meeting, during the Thirty Years War in 1638, when 'your forwardness lost us the day in Germany, where you yourself were taken prisoner'. Nevertheless, Rupert overruled his colleagues and gave orders for the Royalist forces to assemble on Marston Moor on 2 July.

Although both Rupert and Newcastle were in position by late morning, plans to bring the Parliamentarian army to battle that day seemed to have been undermined by the fact that Eythin did not arrive on the field until late afternoon, and then only with 4,000 of the 5,000 troops at his disposal. It is uncertain why his arrival was so delayed, but it may well have been due to his lack of trust in Rupert as his commander. Upon being shown Rupert's plan of battle, he commented dryly, 'By God, Sir, it is very fine on the paper, but there is no such thing in the field.' As the Royalist troops began to stand down, on the assumption that battle would not start until the following day, the Earl of Leven ordered his troops into battle.

While the infantry became heavily engaged in the centre, the parliamentary left wing, commanded by Cromwell, routed the Royalist cavalry on their side of the field. On the right wing, however, the parliamentary horse under Sir Thomas Fairfax was broken by Goring, who then pursued his opponents off the field, and attacked the Scottish baggage train. Although Cromwell had been wounded and briefly withdrew from the battle, he was able to return, rally his troops and link up with Fairfax, who had avoided being swept off the field in Goring's earlier cavalry charge. As Goring's cavalry belatedly returned to the battlefield they found themselves confronted and defeated

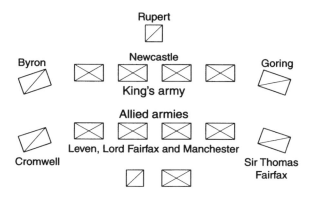

Figure 6.5 The battle of Marston Moor, 2 July 1644

decisively by Cromwell and Fairfax. The parliamentary horse was then rallied again, and directed against the Royalist infantry. Although night had fallen, Newcastle's infantry refused to surrender and continued the struggle. As one contemporary recorded:

> By mere valour for one whole hour [they] kept the troops of horse from entering amongst them by push of pike; when the horse did enter they would have no quarter, but fought it out till there was not thirty of them living, whose hap [*fate*] it was to be beaten down upon the ground. As the troopers came near them though they could not rise from their wounds, yet [they] were so desperate as to get a sword or a pike or piece of them, and to gore the troopers' horses as they came over them or passed them by.

As with many other battles of the Civil War, Marston Moor was largely characterised by confusion amongst its participants. At one stage of the battle, Lord Fairfax and Leven had been convinced that the Royalists had won the day, and abandoned the field accordingly. Rupert also seems to have left the field early, and spent some time hiding from parliamentary troops in an adjacent beanfield! The account of the battle by the Royalist, Sir Arthur Trevor, provides further graphic evidence of the confused nature of seventeenth-century warfare:

> In the fire, smoke and confusion of that day I knew not for my soul whither to incline; the runaways on both sides were so many, so breathless, so speechless, and so full of fears that I should not have taken them for men … not a man of them being able to give me the least hint where the Prince was to be found, both armies both mingled, both horse and foot, no side keeping to their posts. … In this horrible distraction did I court the centre, here meeting with … Scots crying out 'Weys [Woe is] us, we are all undone' … as if their day of doom had overtaken them, and from which they knew not [where] to fly.

As the bloodiest battle in the Civil War, it was also characterised by high casualty rates. There were over 6,000 fatalities, two-thirds of whom were Royalists, and a further 1,500 men were taken prisoner. Yet, Rupert was able to salvage his cavalry, and despite the decisive nature of the parliamentary victory, Marston Moor did not signal the end of Royalist hopes. Divisions amongst the parliamentary ranks, and developments elsewhere meant that the King's position was not as seriously affected as it might have been.

1 What similarities can you detect between the two battles?
2 What key differences were there between the battles of Edgehill and Marston Moor that might have enabled Parliament to win a decisive victory at the latter?
3 What issues do you think needed to be dealt with in order to make both Royalist and Parliamentarian armies more effective?

Why did Parliament win the Civil War?

As we have seen, both sides had certain advantages at the beginning of hostilities. Probably the most important was Parliament's potential access to greater financial resources, which from 1643 they began to exploit with increasing efficiency. Pym oversaw the creation of county committees, made up of Parliamentarian gentry, to oversee the collection of the Weekly Pay, which later became the Monthly Assessment. Ironically, it was a scheme that was modelled on Ship Money, in that a fixed amount was demanded from each county, and local assessors had to calculate the amount for which each household was liable. The effectiveness of the Assessment varied from area to area, but counties such as Kent and Sussex yielded enormous amounts, Kent alone yielding £100,000 in 1645–6. Seizures of estates from 'delinquents', or known Royalists, also provided an important source of revenue, as did the Excise, a sales tax on certain goods such as beer, wine and sugar, again devised by Pym. Overall, it is estimated that Parliament was able to raise over a million pounds a year to keep its armies in the field. This compares very favourably with the Royalists' finances, where money was raised locally and more haphazardly. It tended to be kept and spent there, rather than being made available to a central treasury at Oxford, from where more financial control could have been exercised. As the war began to go against the King, so he found it harder and harder to raise the levels of finance that he needed to keep his armies in the field, and in 1645–6, the collapse of the King's forces owed much to this lack of resources.

Localism was also a problem that both sides faced, but it was probably more damaging to the King's cause than Parliament's. The Royalist successes of 1643, which brought them as close to victory as they were to come, were severely limited because of the localism of their armies. Parliamentary garrisons in Gloucester, Hull and, to a lesser extent, Plymouth, made Royalist troops reluctant to advance on London, while their localities were still under threat. While such caution was understandable, the delays enabled Parliament to recover itself, and the King lost his best chance of winning the war. While such sentiments also limited the effectiveness of Parliament's armies, particularly the Scots, it was less of a problem. Until 1644, Parliament's strategy depended more on defence and therefore did not require its troops to range so far from their locality, and certainly the London militia proved willing, when necessary in the summer of 1643, to campaign at distance under Essex. When Parliament was in a position to move on to the offensive in 1645, it had replaced its regional armies with one national force, which although far from perfect, was less affected by localism than its predecessors.

Both sides were also plagued by political divisions, which had the potential to be far more damaging to Parliament than to the King. That this was not the case is a testament to the skills of Pym, who managed a remarkable balancing act between the two factions until his death at the end of 1643. While friction between figures such as Manchester and Cromwell cannot have helped Parliament's cause, it was again something that was to a large extent overcome with the Self-Denying Ordinance. The Royalists should have been less affected by such problems, but Charles was not always able to provide the decisive leadership to which his position entitled him. There were moderates among the King's supporters, such as Hyde, Falkland and the Earl of Bristol, who favoured a negotiated rather than a military solution to the conflict, whereas Prince Rupert, Lord Digby and the Queen saw the total destruction of their opponents as the only viable option. Further divisions saw Rupert and Digby manoeuvring against each other, and figures such as Newcastle going into exile after Marston Moor, because of his lack of trust in his 'allies' at court.

Military factors also played a part in Parliament's ultimate victory. Scottish intervention tipped the scales heavily in Parliament's favour, and was central to the Royalist defeat at Marston Moor and the loss of the north. There were able generals on the King's side, most notably Prince Rupert and Sir Ralph Hopton, but key to Parliament's victory was the emergence of Sir Thomas Fairfax and Oliver Cromwell. Cromwell's ability, in particular, at the key battles of Marston Moor and Naseby, to maintain his cavalry's discipline, proved crucial in both encounters. The success of the New Model Army in 1645–6 owed much to the leadership of these two men.

The impact of war

The immediate effects of fighting varied a great deal. Some areas such as Norfolk and Suffolk saw very little fighting, whereas a county like Berkshire, which lay between the headquarters of the King in Oxford and Parliament in London, was a constant battle-ground. As well as two large-scale battles at Newbury, and a siege of Reading, there was a high level of military activity there throughout the war, with large numbers of soldiers billeted on civilians.

One aspect of the war's impact that did not depend so much on location was its financial demands on the population. Parliament's demands for weekly pay massively exceeded those of peacetime taxation, with Hampshire, for example being assessed at £39,000 a year, compared with the £6,000 for which it was liable under Ship Money. The Royalist equivalent, the 'Contribution' was set at similar levels, with Oxfordshire's annual charge amounting to £76,800, compared with its Ship Money assessment of £3,500. Although efficiency in collecting money varied from area to area, there can be little doubt that everyone was seriously affected by this enormous and unprecedented demand for regular taxation.

Added to the burdens of direct taxation, was the cost of providing armies with free lodgings and food. Although records were supposed to be kept of the costs to individual householders of billeting soldiers, compensation was rarely paid. These costs varied according to the levels of military activity in the area, but for instance it has been calculated that in Cheshire the cost of billeting may have been as high as £120,000, compared with a total of £100,000 raised in direct taxation during the war. In addition to this were the costs of being plundered by troops from both sides. Most of this kind of activity was small scale and carried out by local garrisons or passing troops, but none the less damaging for those on the receiving end. There were also instances of large-scale pillaging following the capture of towns, by soldiers determined to profit from their victories. Birmingham and Bristol were both sacked by Royalist forces under the command of Prince Rupert, and Reading suffered a similar fate at the hands of Essex's troops.

The resurgence of neutralism towards the end of the war can be seen, to a very large extent, as a reaction against the burdens that war had placed on the civilian community. In 1645, a number of associations sprang up, which together constituted the Clubmen movement. The Clubmen were local groups, often under gentry leadership, committed to protecting their communities from pillage and financial exploitation by either side. Associations were formed in South Wales, and in ten counties of central and southern England, with the Dorset and Wiltshire Clubmen claiming to be able to raise 20,000 men within forty-eight hours to repel outsiders. In the event, the Clubmen proved no match for the King's or Parliament's forces, but their willingness to take up arms to protect their communities is a clear reminder of the fact that it was only for the minority that the Civil War was about matters of principle. The neutralism that was evident in 1642 had never gone away, and most people were more concerned to see an end to war than a victory for a particular side. The Clubmen movement was the result of this sentiment, motivated into action by the continuing burdens and hardship that three years of war had brought with it.

Documents

While the impact of war varied from community to community, it is evident that it had a significant effect upon almost everyone in England and Wales, whether they were combatants or civilians, committed or non-aligned. The documents below concentrate particularly on the impact of war upon the civilian population:

A   The Cavaliers rode up into the town ... the Earl of Denbigh being in the front, singing as he rode, they shot at every door and window where they could spy any looking out, then hacked, hewed or pistolled at all they met, blaspheming, cursing and damning themselves most hideously. ... Having possessed themselves of the town, they ran into every house, cursing and damning, threatening and terrifying the poor women most terribly, setting naked swords and pistols to their breasts; they fell to plundering all the town before them ... forcing people to deliver all the money they had. ... It is conceived that they had £2,000 in money from the town. They beastly assaulted many women's chastity and impudently made their brags afterwards how many they had ravished, glorying in their shame. ... That night few or none of them went to bed, but stayed up revelling, robbing and tyrannising over poor affrighted women and prisoners, drinking [until] drunk, healthing upon their knees, yea drinking healths to Prince Rupert's dog. Nor did their rage here cease, but when on the next day they were to march out of town, they used all diligence in every street to kindle fire in the town. ... The houses burned were about 87, besides multitudes of barns, stables and back buildings. ... And yet for all this, the soldiers told the inhabitants that Prince Rupert had dealt mercifully with them, but when they came back with the Queen's army they would leave neither man, woman, nor child alive.

(A contemporary description of the sack of Birmingham, spring 1643)

B   i)   Mr Hunter, Corporal under Captain Thacker, having taken a horse from Mr. Hart ... hath refused to restore the said horse upon the Committee's order; it is ordered that for his contempt of the said order he shall be committed to the marshal till he restore the said horse and give satisfaction to the committee for his contempt.

    ii) Upon the petition of Richard Backhouse of Stafford, showing that Colonel Lewis Chadwick, Lieutenant Colonel Jackson, and others at the taking of the town, seized upon his house for the public use, and have held it ever since. ... It is therefore ordered that the Treasurer shall pay to the said Mr. Backhouse, the sum of eight pounds yearly so long as the Committee, their officers and servants shall make use of it; and shall likewise pay the arrears of the rent for the time since they first entered upon it.

iii) There is £23 due to John Twyford for his quartering of soldiers, it is ordered that he shall be paid £11 by the solicitors for sequestration, and shall have the public faith of the kingdom for the sum of £12.

iv) The lands of Edward Stanford, esquire, within the county of Stafford, are sequestered for the use of ... Parliament, he being a recusant and in arms against them; yet upon Mrs. Dorothy Stanford, his wife's petition for maintenance out of the said lands, it is agreed by and between the Committee of Stanford ... [that] a fifth part ... of the profits [on those lands] ... shall be paid to the said Mrs. Stanford ... and the rest to the Treasurer at Stanford for the state's use. And because the said Mrs. Stanford is destitute of a house, it is ordered that she shall have the hall called Perry Barr Hall ... Mrs. Stanford shall pay the weekly pay for the lands and profits she holds.

(Extracts from the proceedings for the County Committee for Stafford, January 1645)

C   On New Year's day 1644 ... [Parliamentary troops] came to Bramhall and went into my stable and took out all my horses ... above twenty in all, afterwards searched my house for arms. ...

In May 1644 ... came Prince Rupert and his army, by whom I lost better than 100 pounds in Linens and other goods ... besides the rifling and pulling in pieces of my house. By them and my Lord Goring's army, I lost eight horses and besides victuals [*food*] and other provisions, they ate me three score bushels of oats. No sooner was the prince gone than [Parliamentary troops] hastened their return to plunder me of my horses which the prince had left me.

On Friday the 9th August 1644, information was brought into the sequestrators against me for delinquency. ... They alleged against me that I had joined with the Commissioners of Array at Hoo Heath ... whereunto I affirmatively answered that I was there ... yet nevertheless I did think that ... my restraint from arms might free me from delinquency in that point. ... They ... proceeded further against me in renewing their commands to my tenants to detain their rents from me ... and in conclusion, unless I would agree to give them five hundred pounds ... they intended to proceed against me as a delinquent in all rigor and extremity.

(From William Davenport's account of his sufferings in Cheshire, during 1644)

D   i) The want of Church government, whereby our churches are decayed, and God's ordinances neglected.

ii) For three years we have through much labour and God's blessing gained the fruit of the earth, and had hoped to enjoy the same, but by free quarter [billeting] and plunder of soldiers our purses have been exhausted ... we are disabled to pay our rents, just debts and to maintain our wives in utter ruin.

iii) The insufferable, insolent, arbitrary power that hath been used among us, contrary to all known laws. ...

iv) Now we shall endeavour to defend the frontiers of the county, that all the taxes imposed by Parliament may be abated [*lessened*] in a moderate way.

(The complaints of the Sussex Clubmen, September 1645)

1 What concerns might you have about the reliability of source A?

2 From your reading of source B, what complaints could have been levelled by people in the Stafford area, at the Parliamentarian forces?

3 From the evidence of source B, how far do you think that the county committee for Stafford made concessions to local feelings in the way it administered the area?

4 According to source C, what losses did William Davenport incur during 1644?

5 What does source C reveal about the difficulties of trying to remain uncommitted during the Civil War?

6 From the evidence of source D, what were the issues that motivated the Clubmen movement?

7   The search for a settlement, 1646–9

Table 7.1 Timeline of the main events of 1646–9

1646	April:	King surrenders to the Scots
	July:	The Newcastle Propositions
1647	January:	King handed over to Parliament
	June–August:	Army Revolt
	August:	Heads of the Proposals
	October–November:	Putney Debates
	December:	Charles I signs the 'Engagement'
1648	April–September:	Second English Civil War
	December:	Pride's Purge
1649	January:	Trial and execution of Charles I

The situation in 1646

Charles's surrender to the Scots in April 1646 signalled the end of the Civil War, a war won by Parliament. Yet, what had Parliament actually won? The King had been defeated but among the ranks of those who had fought against him there was little clear idea of what the post-war settlement should look like. The issues of 1641–2 were still unresolved. Many Parliamentarians had fought for religious ideals, but not necessarily the same ones. Some believed that they were protecting the old, traditional Church of England, others wanted to see the introduction of Presbyterianism, or even independence from any kind of Church government. For those who were more concerned with constitutional issues, there was the problem of what balance of power there was to be between the Crown and Parliament. Should a settlement seek to restore the traditional balance of the constitution or to fundamentally reduce the powers of the monarch?

Whatever form of settlement was reached would still need the agreement and co-operation of the King, without whose participation few could envisage a future Government. It would also need the support of at least some of the powerful interest groups within the parliamentary camp, whose agendas were by no means identical. Below is a summary of the main players, who were seeking to influence the shape of any future agreement:

The King: in defeat, Charles was still hopeful of eventual victory, as he asserted to Prince Rupert: 'I must tell you that God will not suffer rebels and traitors to prosper, nor for this cause to be overthrown.' He had surrendered to the Scots in the hope of exploiting divisions between them and Parliament, and remained involved in intrigues with various parties throughout this period.

The Scots: under the terms of the Solemn League and Covenant, the Scots had intervened in the Civil War in winter 1643, in return for the introduction of Presbyterianism in England and financial compensation. By the end of the war, the Scots' leaders were relatively open to the idea of dealing with Charles, and the presence of their army in Newark made them an immediate presence in the English political scene.

Parliament: There were two main groupings within Parliament –

The Peace Party: became known as the 'Presbyterians', although not all of them favoured the introduction of a Presbyterian system. Led by Holles, and including Oliver St John and Lord Saye and Seal, the Peace Party were essentially a moderate group who believed that negotiations with the King were vital to restoring traditional Government. Fearful of social breakdown and revolution, Holles was convinced of the need to restore the unity of King and the political nation as quickly as possible.

The War Party: became known as the 'Independents', due to their hostility to the introduction of Presbyterianism. Led by Vane, Haselrig, Cromwell and Ireton, they had strong links with the army, through which they drew much of their strength. Their approach to negotiations with Charles was more extreme, favouring strict limitations on the King and the maintenance of the New Model Army in peacetime to enforce any settlement.

The New Model Army: the main concern of the army was the payment of the arrears in their wages. By the end of 1646, they were owed around £300,000 and many feared their contribution to Parliament's victory would be rapidly forgotten during peacetime. As one army chaplain declared:

You who have conquered the kingdom, done all this service, and now when you have done all this, might expect your arrears, look to enjoy your liberties, yea and expect preferments, good places as you have well deserved, it may be you shall be cast into a stinking prison.

Although the Army was led by Fairfax, who was a conservative, this was not the case with all its officers, many of whom were not from gentry backgrounds and as a result had less of a stake in maintaining the status quo. There was also a significant radical religious and political element amongst its ranks.

The Levellers: were a radical political group who had emerged during the war, favouring a 'levelling' of society, whereby old social and hierarchical structures would be destroyed. Although their influence in 1646 was relatively limited, the Levellers did draw on support from the lower ranks of the New Model Army, and among a few senior officers, such as Colonel Rainsborough, and offered a dramatic alternative for any future settlement.

The Newcastle Propositions

In July 1646, the King was sent a list of proposals by Parliament, under the leadership of Holles, known as the Newcastle Propositions, the key clauses of which were:

2) That his Majesty ... may be pleased to swear and sign the late solemn League and Covenant. ...
3) That a Bill be passed for the utter abolishing and taking away of all Archbishops, [and] Bishops. ...
5) That reformation of religion, according to the Covenant, be settled by Act of Parliament. ...
13) That the Lords and Commons shall during the space of twenty years arm, train, and discipline all the forces of the kingdom.
16) 57 leading Royalists were named as 'persons who shall expect no pardon for treason' and 48 others who were to 'be removed from his Majesty's counsels'.

Such proposals were not particularly attractive to Charles, as is illustrated by the letter that he sent to his wife in July 1646:

I ... do assure thee that they are such as I cannot grasp without the loss of my conscience, crown, and honour; to which, as I can no way consent, so in my opinion a flat denial is to be delayed as long as may be, and how to make an handsome denying answer is all the difficulty.

Charles's hopes still rested on the premise that over time the differences between his opponents would widen, and that therefore he should avoid giving a definite response to Parliament for as long as possible.

Frustrated by the King's apparent indecision, the Scottish army handed Charles over to Parliament in January 1647, a decision that was facilitated by Parliament paying the first instalment of the money that they owed them. In May 1647, Charles finally responded to the Newcastle Propositions, indicating that they might be acceptable in a modified form. Parliamentary control of the militia should be reduced from twenty to ten years, further discussions should take place over the nature of any Presbyterian system, and there should be no persecution of, or limitations on, his advisers as envisaged in clause 16 of the Propositions. Any potential for further negotiations was however cut short by an unexpected development: the revolt of the army.

The Army Revolt

Together with persuading the King to agree to a settlement, Holles's main concern was to try to diminish the power and size of the army, which posed a considerable potential threat to his position and a huge drain on Government finances. His hopes of achieving this, by demobilising part of it and sending another part of it to deal with the ongoing revolt in Ireland, were undermined by the army's grievances over back pay. When Holles proposed that part of the army be sent to Ireland, they petitioned Fairfax that they would only be willing to do so if their arrears were settled, and pensions provided for war widows. Holles saw this as an opportunity to move against the army on the grounds that it was being misled by 'enemies to the State and disturbers of the public peace'. On 25 May, under Holles direction, the Commons voted to disband immediately the New Model foot regiments, with minimal back pay.

The reaction of the army was almost immediate. Within a few days they had seized control of the King and on 14 June issued a declaration demanding settlement of their back pay, a purge of their opponents in Parliament, new elections, and reinforcing their opposition to Presbyterianism. The army was now a political player in its own right, and was claiming the right to influence and if necessary oppose the government that had created it. Fairfax and other natural moderates had little choice but to go along with their troops' demands, and to hope to control the more extremist elements among them. The army advanced slowly on London, calling for the impeachment of Holles and ten other Presbyterians. Following a war of nerves lasting two months, Holles and the other MPs accused by the army fled and most of the rest of the Presbyterian party swapped sides. On 3 August, Fairfax occupied London without any fighting. The Independents found themselves as the dominant party in Parliament, and it now fell to them to try and find a settlement with the King.

Heads of Proposals

Two days before the army entered London, they had submitted their own version of a future settlement to Charles drawn up by the Army Council, under the leadership of Fairfax and Ireton. These Heads of Proposals put forward the following demands:

1) That parliaments may be biennially called. ...
2) That the power of the militia by sea and land during the space of the ten years next ensuing shall be ordered ... by the Lords and Commons. ... That during the same space of ten years the said Lords and Commons may ... raise and dispose of what moneys ... they shall find necessary. ...
4) That an Act be passed for disposing the great offices for ten years by the Lords and Commons ... and after ten years they to nominate three, and the King out of that number to appoint one. ...
11) An Act to be passed to take away all ... authority and jurisdiction of bishops. ...
12) A repeal of all Acts ... enjoining [*requiring*] the use of the Book of Common Prayer, and imposing any penalties for the neglect thereof. ...
13) That the taking of the Covenant not be enforced upon any. ...
15) (Excluded five Royalists from pardon.) [NB: The Proposals also called for the full payment of arrears for the army]

1   How far did these Proposals differ from the Newcastle Propositions? How might the differences be accounted for?
2   In your view, was this a better or worse deal for the King?
3   How far could you see either the Heads of Proposals or the Newcastle Propositions as a realistic basis for a future settlement?

Although the Heads of the Proposals may have been more palatable to the King than some previous suggestions, it did not necessarily meet the aspirations of the rank and file of the army, particularly those agitators who had stirred the army to revolt in June. Negotiations could no longer be confined to monarch and Parliament; the army were now a vital element in the political mix. Leveller influences were becoming more pronounced, and there were those who wanted to push for a far more radical solution than was envisaged by the leaders, or 'Grandees' of the army. One Leveller manifesto,

The Case of the Army Truly Stated, criticised the 'neglect and treacheries' of MPs in not acting for the benefit of the whole nation, and suggested a solution: that 'all the freeborn at the age of twenty-one years and upwards be the electors'.

The Levellers and the Putney Debates

Under pressure from the radicals, Cromwell agreed to meet army representatives and some civilian Levellers in a church in Putney to discuss their demands, in what have become known as the Putney Debates. The basis for initial discussions was a document produced by the agitators, entitled *The Agreement of the People*. Its key proposals were as follows:

> That, to prevent the many inconveniences arising from the long continuance of the same persons in authority, this present parliament be dissolved. ... That the power of this and all future representatives of the nation is inferior only to theirs who do choose them ... that matters of religion and the ways of God's worship are not at all entrusted by us to any human power. ... That the matter of impressing and constraining any of us to serve in the wars is against our freedom. ... That in laws ... every person may be bound alike, and that no tenure, estate, charter, degree, birth or place do confer any exemption from the ordinary course of legal proceedings.

The main figures in the debates were as follows:

The Grandees: Cromwell, Ireton and Colonel Rich
Army radicals and Levellers: Trooper Sexby, Colonel Rainsborough and Wildman

The following are extracts from the record of the debates:

> Truly this paper does contain in it very great alterations of the very government of the kingdom ... and although the expressions in it are very plausible ... what do you think the consequences of that would be? Would it not be confusion? Would it not be utter confusion?

> (Cromwell)

> I really think that the poorest he that is in England hath a life to live, as the greatest he; and therefore ... I think that it's clear that every man that is to live under a government ought first by his own counsel to put himself under that government; and I do think that the poorest man in England is not at all bound in a strict sense to that government that he hath not had a voice to put himself under.

> (Rainsborough)

> For my part, I think it is no right at all. I think that no person hath a right to an interest or share in the disposing of the affairs of the kingdom, and in choosing those that shall determine what laws we shall be ruled by here ... that hath not a permanent fixed interest [i.e. owns land] in this kingdom. ... That by a man's being

born here he shall have a share in that power that shall dispose of lands here, and of all things here, I do not think it a sufficient ground … I speak because I would have an eye for property. … Now I wish we may all consider of what right all the people should have right to elections. Is it by right of nature? If you will hold forth that as your reason, then I think you must deny all property too, and this is my reason.

(Ireton)

I think that the law of the land in this thing is the most tyrannical law under heaven. And I would fain [*like to*] know what we have fought for.

(Rainsborough)

Some men have ten, some twenty servants. If the master and servant shall be equal electors, then clearly those who have no interest in the kingdom will choose those who have no interest. It may happen that the majority may … destroy property; there may be a law enacted that there shall be an equality of goods and estate.

(Rich)

We have been under slavery; our very laws were made by our conquerors [i.e. via the Norman Conquest]. We are now engaged for our freedom. Every person in England hath as clear a right to elect his representative as the greatest person in England. There is no person that is under a just government, unless he by his own free consent be put under that government.

(Wildman)

We have engaged in this kingdom and ventured our lives, and it was all for this: to recover our birthrights and privileges as Englishmen. … But it seems now, except a man hath a fixed estate in this kingdom he hath no right in this kingdom. I wonder we were so much deceived.

(Sexby)

1   What was the basis of the arguments put forward by i) the Grandees and ii) the Levellers?
2   What would the reaction to these debates have been amongst the political nation – particularly the King, nobility and gentry?

The debates lasted from 28 October to 8 November, and broke up without agreement. However, the Grandees had been alarmed at the views that their opponents had expressed, and were concerned at how far they might undermine conservative support. On 15 November, two army regiments, disillusioned by the apparent failure of the Putney Debates, mutinied at Corkbush Field in Hertfordshire, but were relatively easily dealt with. The ringleaders were arrested and one shot. Military discipline was reimposed and for the time being Leveller influences suppressed.

The Second Civil War

While these divisions continued to hinder his opponents, Charles I continued to negotiate secretly with the Scots. In December 1647, he briefly escaped from parliamentary
custody and concluded a deal with a Scottish delegation, known as the 'Engagement'. It
gave both sides what they wanted. For the Scots a promise to introduce Presbyterianism
into England and suppress all non-conformists; for the King the promise of a Scottish
army in England to defend his 'person and authority' and to restore him to 'his government, to the just rights of the Crown and his full revenue'. Charles consequently felt
able to reject flatly Parliament's latest set of proposals, known as the Four Bills, and
Parliament responded by passing the Vote of No Addresses in January 1648, which
prohibited any new initiatives to be made to Charles. The search for a negotiated settlement had reached a dead end.

The Second Civil War started in April 1648 with the outbreak of a series of rebellions, in South Wales, Essex and Kent, motivated as much by grievances over taxation
and the interference of central Government in local affairs, as by any Royalist sentiment.
These were dealt with by the New Model Army, but were followed by a far more
serious threat in July: a Scottish invasion. However, the Scots' advance was halted in
Lancashire, as they were brought to battle and decisively defeated by Cromwell at the
battle of Preston in August. Although pockets of resistance continued to hold out into
the autumn, Preston was to signal the effective end of the war.

The Second Civil War saw a significant hardening of attitudes towards the King
among many in the army. William Allen's account of a prayer meeting held by the officers of the New Model Army at Windsor, in April 1648, records a resolution:

> that it was our duty, if ever the Lord brought us back again in peace, to call Charles
> Stuart, that man of blood, to an account for that blood he had shed, and the
> mischief he had done to his utmost.

There was a sense that the King had been insincere in negotiations that Parliament had
undertaken in good faith over the previous two years. He had been responsible for
plunging the nation into war once more, and could not be trusted to hold to the terms
of any settlement that might be reached in the future. The stance of the army had radi-
calised, and the autumn was to see the army leaders moving into an alliance with the
Levellers.

However, these were not sentiments that were shared by all. A majority within
Parliament could still not conceive of a settlement without the King, and in September
they revoked the Vote of No Address and reopened negotiations with Charles. The
Army Council's response on 15 November was to publish a *Remonstrance* demanding a
purge of Parliament and the trial of the King, and the army, under the command of
Ireton, began to march on London. Despite their arrival in the capital on 2 December,
on 5 December the Commons voted by 129 to 83 to continue negotiating with
Charles.

The army took action the following day. As MPs arrived at Westminster, they found
the entrance blocked by a large force, under Colonel Pride, who had a list of Members
who were to be barred from future sittings, including some who were to be arrested.
The result of 'Pride's Purge' was that of the 471 MPs who were eligible to sit in the
Commons, 231 were barred. In addition, 45 were arrested, including some notable past

opponents of the King, such as Waller, Strode and D'Ewes. The remaining MPs were known from now on as 'the Rump', although less than half of them were to allow themselves to be involved in the subsequent proceedings to bring the King to trial.

The trial and execution of the King

God has inspired the English to be the first of mankind who have not hesitated to judge and condemn their King.

(John Milton)

On 1 January 1649, the Rump passed an ordinance to bring Charles I to trial. Following the Lords' rejection of the ordinance, they passed a further measure to establish a special High Court of Justice of 135 commissioners and began to proceed without the Lords' support. The nominations for commissioners excluded some prominent Parliamentarians, such as Vane and St John, who refused to serve, and attendance at court was poor. Forty-seven commissioners never appeared at a session, and Fairfax, who evidently had little enthusiasm for the proceedings, only attended once.

The King's trial lasted from 20–27 January. Its sole purpose was to declare the King's guilt and deliver sentence, and this was something of which Charles was well aware. He refused to respond to any of the accusations against him, concentrating on the fact that the proceedings had no validity in law. He claimed that the Commons had no judicial powers to set up such a court, and furthermore that no court had the right to try a monarch. Although technically correct, Charles's defence made no difference to the verdict, or sentence: 'That the said Charles Stuart, as a tyrant, traitor, murderer and public enemy, shall be put to death by the severing of his head from his body.'

On 30 January 1649, Charles was led on to a platform outside the Whitehall Banqueting Hall and was executed. The King's opponents had removed the immediate obstacle to a political settlement, but were now faced with the prospect of what had previously been unthinkable for all but a few radicals: Government without a monarch.

Why was Charles executed?

How are we to explain the execution of Charles I? Was it a necessary act carried out to safeguard the nation from further civil war, or a callous act of brutality, perpetrated by a small, unrepresentative minority against the wishes of the vast majority of the English people? Below is a number of extracts from contemporaries and historians that deal with these issues.

Documents

A   Charles Stuart, being admitted King of England, and therein trusted with a limited power to govern by, and according to the law of the land and not otherwise; and by his trust, oath and office, being obliged to use the power committed to him for the good and benefit of the people, and for the preservation of their rights and liberties; yet, nevertheless, out of a wicked design to erect and uphold in himself an

unlimited and tyrannical power to rule according to his will … the said Charles
Stuart … hath traitorously and maliciously levied war against the present parliament, and the people therein represented. … This court is fully satisfied in their
consciences that he has been and is guilty of the wicked design and endeavours in
the said charge … that he hath been and is the occasioner, author, and continuer of
the said unnatural, cruel, and bloody wars, and therein guilty of high treason.

(The sentence of the 'High Court of Justice', 27 January 1649)

B   All the world knows that I never did begin a war with the two Houses of
Parliament. … They began it on me; it is the militia they began upon. They
confessed that the militia was mine, but they thought it fit to have it from me. And
to be short, if anybody will look at the date of the commissions [i.e. the Militia
Ordinance and Commissions of Array], of their commissions and mine, and likewise to the declarations, [they] will see clearly that they began these unhappy
troubles, not I. … I have forgiven all the world, and even those in particular that
have been the chief causers of my death. … For the people, I truly desire their
liberty and freedom as much as anybody whomsoever; but I must tell you, that their
liberty and freedom consists in having of government; those laws by which their
lives and their goods may most be their own. It is not for having a share in government that is pertaining [belonging] to them; a subject and a sovereign are clear
different things. … Sir, it was for this that I am come here … I am the martyr of the
people.

(Charles's speech from the scaffold, 30 January 1649)

C   The gentlemen that were appointed his judges … saw in him [Charles] a disposition so bent on the ruin of all that opposed him, and of all the righteous and just
things they had contended for, that it was on the consciences of many of them, that
if they did not execute justice upon him, God would require at their hands all the
blood and desolation which would ensue by their suffering [*allowing*] him to escape.
… Some of them afterwards, for excuse … said they were under the awe of the
army, and overpersuaded by Cromwell and the like. But it is certain that all men
herein were left to their free liberty of acting, neither persuaded or compelled; and
as there were some nominated [as judges] that never sat, and others who sat at first,
but dared not hold on, so all the rest might have declined it if they would, as it is
apparent they would have suffered nothing by doing so. … As for Mr. Hutchinson
… he addressed himself to God in prayer … and finding no check, but a confirmation in his conscience that it was his duty to act as he did … proceeded to sign the
sentence against the King.

(Lucy Hutchinson, *Memoirs of Colonel Hutchinson*, 1660s)

D   At the later end of the year 1648, I had leave given me to go to London to see my
father, and during my stay there at that time at Whitehall it was that I saw the
beheading of King Charles the First. … On the day of his execution, which was
Tuesday, Jan. 30th, I stood amongst the crowd in the street before Whitehall gate,
where the scaffold was erected, and saw what was done, but not so near as to hear

anything. The blow I saw given, and can truly say with a sad heart; at the instant whereof, I remember well, there was such a groan by the thousands then present, as I never heard before and desire I may never hear again. There was according to order one troop immediately marching from Charing Cross to Westminster and another from Westminster to Charing Cross purposely to masker [*confuse*] the people, and to disperse and scatter them.

(Account of eyewitness, Philip Henry)

1   According to source A, how had Charles abused his position as King, and why was his execution justified?
2   What further light is shed upon the reasons underlying the decision to execute the King by source C?
3   How does Charles justify himself in source B?
4   How much can be deduced from source D about the public reaction to Charles's execution?

Figure 7.1 Engraving of the execution of Charles I

Historians' views

A   Trial and execution were from the start conceived as integral to each other. There was never any provision for acquittal. ... What right had any man, King or anyone else, to any other treatment when he was preparing, in the middle of a negotiation, to go back on his word and, if he got the chance, to treat the men he was dealing with as traitors? ... The men who brought him to the block, Cromwell and Ireton, were not republicans from choice but from necessity. ... Of the fifty-nine men who, having sat in judgement on the King, eventually put their names to the warrant for his execution by far the most impressive and substantial body was that of the army officers, headed by Cromwell and Ireton.

(Richard Ollard, *This War without an Enemy*, 1976)

B   Throughout the period between the surrender at Oxford and his execution thirty months later, he remained fatally addicted to his old habits of indecision, deception and prevarication. Rather than accepting that those who had defeated him were entitled to impose some restraints upon his future freedom of action as king, he persisted in believing that, as no settlement was possible without him, he would be able to escape the difficult straights in which he found himself without making any meaningful concessions to his opponents. More than anything else, it was this fundamentally unrealistic approach to the attempts of both parliament and army to achieve a compromise which exasperated and infuriated those trying to deal with Charles I and led them finally to conclude that they had no option but to remove him once and for all from the political stage. Charles lost his throne and his life because, in the aftermath of his military defeat, he behaved like a reckless, compulsive and out-of-luck gambler. Refusing all offers to cut his losses, he continued to play 'double or quits' until all his credit was finally spent and he was violently expelled from the casino.

(Christopher Durston, *Charles I*, 1998)

C   The English Revolution – the purge of Parliament in December 1648 and the trial and execution of the King in January 1649 – was carried out by a tiny clique against the wishes of the vast majority of the country. By October 1648 this clique included Ireton among the 'grandees' (though not yet Cromwell ...), rank-and-file supporters of the agitators in the army, civilian republicans, like Henry Marten and Edmund Ludlow, in Parliament, and their militant supporters in the counties. ... The fact that the events of December 1648 to January 1649 were carried out by a minority drawn largely from outside the traditional ruling elite in England and against the wishes of the elite, goes a long way towards explaining the eventual failure of the new English Republic.

(Barry Coward, *The Stuart Age*, 1994)

D   The rump House of Commons asserted that they alone represented the will of the people and unilaterally created a 'High Court of Justice for the Trying and Judging of Charles Stuart'. Although 135 people were named to this tribunal, far fewer actually served. At the end of the trial 67 voted for the death sentence, but only 59 signed the death warrant. Thus the King's death was demanded by a small minority of iron-willed extremists, nowhere near a majority of British people, only about one tenth of the legitimate membership of the House of Commons, not even a majority of the people appointed to the special tribunal.

Although these proceedings are conventionally referred to as a trial, it was more a case of judicial murder. The people who were now determined to do away with the King ... were so convinced of their cause and desirous to cloak their actions in the mantle of legality that they insisted on a public trial. There was never any genuine intention to test the King's guilt or innocence.

(Michael Young, *Charles I*, 1997)

1 In the view of sources A and B, what reasons lay behind the execution of Charles I?
2 According to sources C and D, how much support was there for Charles's execution?

Historians' verdicts on Charles I

It is perhaps inevitable that historians' judgement of Charles I has varied enormously. From the violent 'man of blood, Charles Stuart' during the years of the Republic, he was to emerge in Restoration England as 'King Charles, the Martyr', who had shed his blood for his people and Church. Whig histories predictably portray him as a tyrant and deadly enemy of parliamentary liberty, while Marxist history has tended to see him as the last remnant of an old order, trying to cling vainly on to power and the last vestiges of feudalism. In reaction to these negative portrayals, revisionists have tended to emphasise the positive aspects of Charles's rule and to suggest that his execution was largely a historical aberration. Perhaps, more recently still, the pendulum has begun to swing the other way, with historians being less charitable about Charles's character and his record as a ruler. This approach is reflected in the two extracts below:

A To understand Charles, to give him credit for his virtues, and to take his ideas seriously, is not the same as excusing him. In the end, his faults prevailed and the blame must be his. Two qualities in the end were especially decisive. One was his combativeness. As Russell wrote, Charles was 'a King who invited resistance in all of his three kingdoms, and got what he was asking for'. Charles was too eager to throw down the gauntlet. ... He bristled at dissent. When his will was thwarted, his goal was to force people into submission, not to reach mutual accommodation. From beginning to end, he was Rex Bellicosus [the King of War]. The second decisive quality in Charles' nature was his untrustworthiness. For a person who tended to provoke fights, it was doubly unfortunate that he could not be trusted to honour the terms of the reconciliation. ... Time and again he proved that he could not be trusted to respect any settlement he entered into if someday he became sufficiently powerful to renege. This was the fundamental, unforgivable defect in Charles' character that in the end made his execution necessary. It was truly his fatal flaw.

(Michael Young, *Charles I*, 1997)

B   As a ruler, he was an abject failure. His record speaks for itself. Coming to the throne on a wave of moderate enthusiasm in 1625, within five years he had presided over the complete collapse of the working relationship between crown and parliament and had allowed his armed forces to suffer humiliating reverses in both Spain and France. During his personal rule in the 1630s the outward calm in the nation masked a growing resentment over his fiscal and religious policies. In particular, through his ill-advised patronage of William Laud and Arminianism he alienated large numbers of Englishmen and women from his rule and in the late 1630s provoked an all-out rebellion by his Scots subjects. ... By 1642 he had lost control of all three of his British kingdoms. ... In the last years of his life his refusal to take seriously the various proposals which would have allowed him to regain his throne with reduced powers left his enemies with little choice but to remove him permanently. ... He himself was primarily responsible for precipitating the successive catastrophes that were visited upon the British peoples and for bringing about his own unhappy and untimely end.

(Christopher Durston, *Charles I*, 1998)

1   According to Young, what two aspects in Charles's character were decisive in his downfall?
2   On what grounds does Durston consider Charles I to have been 'an abject failure' as a ruler?
3   How convinced are you by Durston's judgement? What alternative case could be put forward?

8 The European context

Although not part of continental Europe as such, England was still profoundly influenced by developments on the European mainland. Although a proper survey of the European context is the subject for a book in its own right, there are certain key areas that can perhaps be identified as having a particular impact on English affairs, namely the Thirty Years War; the growth of the Dutch Republic; and the ambitions of Louis XIV.

The Thirty Years War

What is now known as the 'Thirty Years War' was in fact a series of conflicts that raged through central and northern Europe between 1618 and 1648. Despite the fact that England played only a minimal role in the Thirty Years War, it had a significant impact on the English political scene, not least in its ability to maintain and increase the sense of an ongoing international Catholic threat. Religious, territorial and dynastic motivation all played their part in provoking and prolonging the fighting, whose main legacy, apart from an almost unparalleled level of destruction in Germany, was the emergence of France to replace Spain as Europe's foremost power.

The war's origins are to be found in the Bohemian Revolt (1618–20). A mixture of Czech nationalism and Protestantism led to the famous 'Defenestration of Prague', in which the ministers of the Catholic monarch, Ferdinand, were thrown from the windows of the royal palace in Prague. Ferdinand was declared to have been overthrown and the Bohemian throne was instead offered to the Protestant Elector Palatine, Frederick. His acceptance of the Bohemian crown led to direct conflict with Ferdinand, who was also Holy Roman Emperor. In addition to any dynastic considerations, Frederick's actions also had a religious significance. By seizing the Bohemian throne, he had upset the fragile balance within the Empire between Protestant and Catholic Electors (see below). Ferdinand's response was as decisive as it was inevitable. He invaded Bohemia and defeated Frederick's forces at the battle of the White Mountain (1620). This victory was followed up swiftly, as imperial armies seized the Upper Palatinate in 1620 and the Lower Palatinate in 1623.

(The Holy Roman Empire was made up of a series of separate states, all of which enjoyed a great deal of independence, but also owed allegiance to the Emperor. The office of Emperor, although traditionally held by the Habsburgs, was an elected one. There were seven Electors, three of whom were churchmen and four of whom were princes. On the eve of the Bohemian Revolt, the make-up of the Electors was as shown in Figure 8.1.)

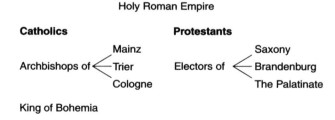

Figure 8.1 Map of the Thirty Years War and table of Electors of the Holy Roman Empire

However, Frederick's defeat did not signal the end of the fighting. Other Protestant states in northern Germany were concerned by the prospect of a resurgent and aggressive Holy Roman Empire. Together with Denmark, they resorted to armed force. The Danish War (1625–9) was to see northern Germany overrun by Spanish and Imperial armies, and Denmark forced to withdraw from the hostilities. However, the apparent triumph of the Habsburg armies was soon thrown into doubt, with the intervention of Sweden in 1630. Under the leadership of the new Protestant champion, King Gustavus Adolphus, the Swedes won a series of dramatic victories, breathing new life into the

Protestant cause. Despite Adolphus's death in 1632, Sweden continued as a major player in the fighting until the end of the war in 1648.

Whereas Denmark and Sweden's involvement in the war was due at least in part to religious motivation, France's entry into the conflict in 1635 was due entirely to strategic concerns. Under the direction of Cardinal Richelieu, its main aim was to limit the power of its traditional Habsburg rivals, while extending its own borders and influence at their expense. This initially led to funding Swedish intervention, and later to direct military action in support of the Protestant states. Ultimately, France was the main beneficiary of the conflict, with the Treaty of Westphalia (1648) upholding its claims to imperial lands, and signalling the beginning of its ascendancy and the decline of both Spain and the Empire as major European powers.

Although English involvement in the Thirty Years War was marginal at best, the conflict still had important knock-on effects in England. As we have seen, the Palatinate crisis had a destabilising effect on relations between Crown and Parliament in the early 1620s, as James I tried to resist the pressure to become involved to aid his son-in-law via direct military intervention. As Europe divided along largely religious lines, James continued to pursue a Catholic match for his son, Charles, a policy that caused considerable disquiet among his Protestant subjects. The belated switch to an aggressive approach in foreign relations, seen in Mansfeld's expedition to the Palatinate, was unsuccessful and did little to foster domestic unity in England.

Buckingham pursued a more ambitious foreign policy, which saw a degree of direct involvement in the Thirty Years War. Alliances with the Danish and the Dutch, and direct military action against Spain, and later France, however, were no more successful. The enormous cost and failure of Buckingham's various initiatives destabilised parliamentary relations and were in part responsible for Charles's eventual decision to rule without Parliament after 1629.

Although the Thirty Years War had little direct impact on England after Buckingham's death, its influence continued to be felt. The war saw horrific levels of destruction and barbarity directed towards the civilian population of Germany. Stories of atrocities perpetrated by the Imperial armies, such as the sack of Magdeburg in 1631, in which around 25,000 of her 30,000 Protestant inhabitants were massacred, helped fuel anti-Catholic sentiment. Pamphleteers drew attention to the continuing threat of the Counter-Reformation in mainland Europe, and to the links between Catholicism and tyranny and violent oppression. The fear of Catholicism, which gave Pym and Parliament so much of their support during the early 1640s, was not born out of a vacuum, but, at least in part, out of what contemporaries perceived as the religious conflicts of the Thirty Years War.

The Dutch Republic

The seventeenth century was to see the emergence of the Dutch Republic as a new power in western Europe. Its status rested above all on its commercial strength. Trade was the cornerstone of Dutch commerce and her merchants were involved in carrying goods in the Baltic, Atlantic and Mediterranean as well as in developing routes to and from the East Indies. It had an enormous merchant fleet, estimated at around 568,000 tons by 1670, larger than all the other trading powers put together. In addition, it also had a well-developed financial system, with the banking houses of Amsterdam providing the credit and the means of exchanging currency required to sustain such a level of commercial activity. It was also notable for its unique political make-up. The United Provinces of the Dutch Republic were made up of seven separate provinces, who each retained a great deal of autonomy over their own affairs. Although there was a *Stadtholder*, who performed the role of Head of State, effective power rested in an elected body, the States-General, who above all represented the interests of the Republic's merchant class.

The rise of the Dutch Republic was due in part to the broader international situation. Most of its energies since 1560 had been devoted to war with Spain, as it struggled to break away from Habsburg control. In 1609, it finally won a breathing space in the Truce of Antwerp, which was effectively prolonged by Spain's military and financial commitments during the Thirty Years War. The Dutch were able to take advantage of this by attacking Spanish colonies and developing their trading muscle while their former adversary was absorbed in the epic struggles in Germany. Under the Treaty of Münster (1648), Spain finally acknowledged Dutch independence and the Republic's security seemed assured for the first time.

However, Dutch prosperity brought with it the jealousy and hostility of its neighbours. As the French minister, Colbert, observed, 'commerce causes a perpetual combat in peace and war amongst the nations of Europe, as to who shall win the most of it'. According to his calculations, of the 20,000 trading vessels in Europe, 'the Dutch have 15,000 to 16,000, the English about 3,000 to 4,000, and the French 500 to 600' – a situation both the English and the French found unsatisfactory. Economic pressure was brought to bear on the Dutch, first by the English, in the form of a series of Navigation Acts, aimed at restricting the flow of Dutch trade with England and her colonies. These commercial tensions led in turn to armed conflict, with the outbreak of three Anglo–Dutch wars, in 1652–4, 1665–7 and 1672–4.

The most serious threat to the Republic was to come not from England, however, but rather from the France of Louis XIV. Dutch naval superiority and trading strength were seen as major obstacles to the ambitions of Louis to develop a French supremacy over Europe. Colbert's attitude was uncompromising:

> As we have crushed Spain on land, so we must crush Holland at sea. The Dutch have no right to usurp all commerce … knowing very well that so long as they are the masters of all trade, their naval forces will continue to grow and to render them so powerful that they will be able to assume the role of arbiters of peace and war in Europe and to set limits to the king's plans.

Trade tariffs were progressively introduced against the Dutch during the 1660s and early 1670s, and war was to follow in 1672.

However, the Franco–Dutch war of 1672–9 was not only the result of the struggle for trade. In 1668, the Dutch had formed a Triple Alliance with Sweden and England, designed to protect their borders by preventing further French penetration into the Spanish Netherlands. Louis was incensed at what he saw as the treachery of the Dutch, whose struggle for independence from Spain had been supported by France, and whom he had previously regarded as reliable allies. Having bought the support of Charles II of England at the Treaty of Dover, Louis declared war against the Dutch, his armies making dramatic advances and almost achieving complete victory. It was at this moment of crisis that the young William of Orange was to emerge as the saviour of the Republic. Replacing Jan de Witt, who had been lynched by a mob on the streets of

Amsterdam, as leader of the war effort, he ordered the breaching of the dykes that stopped the French advance in its tracks. This ruinous tactic bought William the time he needed to reorganise his forces, and to win the support of the Holy Roman Emperor, Leopold. Faced by an impassable barrier of water, a newly determined enemy and attack from Germany, the French were unable to recover the military initiative. Prolonged warfare was eventually brought to an end with the Treaty of Nijmegen in 1679, although, in William, Louis XIV was to continue to face a most uncompromising and determined enemy.

In 1688, the Dutch intervened directly in English affairs, with the overthrow of its Catholic monarch, James II. It was probably the desire to harness extra resources against France, rather than any sense of Protestant duty as such, that led William of Orange to invade England and alongside his wife, Mary, accept the English throne. With his position in England secure, William was to dedicate his energies to mobilising England and the Dutch Republic against Louis, but also to building a European-wide alliance to curb French power.

Louis XIV

By the end of Louis XIV's minority in 1660, it was apparent that France had assumed the status of Europe's foremost power. As we have seen, the Treaty of Westphalia had already pointed to the beginnings of Spanish decline and the emergence of France, a trend further developed by the foreign policy of his minister, Cardinal Mazarin, in the intervening years. However, it was not until the reign of the 'Sun King' himself, (as Louis XIV was styled) that French ascendancy in Europe was really established.

When Louis assumed the throne, he found himself as monarch of the wealthiest and most heavily populated country in Europe. Although Mazarin had failed in his attempt to get Louis elected as Holy Roman Emperor in 1656, the young king's position was enhanced by the fact that he was married to the Infanta of Spain, thereby gaining a claim to the Spanish empire. While the aim of his predecessors had been to limit Spanish power and prevent it from threatening France's own survival, Louis was able to think in much more ambitious terms: the absorption of Spain and the creation of a new French empire. It was these ambitions that were to set the tenor of much of his reign.

Louis's immediate aims seem to have been more modest. Putting Marazin's view, that the only way to 'provide an impregnable rampart for Paris' was to occupy the Low Countries, into practice, Louis claimed a right to the Spanish Netherlands on the grounds of his wife's bloodline. Failure to reach a negotiated settlement with Spain led to Louis's invasion in 1667, and the capture of much of the southern part of the country. However, at this moment of seeming triumph, the French advance was halted by the formation of the Triple Alliance of the United Provinces, England and Sweden. They accepted Louis's right to keep the cities he had captured, but were pledged to oppose any further advances north. In the face of the combined opposition of three major maritime powers, Louis was forced to back down, but his anger towards the Dutch was intense. He considered their action to be a betrayal of their previous friendship, and was determined to exact his revenge. Allying with England at Dover in 1670, he then proceeded to buy the neutrality of Sweden and various German states. In 1672, he was in a position to launch his invasion, which was only halted at the brink of victory by the Dutch breaking the dykes and flooding much of their country.

This expedient gave his opponents time to organise. By 1674 the Dutch had been joined in a Grand Alliance against France by Spain, the Empire and a number of German princes. This development was a significant one: for much of the rest of his reign, Louis was to face the opposition of most of Europe's major powers, usually allied against him. Although peace was made with his enemies in 1679, war was to break out again in 1688. This time the anti-French League of Augsburg included the Empire, Spain, the Dutch Republic, some German states, and Sweden. With William of Orange's accession as King of England, the alliance against France was to gain a further impetus. Fighting ranged from the Netherlands, to the borders of Spain, and from Ireland to northern Italy, lasting until the Peace of Ryswick in 1697. Yet, despite the cost and inconclusiveness of the war, Ryswick was to prove little more than a respite, with war breaking out again in 1702.

This renewal of hostilities was prompted by the death of Charles II of Spain, and the competing claims of those who wished to succeed him. The annexation of the Spanish empire had long been the central aim of Louis's foreign policy, and a major element in the opposition of most of the rest of Europe against him. Louis's claim of the Spanish throne for his son was to plunge Europe into another phase of major warfare, which was not concluded until 1710.

The figure of Louis XIV dominates any study of latter seventeenth-century Europe, and as such he had a profound impact on English foreign and domestic policy. One can only speculate on how far Charles's domestic problems in the 1670s had their root in the Treaty of Dover and the subsequent French alliance. How far were James II's Catholicising policies undermined by Louis's Revocation of the Edict of Nantes in 1685? How far did fear of Louis influence William of Orange's decision to intervene in English affairs? And how far did war against France after William's accession determine the shape of the Glorious Revolution Settlement? Without the part played by Louis XIV's France on the European stage, it is most unlikely that events would have unfolded as they did in England.

9 The Republic, 1649–60

The rule of the Rump, 1649–53

Some six weeks after the execution of Charles I, the Rump passed 'The Act Abolishing the office of King'. It dispensed with the institution of monarchy, on the grounds that it was something 'unnecessary, burdensome and dangerous to the liberty, safety and public interest of the people', and 'that for the most part, use hath been made of the regal power and prerogative to oppress, impoverish and enslave the subject'. The House of Lords, who had refused to support proceedings against the King, was also to be dispensed with as it had shown itself to be 'useless and dangerous to the people of England'. Authority was now to be vested solely in the Rump, working alongside a council of State made up of its own members. The new republic was declared to be a 'Commonwealth and Free State'.

Although radicals initially welcomed the Rump's actions, it soon became apparent that they were not going to be the door to further reform. The attack of the Leveller, John Lilburne, on the Rump in a pamphlet, *England's New Chains Discovered*, in March 1649, signalled the breakdown of the alliance between them. Calls for the Rump to be dissolved and replaced by a new Parliament elected on the basis of universal male suffrage were ignored, and instead the Rump ordered the suppression of the Levellers. Several prominent Levellers, including Lilburne, were arrested, and Leveller mutinies in the army were put down by Cromwell in London and at Burford.

The Rump's resistance to radicalism is best explained in terms of them being republicans more by circumstance than by conviction. Most of the Rump were members of the gentry and JPs, and had a strong vested interest in opposing radical reform. Although they may have supported the execution of the King on the grounds of necessity, they were still firm believers in hierarchy and were fearful of the anarchy and social breakdown that radical groups, such as the Levellers, seemed to be working towards. The Rump, therefore, had been reluctant revolutionaries, who were now eager to retreat back into conservatism.

Ireland and Scotland

The Rump's most pressing concern, following its repression of the Levellers, was to deal with the situation in Ireland. Ireland had never been pacified following the revolt in 1641, and the situation was made more serious by an alliance between the Catholic rebels and Royalist forces under the Duke of Ormonde. Fearing that Ireland could be used as a base for invasion by the late King's son, Charles II, Cromwell was sent there with a large force to deal with the threat.

Cromwell's success in his Irish campaigns was due in part to the fact that he had a well-disciplined and paid army under his control. He had dealt ruthlessly with the Leveller mutinies and ensured that all wage arrears were paid before the army left for Ireland, from the proceeds of the seizure of Crown lands. The army was further strengthened by racial and religious sentiment. In Cromwell's mind, the Irish were an uncivilised nation of papists whose atrocities against Protestant settlers in 1641 were to be avenged. The sieges of Drogheda and Wexford, in September and October 1649 respectively, were followed by brutal massacres of their civilian populations. To Cromwell, such actions were wholly justified. In his mind this was:

> the righteous judgement of God upon these barbarous wretches, who have stained their hands in so much innocent blood; and it will tend to prevent the effusion of blood for the future. … It was set upon some of our hearts … by the spirit of God.

In 1650, Cromwell was recalled by the Rump to deal with a new threat from Scotland, and left Ireton behind in Ireland to complete its pacification. With Fairfax's resignation as commander-in-chief, Cromwell took over command of the army and the responsibility of dealing with the Scots, who had allied themselves with Charles II. Cromwell invaded Scotland in the summer and defeated the Royalist forces at Dunbar, although he was unable to follow up his victory. The culmination of what is known as the Third Civil War followed a year later, when Charles II's army invaded England and was crushed by Cromwell at the battle of Worcester, in September 1651. Although Charles escaped to the continent, the battle of Worcester marked the end of the civil wars and an end to any serious military threats to the Commonwealth. From now on it could devote its energies to searching for a political settlement.

The difficulties faced by the Rump

Although many historians have criticised the Rump for its relative inaction between 1649 and 1653, the circumstances under which it was working were far from ideal. It lacked the support of much of the political nation, who were alienated from it by its involvement in regicide, and it clearly lacked legitimacy. It was the only one remaining part of the traditional three estates of Parliament. Its members had been elected back in 1641, and, of those, many had been purged by the army. In the circumstances, its claim to rule by the authority of the people was difficult to maintain. Its unpopularity was compounded by the activities of the county committees and the continuation of high levels of taxation that a standing army required. It needed fresh elections to help legitimise its position, but dared not risk them as they would almost certainly produce an anti-army and possibly even a Royalist majority.

The Rump's reaction to its situation was to avoid any dramatic reform, while trying to portray itself as a guarantor of social and political stability, and thereby gradually win over the support of the conservative élites. This approach had to be balanced with the demands of the army, particularly for further religious reform, on whose support the Rump was dependent for its continued existence.

The new Government's room for manoeuvre was further limited by the financial constraints under which it was working. Initially it enjoyed huge windfalls from the seizure of Crown lands, as well as lands belonging to the bishops and cathedral chapters, and the estates of some 780 leading Royalists, but this was quickly swallowed up by the debts accrued by Parliament in the 1640s, and in paying off the arrears of the army. The political situation dictated that it dare not disband the army, and the costs of maintaining a sizeable standing army were further increased by the wars in Ireland, Scotland and against the Dutch. Taxes were increased and the assessment and excise continued to be levied, but even so the Rump was unable to meet its financial obligations. By April 1653, it was facing a short-fall in revenue of £700,000.

The achievements of the Rump

In the domestic sphere, the Rump introduced some cautious changes. It went some way to meeting the old Leveller demands for law reform by changing the language used in proceedings from old French and Latin to English, although more radical Puritan proposals, such as reforming the law codes along biblical lines, were rejected. Other proposals, for reducing legal fees and improving access to the courts fell foul of the substantial block of lawyer MPs in the Rump, between 60 and 70 of a total membership of 211, who felt their interests threatened by such reforms.

The Rump's approach to religious reform was equally cautious. The breakdown of the national Church that had followed the abolition of bishops was a cause of great concern to many MPs, and to the traditional élites in the localities. Although the Rump did repeal the Act making regular church attendance compulsory, it could not bring itself to meet the calls of the Independents and the army, for full religious toleration. With the rise of religious sects such as the Ranters and the Quakers, whose teachings were perceived as a threat to social hierarchy, such toleration was considered most undesirable. The fear of social and political instability was reflected in the reintroduction of censorship, for the first time since royal control over the press broke down in 1641, under the direction of John Milton. In a further measure designed to counter such groups, a Blasphemy Act was also introduced in 1650.

A similar concern to limit social evils led to the introduction of an Adultery Act. It gave a duty to JPs to take action against adulterers, a task previously belonging to the Church courts, which had been abolished. Although such measures won the approval of Puritan critics, the Rump was still attacked for not doing more to promote the cause of a further 'godly' reformation. A bill for the 'Propagation of the Gospel', designed to supervise clerical appointments and ensure the spread of orthodox Protestant teaching throughout the whole country, failed to gain the Rump's approval, and existing commissions for this purpose in Wales and the north were not renewed.

Perhaps the Rump's most successful sphere of activity was in that of foreign affairs. The introduction of the Navigation Act in October 1651 required that all imports to England had to be carried in English ships, or in ships of the country from where those imports originated. This was a measure aimed at the Dutch, whose trading activities in the East and West Indies, as well as North America and West Africa, had been a source of tension for some time. War followed in 1652, in which the English fleet, under the command of Robert Blake, decisively defeated the Dutch in a number of engagements. Large amounts of Dutch shipping were seized, and by the end of 1653 the United Provinces were forced to open negotiations to bring about an end to hostilities.

The end of the Rump

It was, however, the Rump's inability to grasp the nettle of constitutional reform that led eventually to its downfall. Although the Rump had agreed to its own dissolution in September 1651, it had reserved the right to decide on what and who should succeed it. Although it is unclear now what it was actually proposing, Cromwell lost patience with the Rump and decided to take action. Whether frustrated by its inaction, or concerned about the manner in which the Rump proposed to hold elections, Cromwell entered the House in April 1653, accompanied by some of his troops, and forcibly ended their sitting, exclaiming: 'You have sat here too long for the good you do. In the name of God, go!'

In a moment of great irony, the army that had been created by Parliament to protect its liberties, and that had already purged that Parliament once before in 1648, had finally turned on its creator and assumed responsibility for rule itself. The Commonwealth's well-being now rested with its army, and more specifically in the hands of its commander-in-chief, Oliver Cromwell.

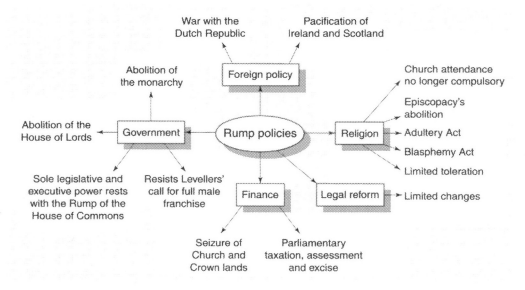

Figure 9.1 Policies of the Rump, 1649–53

The record of the Rump: the reaction of contemporaries

The dissolution of the Rump excited considerable comment among contemporaries. They were divided as to how well the Rump had provided effective government, and as to what Cromwell's real motivations were in closing down the assembly. The sources below give some idea of the divergence of opinion:

A   [Cromwell] loaded the Parliament with the vilest reproaches, charging them not to have a heart to do anything for the public good, to have espoused [*promoted*] the corrupt interest of Presbytery and the lawyers, who were the supporters of tyranny and oppression, accusing them of an intention to perpetuate them in power … and thereupon told them that the Lord had done with them, and had chosen other instruments for the carrying on of his work. … This he spoke with so much passion and discomposure of mind, as if he had been distracted [*mad*].

(Edmund Ludlow's account of the dissolution of the Rump, 1650s)

B   The dissolution is viewed with admiration rather than surprise and gives general satisfaction. The popular voice and the press shows how much the nation disapproved the administration of the parliament, which is principally reproached for having constantly promised law reform but never having done anything, and with having broken faith with those who advanced considerable loans during the civil wars. While instead of seeking to relieve the people, as they promised, they always deceived and taxed them more and more and finally they saddled the country with a troublesome and expensive war with Holland.

(Report by Paulucci, Venetian Ambassador, May 1653)

C   We continued four years before we were put an end to. In which time, I appeal to all, if the nation that had been blasted and torn began not to exceedingly flourish. At the end of the four years, scarce a sight to be seen that we had had a war. Trade flourished; the City of London grew rich; we were the most potent by sea that was ever known in England. Our navy and armies were never better. … What care did the Parliament then take to furnish their army from London with all necessaries, by land and in ships; all provided with the greatest diligence. None but a numerous company of good and honest hearted men could have done the like.

(Speech by Arthur Haselrig, February 1659, quoted in the diary of Themes Burton)

D   The parliament had now, by the blessing of God, restored the commonwealth to such a happy, rich, and plentiful condition, as it was not so flourishing before the war, and although the taxes that were paid were great, yet the people were rich and able to pay them … [dissolution was justified] by making false recriminations of the parliament-men, as that they meant to perpetuate themselves in honour and office, that they had gotten vast estates, and perverted justice for gain … and a thousand such like things, which time manifested to be false.

(Lucy Hutchinson, *Memoirs of Colonel Hutchinson*, 1660s)

1   According to Ludlow, why did Cromwell dissolve the Rump? How sympathetic does he seem towards Cromwell's actions?
2   How far does the report of the Venetian Ambassador support Cromwell's claims?
3   What alternative arguments are put forward in Sources C and D?
4   Comment upon the reliability of Sources A–D.

Oliver Cromwell

Background

Born in Huntingdon in 1599, Oliver Cromwell's first forty years were unremarkable. His family were of gentry stock, his early life was largely spent farming and sitting as a JP. Although elected as MP for Huntingdon in 1628, he took no notable part in the parliament of 1628–9 and it was not until his election as MP for Cambridge in 1640 that he became more active in national affairs.

Cromwell's Puritanism and dislike of prerogative government put him firmly in Pym's camp, although he was not a leading Parliamentarian at this stage. His first speech in the Long Parliament was to attack the Star Chamber, and he went on actively to support the Triennial Bill, the Root and Branch petition, and the Militia Ordinance, which marked him out as one of the more radical of the King's opponents. His commitment to the parliamentary cause was further underlined by his seizure of Cambridge Castle and the colleges' plate for Parliament in July 1642, before the actual outbreak of hostilities the following month.

It was the Civil War that witnessed Cromwell's rise to national prominence. In 1643, he secured Lincolnshire for Parliament, leading his own regiment, the 'Ironsides', men chosen not only for their fighting abilities, but also their willingness to 'stand for the liberty of the gospel and the laws of the land'. His abilities were recognised with his promotion to lieutenant-general in January 1644, and his leadership of the Parliamentary cavalry played a crucial part in the victory at Marston Moor that summer. Cromwell's importance to the parliamentary war effort was illustrated by his exemption from the Self-Denying Ordinance in 1645, and his appointment as second-in-command, under Fairfax, of the New Model Army. It was his cavalry that again proved instrumental to Parliament's decisive victory at Naseby in June 1645.

After 1646, Cromwell became increasingly important as a political figure, taking part in the Army Revolt of 1647, and playing a leading role in the Putney Debates and the subsequent suppression of the Levellers. His position was further enhanced by his victory over the Scots at the battle of Preston in 1648, and he was to be a pivotal figure in the decision to bring Charles I to trial. The pacification of Ireland and the defeat of the Scots in the Third Civil War, at Dunbar and Worcester, owed a great deal to his military prowess, and with the retirement of Fairfax in 1650, his control over the army was complete.

By 1653, with the dissolution of the Rump, Cromwell was the most powerful military and political figure in England. His rise owed much to his military skills, and the loyalty that he managed to inspire in his troops, but also in an unshakable conviction that he was an agent of God's will. It was this belief in 'providentialism' that underpinned much of Cromwell's career.

The Parliament of Saints, 1653

With the dissolution of the Rump, Cromwell was faced with a political vacuum. Although he seemed to have had few qualms about using the army to dispense with the Rump once he was convinced that such a course of action was justified, Cromwell had little interest in establishing direct military rule. His answer was to create a new governmental body, the Parliament of Saints. Due to the fact that the people, in Cromwell's view, needed 'to forget monarchy' before elections could be carried out safely, the Parliament of Saints was a nominated assembly, whose 140 members were selected by the army's Council of Officers. The idea originated with Major-General Harrison, a Fifth Monarchist, who pressed Cromwell to create an assembly of Puritan 'saints', gathered from the various Independent and Separatist churches. In the event, not all the nominees would have fitted Harrison's description of 'saints', although a substantial number were. The majority were landowners of gentry backgrounds, whose instincts were relatively conservative.

Some members, however, had a clear agenda for reform, which drew on the programmes of the Levellers and other radical groups. They wanted to reform the law using the principles of the Old Testament, and reduce it in size and complexity, as had been done in New England; to abolish tithes and the rights of holders of impropriated tithes; and they even suggested economies within the army. Such a programme cut against the interests of important groups on whose support Cromwell depended, and as such could not be allowed. Most disturbing was the threat to tithe-holders, most of whom were gentry, which was seen as an unacceptable attack on property. With Cromwell's encouragement, the moderates in the assembly met early on the morning of 12 December and voted the Parliament's dissolution before the radical members had arrived. When the radicals attempted to hold a session anyway, they were cleared from the House by armed troops. The Parliament of Saints' hope for a godly reformation foundered on the rocks of conservatism. As Cromwell complained, the radicals programme had attacked 'liberty and property. ... Who could have said that anything was their own if they had gone on?'

The Protectorate, 1653–8

> I am as much for government by consent as any man, but where shall we find that consent?
>
> (Oliver Cromwell, 1656)

The Instrument of Government

With the failure of the Parliament of Saints, Cromwell accepted the suggestion put forward by another of his generals, John Lambert. This was a written form of constitution, known as the Instrument of Government, which laid down the respective powers and rights of the executive and legislature as follows.

The Executive:
- Executive power to be held by a Lord Protector (i.e. Cromwell), with the assistance of a Council of State. On his death, a new Protector would be elected by the Council.
- Vacancies on the Council to be filled by the Protector, choosing from nominees suggested by the Council and Parliament.
- Officers of State to be chosen with the approval of Parliament.
- The executive was to be in control of the armed forces, and a regular revenue was to be provided to maintain an army of 30,000. In addition, £200,000 was to be provided for the costs of running the Government. Any additional funds would depend on parliamentary approval.

Figure 9.2 Engraving of Cromwell's Triumph over Error and Faction (1658)

The Legislature:

- Parliament was to be called at least once every three years, and could not be dissolved without its own consent.
- Its bills could be delayed by the Protector by up to twenty days, but thereafter they would automatically become law.
- The voting franchise was limited (in county seats it was changed from holding land worth 40 shillings or more per year, to those whose total wealth was calculated at £200 or more) thereby reducing the size of the electorate.

The Instrument also laid down articles on the practice of religion, which allowed freedom of worship to all, with the exception of Catholics, Episcopalians (those supporting the institution of bishops), and those who 'hold forth and practise licentiousness', a catch-all phrase for sects such as the Ranters and Quakers.

---

1   How far do you think the Instrument fulfils the aspirations of Parliamentarians such as Pym, during the constitutional struggles of 1640–1?
2   How workable would you judge the Instrument to have been as a framework for government? Are there any concerns that you think contemporaries might have had over it?

The Instrument in practice

The most immediate effect of the Instrument was to allow a much wider degree of religious toleration. For the first time, the content and style of church services were not laid down by law, but rather each congregation was able to order its affairs as it saw fit. The only limit on this were commissions that were set up to exercise a degree of control over the clergy. A Commission of Triers was established in London to ensure that candidates for the ministry met certain standards of morality and godliness; and, in each county, a Commission of Ejectors was set up to expel ministers and schoolmasters who were found guilty of immorality. Although in theory the Instrument did not extend toleration to Catholics or Episcopalians, in practice both were given a great deal of freedom.

Although the Instrument was drawn up in December 1653, Cromwell ruled directly by ordinance for the next nine months. When the first Protectorate Parliament finally met in September 1654, some of its members quickly made it clear that they did not necessarily share Cromwell's view of their powers, as laid down in the Instrument. Over 100 MPs who were elected had previously sat in the Long Parliament, the Rump of which had been forcibly dissolved by Cromwell, some sixteen months earlier. Their choice of William Lenthall as Speaker, who had also performed that role in the Long Parliament, suggested that many MPs saw the new institution as a continuation of the old one. Although Cromwell did have supporters in Parliament, it was his opponents who seized the initiative, and started to attack the division of powers outlined in the Instrument.

Cromwell's response, which was to surround the House with troops and demand a recognition of the Instrument in its original form, prompted a walk out by Haselrig and around a hundred other members. However, other opponents remained and continued to call for limitations on the Protector's powers, in particular parliamentary control over the militia and appointments to the Council of State. In addition, some conservatives who were concerned over the proliferation of radical religious sects, started to demand changes to the Instrument's provision for religious toleration. Cromwell's reaction was characteristic and decisive. In January 1655 he dissolved Parliament, and returned to rule by Ordinance, or decree.

The major-generals, 1655–6

In the spring of 1655, a Royalist rising broke out in Wiltshire and, although it was easily suppressed, Cromwell decided that it was indicative of the need for greater control over the provinces. He imposed direct military rule on the country, by dividing it into eleven districts, each under the control of a major-general. They were responsible not only for maintaining internal security, but also for the enforcement of a series of instructions that required them to suppress immorality and ensure order and godliness. In the light of the financial strains placed on the Government by the existing army, the major-generals were to be aided in their task by a new militia, to be paid for by a 10 per cent tax on the estates of known Royalists, known as 'decimation'.

The effectiveness of the major-generals scheme varied from area to area, and from individual to individual. In Lancashire, Major-General Worsely claimed to have closed over 200 alehouses in the Blackburn area alone, and, in Lincolnshire and Nottinghamshire, Major-General Whalley seems to have been particularly enthusiastic in his suppression of Royalist sympathisers, and traditional entertainments such as cockfighting, stage-plays and horse-racing. Other major-generals, however, such as Goffe in the southern counties, seem to have applied themselves to their task with less relish. Perhaps the most important limitation on the major-generals was the resentment felt towards them by the local élites in the counties. They were seen as outsiders imposed by central government, who were undermining the position and role of the gentry. Without the co-operation of this class, the success of the major-generals was bound to be limited.

The limitations of this system of rule were exposed with the outbreak of war with Spain in 1656. The Government's income from assessments and customs was already insufficient for its peacetime commitments, and it was evident that, in order to fight a war, parliamentary taxation would be needed. Like Charles in 1640, Cromwell had little choice but to recall Parliament.

The Second Protectorate Parliament, 1656–8

The reaction to this period of military rule was characterised by the widespread election slogan: 'No courtiers, no swordsmen, no decimation'. When Parliament reassembled in September, tensions were immediately heightened by the Council of State's decision to exclude over a hundred MPs who they suspected would be critical of the regime. This in turn led to the withdrawal of around sixty more members in protest. Although the remainder duly voted £400,000 for the Spanish war, they went on to demonstrate their concern over the policy of religious toleration by attacking the Quaker, James Naylor, who was accused of having claimed to be Christ. Although Cromwell saved his life, he was unable to prevent him from being savagely punished by Parliament. Like his Stuart predecessors, he was forced to make concessions to ensure parliamentary supply.

It was evident to both Cromwell and many MPs that the Instrument needed amendment if a more workable settlement was to be found, and a set of proposals along these lines was put forward by Parliament in the spring of 1657, in the *Humble Petition and Advice*. The most dramatic proposal was that Cromwell should accept the throne, which after some hesitation the Protector declined, probably on the grounds that the army was against the idea. However, the rest of the suggested amendments were accepted. They were as follows:

- The Protector should be able to appoint his successor, thus opening up the possibility that the post would become hereditary.
- Parliament would consist of two Houses, the second House of which would consist of individuals nominated by the Protector.
- Nobody elected to the Commons could be excluded from it.
- Appointments to the Council were to be approved by Parliament.
- An annual revenue to be provided of £1 million for the armed forces, and £300,000 for costs of Government.
- A 'Confession of Faith' to be agreed by the Protector and Parliament, which no one would be able to 'revile or reproach' without facing punishment.

Cromwell's acceptance of the Humble Petition was intended to lead to more harmonious relations with Parliament. However, any such expectations were dashed when Parliament reassembled for its second session in January 1658. Cromwell's strength in the Commons had been weakened by the elevation of many of his supporters to the new upper House, and the readmission of the excluded members, many of whom were republicans, prompted a concerted attack on the new constitution. The validity of the 'other House' was questioned, as were Cromwell's enhanced powers. Arthur Haselrig accused Cromwell of trying to return the Commons to slavery, and Sir Henry Vane declared that he saw the Protector as being 'not many steps from the old family' (i.e. the Stuarts). With the circulation of a petition within London calling for the abolition of the second chamber and the Protectorate, Cromwell took action. Two weeks into the new session he dissolved Parliament, exclaiming: 'I think it high time that an end be put to your sitting; let God be the judge between you and me.'

From February to September 1658, Cromwell returned to rule by Ordinance, governing with the assistance of his Council. Despite several attempts at finding a political settlement that would be workable and acceptable to his parliaments, Cromwell found himself further from any settlement than ever.

Religious policy

For Cromwell, religious division had been at the heart of the conflicts of the 1640s. It was now his responsibility to foster conditions that would allow the emergence of a broad Protestant consensus and godliness within England. He saw compulsion in religion as being something that was fundamentally undesirable. Having overthrown the tyranny of Charles and his bishops, he fervently opposed those who strove to replace it with alternative forms of religious control. As he asserted:

> Those that were sound in faith, how proper was it for them to labour for liberty, for a just liberty, that men should not be trampled upon for their consciences! … What

greater hypocrisy [is there] than for those who were oppressed by the bishops to become the greatest oppressors themselves, so soon as their yoke was removed?

Although Cromwell favoured a broad religious toleration, it did have its limits. Toleration was not to be extended to Catholics, nor to those sects that 'make religion a pretence for arms and blood'. Subversive sects that threatened duly appointed Government were to be suppressed, but otherwise any who would 'continue quiet and peaceable, they should enjoy conscience and liberty'. Such an approach led to Cromwell coming under fire from both sides of the religious divide. To conservatives, who favoured the introduction of a Presbyterian system to ensure religious order, his views threatened chaos; to the members of the sects (including many in the army), they were still denied the freedom for which they strove. As Cromwell himself noted, 'I have had buffets and rebukes, on the one hand and the other; some censuring me for Presbytery; others as an encourager of all sects and heresies.'

In the promotion of this policy of toleration within limits, Cromwell and the Council issued two ordinances in 1654, aimed at ensuring the suitability of church ministers. In March, a central commission of thirty-eight men (later known as 'Triers') was established to ensure that all new appointees to church livings were 'men of known integrity and piety, orthodox men and faithful'. This was followed by the establishment of local commissioners (later known as 'Ejectors'), who were to deal with those ministers already in posts, who were guilty of 'ignorance, insufficiency, scandal in their lives and conversations or negligence in their respective callings'. The aim behind these measures was not to try to enforce a rigid uniformity in beliefs or practice, but to produce a loose framework of State control, which maintained minimum standards and excluded those who might threaten the religious peace that Cromwell wanted to bring about. The inclusiveness of Cromwell's aims is demonstrated by the efforts to which he went, to try to ensure that the commissioners came from as many different groups as possible, including Presbyterians, Baptists and Independents. Even though religious toleration was not absolute under Cromwell, his stance was still remarkable by contemporary standards. Under his government, there was a far greater degree of religious freedom than under any other regime in seventeenth-century England.

Another interesting aspect that sheds light on the Protector's approach to religious policy was the readmission of Jews into England. Prohibited from living, trading or worshipping in England since the thirteenth century, the Council of State was petitioned to allow the return of Jews into the country. While the support the proposal attracted was in part due to the economic benefits that any such influx might bring, Cromwell's enthusiasm was founded more in theological considerations. Rather than being motivated by notions of religious toleration, Cromwell pointed out biblical texts that indicated that the return of Christ and the arrival of the millennium (his thousand-year rule on earth) was dependent on the conversion of the Jews. This millenary enthusiasm, usually more normally associated with the sects, was also an important part of Cromwell's religious make-up. His firm conviction of God's providence led him to pursue those policies that he believed would lead England nearer to God's new kingdom on earth.

Documents: the judgement of his contemporaries

Contemporary opinion over Cromwell was predictably divided. Many groups had very obvious axes to grind, from Royalists and republicans to radicals and conservatives, although the Protector did have his supporters. The issue of his motivation and his sincerity in claiming religious inspiration for his actions are dealt with in the extracts below.

A   [Cromwell had been] long famous for godliness and zeal in his country, of great note for his service in the House; accepted of a commission at the very beginning of the war; wherein he served his country faithfully and it was observed that God was with him and he began to be renowned; insomuch that men ... [had] an expectation of greater things and higher employments whereunto divine providence had designed him for the good of this kingdom.

(Joshua Sprigge, *Anglia Rediviva*, 1647)

B   You shall scarce speak to Cromwell about any thing, but he will lay his hand on his heart, elevate his eyes, and call God to record, he will weep, weep and repent, even while he doth smite you under the first rib.

(A Leveller pamphlet, *The Hunting of the Foxes*, 1649)

C   I must speak of his religion. While in general he displays a most exemplary exterior, yet it cannot be known what rite [*type of religion*] he follows. ... The moment Cromwell was elevated to power, he not only broke off with the Independents, but condemned and persecuted them. Thus he has changed his creed in accordance with the interests of state, and he thinks it suits his policy that 246 religions should be professed in London, all alike in hostility to the Pope, but differing greatly from each other and incompatible. This division into so many sects makes them all weak, so that no one is strong enough to cause him any apprehension.

(A report by the Venetian ambassador in England, 1656)

D   I am a man standing in the place I am in, which place I undertook not so much out of hope of doing any good, as out of a desire to prevent mischief and evil, which I did see was imminent upon the nation. I saw we were running headlong into confusion and disorder, and would necessarily run into blood ... I am ready to serve not as a King, but as a constable. For truly I have as before God thought it often, that I could not tell what my business was ... save by comparing it with a good constable to keep the peace of the parish.

(Cromwell to a parliamentary committee, 1657)

E   Cromwell and his army grew wanton with their power, and invented a thousand tricks of government which, when nobody opposed, they themselves fell to dislike and vary every day. ... He made up several sorts of mock parliaments, but not finding one of them absolutely for his turn, turned them off again. ... True religion was now almost lost, even among the religious party, and hypocrisy became an epidemical disease. ... He at last exercised such an arbitrary power that the whole land grew weary of him.

(Lucy Hutchinson, *The Memoirs of Colonel Hutchinson*, 1660s)

F   If after so many others I may speak my opinion of Cromwell, I think that, having been a prodigal in his youth, and afterwards changed to a zealous religiousness, he meant honestly in the main course of his life till prosperity and success corrupted him. ... Hereupon Cromwell's general religious zeal giveth way to the power of that ambition which still increaseth as his successes do increase. ... He meaneth well in all this at the beginning, and thinketh he doth all for the safety of the godly and the public good, but not without an eye for himself.

(Richard Baxter, *Memoirs*, 1680s)

1   How might you account for the difference in opinion towards Cromwell expressed in sources A and B?
2   What was the purpose of Cromwell's policy of religious toleration, according to source C? Do you have any reservations about this analysis?
3   How might a Leveller have commented on the views expressed by Cromwell in source D?
4   How similar are the analyses of Cromwell's Protectorate put forward in sources E and F?
5   What concerns might you have over the reliability of sources E and F?

Foreign policy

His greatness at home was but a shadow of the glory he had abroad. It was hard to discover which feared him the most, France, Spain, or the Low Countries.

(Clarendon, *History of the Rebellion*, 1670s)

As such glowing praise from a Royalist historian would suggest, it was in the field of foreign policy that Cromwell enjoyed his greatest success. His military skill had already helped to ensure the obedience of Ireland and Scotland by 1651, and his Protectorate was to see an expansion of English influence and power to its highest point in the seventeenth century.

When Cromwell took over the reigns of Government in 1653, England was already committed to a war against the Dutch. This was concluded on advantageous terms in April 1654, and despite continued strains over trading interests, peace was maintained thereafter. Treaties with Sweden and Denmark opened up the Baltic to English merchants, whilst consolidating relations with Europe's other Protestant powers. Cromwell laid great emphasis on the importance of creating a European-wide Protestant alliance, and was active in mediating between the Swedes and the Dutch over trading conflicts. However, the religious element in Cromwell's foreign policy did not preclude other considerations, as can be seen from the treaty with Catholic Portugal in July 1654, which allowed English trade with Portuguese colonies. There was also a strategic aspect to this alliance, as there was with the treaty with France in October 1655, as both countries were traditional enemies with Spain, with whom England had come into conflict.

War with Spain broke out officially in October 1655, although it was provoked by an English expedition earlier in the year, against Spanish colonies in the Caribbean. Although the expedition failed to achieve its goals and attracted criticism for its high cost, it did manage to capture Jamaica, which was to prove an invaluable asset in the future. The Spanish war proved to be extremely popular, since not only was it successful but also it was directed at a traditional, Catholic enemy. An expedition against Malaga and a naval victory against the Spanish fleet off Cadiz, in July and September 1656 respectively, were followed by a blockade of the Spanish coast. The English fleet, still under the command of Blake, underlined their dominance of the seas in another engagement in April 1658, in which they sank the Spanish treasure fleet off Santa Cruz. Closer to home, an Anglo-French force defeated the Spanish at the Battle of the Dunes in June 1658, winning control of Dunkirk, which had previously been used as a base for Spanish privateering in the English Channel.

By his death in September 1658, Cromwell had seen England's international stock rise dramatically. In 1649, the Commonwealth had been isolated and widely condemned as regicidal, even in Protestant nations such as Sweden and Holland. During Cromwell's period of rule, England had improved its international standing and trade through a series of treaties, and had successfully prosecuted a war against Spain. Cromwell was able to achieve more than either of his Stuart predecessors in the field of foreign policy. He did so through a combination of diplomacy and effective military force; and by identifying religious with national interests when possible, and ignoring them when it was not expedient.

Oliver Cromwell: an assessment

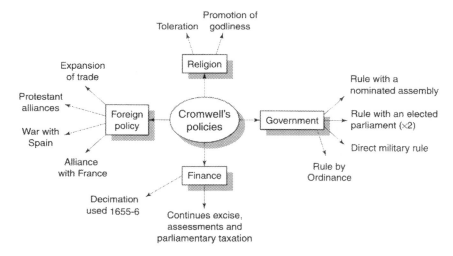

Figure 9.3 Policies of Cromwell, 1653–8

Oliver Cromwell died on 3 September 1658, and was succeeded as Protector by his son, Richard. It is a testimony to the strength of Cromwell's government that the succession was unopposed and that his death did not provoke any immediate instability. The fact that within eight months the Protectorate had disintegrated, and by May 1660 the monarchy had been restored, can be seen as a legacy of his rule, or a testimony to it. Was it a sign of the failings of his rule that Charles II was restored so soon after his demise? Or does it show how effectively Cromwell ruled that such a restoration could only be achieved once he had disappeared from the political scene?

Historians' views

Historians have been greatly divided over Cromwell, both in terms of what motivated him, and as to whether or not he is a figure of any long-term significance. To some he was an insincere, power-hungry figure, hiding his true intentions behind a mask of religion. To others, he has been seen as the founder of the British Empire; a champion of parliamentary democracy; the betrayer of parliamentary democracy; or the driving force of the bourgeois revolution. To others still, he is a confused, yet stubborn, figure, torn by the contradictory forces of his religious radicalism, and his social conservatism. For some, his achievements long outlived him; for others, they were swept away with the Restoration. A sense of the variety of opinion is provided by the extracts below.

A   Cromwell ... could never have done that mischief without great parts of courage, industry and judgement. ... Without doubt, no man with more wickedness ever attempted anything, or brought to pass what he desired more wickedly, more in the face and contempt of moral honesty; yet wickedness such as his could never have accomplished those trophies, without the assistance of a great spirit. ... To reduce three nations which perfectly hated him to an entire obedience ... [and] his greatness at home was but a shadow of the glory he had abroad. ... In a word, as he had all the wickedness ... for which hell-fire is prepared, so he had some virtues which have caused the memory of some men in all ages to be celebrated; and he will be looked upon by posterity as a brave, bad man.

(Clarendon, *The History of the Rebellion*, 1670s)

B   Peace reigned. Law and order were enforced with a strong, perhaps too strong, a hand. The country recovered its prosperity, and in many ways there was a deal of progress made. ... Above all, religious difficulties were in a large measure overcome. Cromwell himself stood for all-round toleration, and for the first time since the Reformation the many sects enjoyed complete freedom of religion ... Cromwell's failure was not a failure of authority. He was never in serious danger of being overthrown. It lay rather in this, that he did not arrive at any adequate arrangement by which the people could have a say in the administration. He, the arch-enemy of despotism, could not bring himself to bring democracy its head. The result was that his rule failed to express the true wishes of the people. It grew more and more unpopular as time went on; and with the author's death the fabric of government which he had designed went utterly to pieces. The Protectorate proved too feeble to survive, because the Protector himself had been too strong.

(Cyril Robinson, *A History of England*, 1920)

C   For good and for evil, Oliver Cromwell presided over the great decisions which determined the future course of English and world history. Marston Moor, Naseby, Preston, Worcester – and regicide – ensured that England was to be ruled by Parliaments and not by absolute kings; and this remains true despite the Protector's personal failure to get on with his Parliaments ... the man who almost emigrated to New England in despair of old England lived to set his country on the path of empire, of economic aggression, of naval war. He ruthlessly broke the resistance not only of backward-looking royalists but also of those radicals whose programme for extending the franchise would have ended the exclusive political sway of Cromwell's class, whose agrarian programme would have undermined that class's economic power. ... The British empire ... a free market ... Parliamentary government ... religious toleration ... relative freedom of the press, an attitude favourable to science ... none of these would have come about in quite the same way without the English Revolution, without Oliver Cromwell.

(Christopher Hill, *God's Englishman*, 1970)

D   Cromwell's character remains very much an enigma, but it is clear that much of the praise lavished on him then and later is misplaced. In the early 1650s he alone stood between the English people and a peaceful and permanent settlement; without his military genius, the republic would have foundered in its first two years; single-handed he postponed the inevitable restoration of the monarchy for another ten. Moreover, his increasing authoritarianism so weakened the cause for which he had struggled, that after his death his bewildered and demoralised successors had to recall Charles II on his own terms, without imposing on him the conditions that would have made the introduction of authoritarian government impossible, and the Revolution of 1688 unnecessary.

(J.P. Kenyon, *Stuart England*, 1985)

E   Not all contemporaries scorned Oliver's achievements. As hostile an observer as Clarendon could acknowledge that 'bad, brave man', for Cromwell's soldiers and sailors had made England the most respected military power in Europe. ... More generally, Cromwell had astonished the world ... by showing that a strong state could be built, as it seemed, from scratch. ... Oliver of course prided himself on his efforts not only as an Englishman, but as a Christian. He had ensured freedom of worship for the godly and brought good men into public life. Others too could praise him, and not merely in retrospect – even in 1656 Richard Baxter could 'bless God for the change that I see in this country'.

(Derek Hirst, *Authority and Conflict: England, 1603–1658*, 1986)

F   Cromwell repeatedly called himself a seeker. He did not know exactly what God's will was for him or England. He simply believed that God had a purpose for England. ... Cromwell had been called to lead God's new chosen people from under the yoke of popery and tyranny to a new freedom. Cromwell cared about ends not means. ... He was, he said in 1647, 'not wedded or glued to forms of government', or as he put it ten years later as he pondered the offer of the Crown, 'not scrupulous about words or names or such things'. ... He turned to different groups of the godly in turn, trying out their scheme for government. But as each form failed to bring his vision any closer to realisation, he jettisoned or cast out its proponents. ...

In the regicide and its aftermath, therefore, we must recognise the greatest paradox of all. In confronting and destroying Charles I, Oliver Cromwell was concerned not to establish constitutional government ... in which those who exercised authority were accountable to those they governed. The destruction of divine right kings was to make room for a divine right revolutionary.

(John Morrill, 'Introduction', in *Oliver Cromwell and the English Revolution*, 1990)

1   What positive and negative criticisms of Cromwell are made by the authors of sources A and B? Why do you think they might hold the views that they do?
2   According to source C, how significant was Cromwell as a historical figure?
3   To which 'school' of historical thought does the analysis in source C seem to belong? Explain your answer.
4   How far do sources D and E contradict source C?
5   How does the author of source F seek to explain Cromwell's apparent political inconsistency?
6   In the light of the extracts above, and the other material in this chapter, how far do you agree with Kenyon (source D) that much of the praise Cromwell has received is 'misplaced'?

Radicalism

One of the most interesting features of this period from a social, political and religious point of view is the emergence of radical groups, such as the Levellers, Ranters and Diggers. As many conservatives had feared, the political upheaval of civil war gave some an opportunity to challenge the traditional hierarchical systems that underpinned seventeenth-century society. Although most of Parliament's supporters were not looking to innovate or radically change society, a minority were inspired by the events of the 1640s to do just that. Freed from the constraints of Government censorship, which had collapsed in 1641, this period saw an enormous outpouring of printed literature, much of it in pamphlet form, often from small, private presses. Newspapers were also published in large numbers, reflecting a wide range of political opinion, and by 1645 there were over 700 of them! For the first time, circumstances allowed for a free interchange of ideas, some of which questioned the fundamental structures and beliefs of society.

The political climate of the late 1640s and 1650s continued to foster the exchange of new ideas and growth of radicalism. With the abolition of the monarchy, bishops and the House of Lords, the way was opened for some to challenge the whole traditional, hierarchical structure of society, and to question the distribution of wealth and power. The breakdown of any national Church structure, and the introduction of religious toleration saw the rise of a large variety of religious sects, some of whom applied their religious ideas to the political and social sphere. The political philosopher, Thomas Hobbes, was of no doubt that this climate of religious toleration had dangerous consequences:

> every man, nay, every boy and wench that could read English, thought they spoke with God Almighty, and understood what he said ... this license [*freedom*] of interpreting Scripture was the cause of so many sects as have lain hid till the beginning of the late King's [Charles I's] reign, and did then appear to the disturbance of the Commonwealth.

It would be a mistake to try to distinguish too precisely between the political and religious radicalism of this period. Even groups like the Levellers and Diggers, whose programmes seemed to have mainly secular aims, were influenced and moulded by their religious beliefs. There was a widespread belief among radical groupings in 'providence', the idea that the events that they were experiencing were all part of God's plan for the nation. Closely linked to this was a belief that it was their duty to prepare England for the imminent return of Christ and his thousand-year rule, or millennium, prophesied in the book of Revelation. This millenary enthusiasm was particularly evident in the ideas of the Fifth Monarchists, but was shared by many others among the godly.

The best known of the radical groups during this period were the Levellers. They believed that society needed to be 'levelled' by introducing a full male franchise, regardless of wealth or social status. In addition they wanted to reform the law by removing the 'Norman Yoke', which had been placed on the country after the Norman Conquest, tilting the law in the favour of the landowners and those in power. They emerged in London during the Civil War, and were a significant political group in the post-war years, particularly within the New Model Army. However, although the Levellers may be the best known of these groups, they were by no means the most radical. Below, four other groups of particular interest are dealt with, namely the Diggers, the Ranters, the Fifth Monarchists and the Quakers.

The Diggers

Although the Diggers were not as numerous or influential as the Levellers, their ideas were more extreme. They called themselves the True Levellers and wanted to apply the levelling principle not only to political rights but also to the ownership of property. The dominant figure in the Digger movement was Gerrard Winstanley, who spent the Civil War in London and developed his radical views there. In 1649, he led a group of Diggers to occupy some common land on St George's Hill, near Weybridge, in Surrey, and set up a community farm there. Other Digger communes were established during 1650, although they were all suppressed by local landowners, who found their beliefs and their willingness to put those beliefs into action deeply threatening.

Documents

An insight into the beliefs and the agenda of the Diggers is provided by extracts from the writing of their founder and theorist, Gerrard Winstanley:

A   In the beginning of time ... man had domination given to him over the beasts, birds, and fishes; but not a word was spoken in the beginning that one branch of mankind should rule over another. But ... the earth (which was made a common treasury for all, both beasts and men) was hedged into enclosures by the teachers and rulers, and the others were made servants and slave; and that earth, that is within this creation a common storehouse for all, is bought and sold and kept in the hands of a few, whereby the creator is mightily dishonoured. ...

    The work we are going about is this, to dig up George's Hill and the waste ground thereabouts, and to sow corn, and to eat bread together by the sweat of our brow. ... Not enclosing any part into any particular hand, but all as one man working together as sons of one father, members of one family; not one lording it over another, but all looking upon each other as equals in creation; so that our Maker may be glorified in the work of his own hands, and that everyone may see that he ... equally loves his own creation. ...

    Those that buy and sell land and are landlords, have got it either by oppression or murder or theft; and all landlords live in breach of the seventh and eighth Commandments: 'Thou shalt not steal or kill.'

(Gerrard Winstanley, *The True Levellers' Standard Advanced*, 1649)

B   Sir,

    God has honoured you with the highest honour of any man since Moses' time, to be the head of a people who have cast out an oppressive Pharaoh. For when the Norman power had conquered our forefathers, he took the free use of our English ground from them, and made them his servants. And God hath made you a successful instrument to cast out that conqueror, and to recover our land and liberties. ... That which is yet wanting on your part to be done is this, to see the oppressor's power cast out with his person; and to see that the free possession of the land and liberties be put into the hands of the oppressed commoners of England. ...

    Buying and selling did bring in and still doth bring in, discontent and wars, which have plagued mankind sufficiently for so doing. And the nations of the world will never learn to beat their swords into ploughshares, or their spears into pruning hooks, and leave off warring, until this cheating device of buying and selling be cast out with the rubbish of kingly power. ... No man can be rich, but he must be rich by his own labours ... but rich men live at ease, feeding and clothing themselves by the labours of other men, not by their own; which is their shame, and not their nobility ... they are not righteous actors on this earth.

(Gerrard Winstanley, *The Epistle to Oliver Cromwell*, 1652)

1   What does Winstanley attack in source A?
2   How should society be structured and ruled, according to source A?
3   What other issues does Winstanley identify in source B, which require reform?
4   From the evidence of sources A and B, what obstacles were the Diggers likely to face in trying to put their ideas into effect?

The Ranters

Another group that emerged in the late 1640s were the Ranters. Even more than the other radical groups, their views and practices gained them a notoriety that was out of proportion to their actual numbers. The Ranters' beliefs were 'antinomian', in other words they believed that as Christians they were now free from sin, and therefore could indulge in whatever practices they chose, without endangering their salvation. Some went further and asserted that God was not only revealed in the created world, but was actually to be found in it. Therefore it was possible for them to indulge in any activity within the created world, without falling into sin.

Documents

Contemporary accounts of the Ranters provide a wealth of comment and criticism of the sect. Their activity was the subject of numerous pamphlets, both from the Ranters themselves, and from their opponents. Extracts from two such publications are provided below:

C   God having reserved some better things for us that walk in God, and tread upon God, and are covered with God. ... That they see nothing but God and behold him in the face of everything ... that they lie one with another in God and are not ashamed, because God is in them: That they whore in God, that God is the whore and the whoremaster, and they depart not from him in any of their ways, and now like little children they can play together, lie together, dance together, swear together, drink together ... and yet think no evil and do no evil, knowing ... their sins are forgiven them, and there is no guile found in these men's mouths. ... The Lord is now receiving into one ... yea the whoremonger and the thief sweetly embracing, kissing, hugging ... Lord where shall we go from thy presence? Thou are in hell, heaven, the sun, moon, stars, in the grass ... when we go to a whore-house we meet thee, and when we come away thou comest away with us.

(From the introduction to a Ranter pamphlet, *A Justification of the Mad Crew*, 1650)

D   Two of the Ranters which were taken in More Lane, viz Joe Collins and Thomas Reeve were indicted [for] blasphemy ... that the like was never heard before ... [of] the Diabolical practices of these wretched creatures. ... I shall give you some particulars:
       That this Collins, Reeve, and others were sitting at table, eating a piece of Beef, one of them took it in his hand, tearing it assunder said to the other, 'This is the flesh of Christ, take and eat'. The Other took a cup of ale and threw it into the

The Ranters Declaration, 2

WITH

Their new Oath and Protestation ; their strange Votes, and a new way to
get money ; their Proclamation and Summons ; their new way of Ranting,
never before heard of ; their dancing of the *Hay* naked, at the white *Lyon* in
Petticoat-lane ; their mad Dream, and Dr. *Pockridge* his Speech, with their
Trial, Examination, and Answers : the coming in of 3000. their Prayer and
Recantation, *to be in all Cities and Market-towns read and published* ; the
mad-Ranters further Resolution ; their Christmas Carol, and blaspheming
Song ; their two pretended-abominable Keyes to enter Heaven, and the
worshiping of his little-majesty, the late Bishop of *Canterbury* : A new and
further Discovery of their black Art, with the Names of those that are pos-
sest by the Devil, having strange and hideous cries heard within them, *to
the great admiration of all those that shall read and peruse this ensuing subject.*

Licensed according to order, and published by M. *Stubs*, a late fellow-Ranter

Imprinted at London , by J. C. MDCL.   *1650*

Figure 9.4 Title page of *The Ranters' Declaration* (1650)

chimney corner, saying 'There is the blood of Christ' ... and blowing through two pieces of tobacco pipes, he said 'That was the breath of God'. There was also proved many other blasphemous words and uncivil behaviour, as the kissing of one another's breeches ... they were fined and are sentenced to suffer for this first offence six months imprisonment.

Shakespeare and Glover are referred for a trial ... some have confessed that they have often had meetings, where at both men and women presented themselves stark naked one to the other, in a most beastly manner. And after satisfying their carnal and beastly lust, some have a sport they call whipping of the whore: others call for music, and fall to revelling and dancing.

(From an anti-Ranter pamphlet, *Strange News from Newgate*, 1651)

5   Summarise the argument put forward by the author of source C.
6   Comment upon the utility and reliability of source D, in terms of its use for a historian studying the Ranters.

The Fifth Monarchists

The Fifth Monarchists, like many other groups, drew inspiration for their political ideas from the Bible. They believed that the second coming of Christ was imminent, and that it was their task to prepare England for his millennium, or thousand-year reign. Their name was drawn from the book of Daniel, which prophesies the destruction of four earthly monarchies, before the establishment of a godly Fifth Monarchy. This belief in millenarianism was widely held by Puritans, but the Fifth Monarchists were distinguished by their conviction that all earthly structures of Government were sinful, and needed to be removed to facilitate Christ's return. The Fifth Monarchists therefore were a politically active group that were looking for opportunities to put their ideas into action. Their finest hour came with the creation of the Parliament of Saints in 1653. One of Cromwell's generals, Thomas Harrison, persuaded him to summon a nominated Parliament, to rule England on 'godly' principles. It included a small, yet well-organised and committed group of Fifth Monarchists, whose programme of radical reform in State and Church dominated proceedings. However, their ideas were too unpalatable for the conservative leadership of the army, including Cromwell, and the Parliament was dissolved after only a few months. After this, some Fifth Monarchists resorted to direct political action, in the form of two revolts, the first against Cromwell's Protectorate in 1657, and later against the restored monarchy in 1661.

The Quakers

The Quakers were another group who had their origins in the late 1640s. Like other religious separatists, they rejected the notion of Church government but went further by questioning the need for ministers in church life. They believed that each individual should follow their own conscience, or 'inner light', which was provided by the Holy Spirit, rather than automatically accept what was told them by ministers or preachers. Their name came from their habit of quaking in meetings whilst under the influence of the Holy Spirit. Under the leadership of George Fox, the Quakers were regarded as a radical and dangerous group, who refused to accept social conventions such as showing respect to their superiors. They insisted on addressing everyone in the same terms, regardless of social rank, and would not take off their hats to indicate respect to people of a higher social status. In addition they refused to take oaths of any kind, and some were prepared to disrupt public meetings, such as church services to demonstrate over certain issues.

Document

The following deals with a debate in Parliament, in which MPs discuss a petition by the Quakers for the release of a number of their fellows currently in prison:

E

COLONEL GROVESNOR: I took notice of a great number of people called Quakers, in the Hall yesterday and today. I wish you would take some course with the petition that had laid a long time before you; and that they be dispersed.

MR ANNESLEY: They are a fanatic crew. I would have their petition referred to a committee, to put it off your hands.

MR FOWELL: I move to whip them home as vagrants.

MR DANBY: I move that a law be provided to suppress that railing [*criticizing*] against ministers. He instanced what Mr Bulkeley and Dr Reynolds had overheard some of them say: 'the priests and lawyers are bloody men, give them blood to drink'.

MR SWINFEN: Order them, every one of them, to go to their calling, and apply themselves to the law, which is their protection. ...

MAJOR-GENERAL KELSEY: No reasoning by scripture will convince them. ... The justices of the peace do well to imprison them. Disturbers of the peace, they deserve it. They will not conform to the law. ...

COLONEL WEST: I cannot justify them in their affronts to the ministers. ...

MR STEWARD: They complain not of anything done contrary to the law, but according to the law. Though they seem but a small number, yet lesser beginnings have grown to great heights. In their books I find a denunciation of judgement. They will easily believe that they are the persons appointed by God to execute this judgement. They are not of that simplicity as is moved, but wolves under sheep's clothing.

[After the debate, the petitioners were instructed to return home, and 'submit themselves to the laws of the nation, and the magistrates they live under'.]

(Taken from the proceedings of the Third Protectorate Parliament, April 1659)

7   What grounds for hostility towards the Quakers are revealed in this source?
8   Why do you think that Parliament was so unsympathetic to the Quaker's petition?

Table 9.1 Summary: Radical groups

Radical group	Aims and beliefs	Degree of influence/fate
Levellers	• 'Levelling' society • Legal reform • Universal male suffrage • No military conscription • The Government's power is derived from the will of the people	• Influential in the army (particularly 1646–9) • Putney Debates • Supported Pride's Purge and the execution of Charles I • Suppressed after mutinies in 1647 and 1649
Diggers ('True Levellers')	• 'Levelling' society, property and wealth • Communal living • Common ownership of land • Anti-capitalist	• Limited influence • Perceived as a threat to society – suppressed
Ranters	• Freedom from traditional moral restrictions	• Limited influence • Perceived as a threat to morality – suppressed
Fifth Monarchists	• Removal of earthly Government structures to prepare for Christ's return	• Parliament of Saints • Role of Thomas Harrison in Government under Cromwell • Suppressed after revolts in 1657 and 1661
Quakers ('Friends')	• Did not recognise ranks within society • Answerable only to the Holy Spirit (the 'inner light')	• Seen as a threat to society – suppressed • Despite persecution, continued to flourish after the Restoration

10 Charles II, 1660–73

The Restoration

The collapse of the Republic

When Richard Cromwell succeeded his father in September 1658, the prospect of a restoration of the monarchy still seemed a distant one. Yet, although his succession was unopposed, the new Protector's long-term position was undermined by the fact that he had no real links with the army. His father's strength had relied heavily upon his control of the military, yet Richard was unable to command the same degree of loyalty or authority over them. His reaction was to side with anti-army MPs, led by Haselrig and Vane, who proposed in April 1659 that both the political activities of the army and the extent of religious toleration should be restricted. The army's response was swift and decisive. The day after Parliament had finished voting on the proposals, the army, led by Generals Fleetwood and Lambert, forced Richard to dissolve it and then to abdicate himself. The Protectorate was at an end.

The army was now faced with the issue of how to establish an alternative Government, and it is an indication of how few options they had that the generals decided to recall the Rump. However, the body that had been expelled by the army in 1653 for failing to meet its expectations was hardly any more likely to fulfil them in 1659. Predictably, the Rump and army soon fell out as the former attempted to reduce the army's power and make it subservient to Parliament. The Rump's declaration that all acts and ordinances passed since its previous dissolution were illegal, and its attempted arrest of Lambert, stung the army into action. On 13 October 1659, the Rump was once again forcibly dissolved.

With no other options open to them, the army was forced to fall back on military rule and government passed into the hands of a Committee of Safety, headed by Fleetwood. However, this proved to be even less satisfactory than its predecessors, as it was unable even to guarantee the loyalty of the army. Since 1649, the army had been a largely unified body, either in its support for Cromwell, or in its opposition to civilian alternatives, but its response to Fleetwood's seizure of power was different. General Monck in Scotland declared for the Rump, as did the army in Ireland and the Navy, and Portsmouth was seized by Haselrig and some republican supporters. For the first time the country was faced with the real possibility of a renewal of civil war, between opposing army factions. The lack of any legitimate, strong government threatened to drag the country into chaos. That civil war did not develop was due to the resignation of Fleetwood at the end of December, who realised that the situation had slipped out of his control, and the arrival of Monck and his army in England.

Negotiations for the Restoration

Monck crossed the border into England on 1 January 1660, with 10,000 troops, promising to deliver the country from 'the intolerable slavery of sword government' and to restore 'civil authority'. The exact nature of Monck's intentions was not clear at this stage, but he had caught the mood of the nation well. Fairfax declared his support for Monck, began enlisting supporters, and seized the north on his behalf. Opposition to Monck melted away and by February he was in control of London. He recalled the Rump, but also recalled many of the Presbyterian members who had been purged in 1648 for wanting to continue negotiations with Charles I. With the return of these moderates, Monck was able to persuade Parliament to dissolve itself and agree to new elections. The political stalemate had been broken by using traditional, constitutional forms, and with the return of the Presbyterians had come many who, according to parliamentary records, were 'well-affected to kingly government'.

While preparations were being made for elections, Monck turned his attentions to secret negotiations with Charles II, over the restoration of the monarchy. These were to lead in turn to Charles's Declaration of Breda, on 4 April. Largely drafted by his chief adviser, Sir Edward Hyde, the Declaration was extremely well-judged: designed to minimise any fears over the restoration of the monarchy, while remaining vague enough about any details to allow Charles room for future manoeuvre. There were four main issues with which it dealt. An amnesty for all was declared, except for anyone subsequently excluded by Parliament; freedom of religion was granted to all, providing they did 'not disturb the peace of the kingdom'; the issue of future ownership of lands lost by Royalists and now in the possession of others should 'be determined by Parliament'; and all arrears of pay would be settled with 'the officers and soldiers of the army under the command of General Monck'.

The Convention Parliament met on 25 April, and was dominated by Royalist sentiment. Hardly any individuals associated with the Rump or the army were elected, and it was little surprise that, on 1 May, MPs voted for a restoration of the traditional form of government, that is 'by King, Lords, and Commons'. On 29 May 1660, Charles II entered London amid scenes of great rejoicing. The monarchy was seen by most people as a guarantee of future stability and good government, after years of political, social and religious upheaval. How realistic these expectations were remained to be seen.

Contemporary reactions

An idea of the extent of public enthusiasm for Charles II's restoration is provided by the sources below, although it is interesting to note that republican sentiments were not completely extinguished by the King's return.

A   His Majesty entered … the City of London at the bridge, where he found the windows and streets exceedingly thronged with people to behold him, and the walls adorned with hangings and carpets of tapestry and other costly stuff, and in many places sets of loud music, all the conduits as he passed running with claret wine … also the trained bands of the city standing along the streets as he passed, welcoming him with loud acclamations. ... His majesty entered Whitehall at seven o'clock, the people making loud shouts, and the horse and foot several volleys of shots, at this his happy arrival; where the House of Lords and Commons of Parliament received him, and kissed his royal hand. At the same time the reverend bishops ... with divers of the long oppressed clergy, met in that royal chapel at Westminster and there also sang the Te Deum, in praise and thanks to Almighty God for this his unspeakable mercy in the deliverance of his Majesty from many dangers, and so happily restoring him to rule these kingdoms according to his just and undoubted right.

(Anonymous pamphlet, 1660)

B   This day, his Majesty, Charles the Second came to London, after a sad and long exile and calamitous [*disastrous*] suffering, both of the King and Church, being seventeen years. This was also his birthday, and with a triumph of above 20,000 horse and foot, brandishing their swords, and shouting with inexpressible joy; the ways strewed with flowers, the bells ringing, the streets hung with tapestry, fountains running with wine; the Mayor, Aldermen, and all the Companies, in their liveries, chains of gold, and banners; Lords and nobles, clad in cloth of silver, gold, and velvet; the windows and balconies, all set with ladies; trumpets, music, and people flocking, even so far as from Rochester ... I stood in the Strand and beheld it, and blessed God. And all this was done without one drop of bloodshed, and by that very army which rebelled against him: but it was the Lord's doing, for such a restoration was never mentioned in any history ... nor so joyful a day and so bright ever seen in this nation.

(John Evelyn's diary, 29 May 1660)

C   News being brought to Dover of Charles Stuart's being put to sea, Monck with his guard marched to Dover to meet him; where upon his landing ... Charles Stuart owns Monck to be his father, embracing and kissing him. And truly they were brethren in iniquity [*wickedness*], in treachery and falsehood near allied. ... It was so ordered that he should make his entrance into London upon the day of his birth, which was the 29 May. As he came on the road, the giddy multitude, promising themselves all the happiness imaginable, made bonfires, burning the [coats of] arms of the Commonwealth, the badges of their own freedom. ... And it is no less remarkable that this cowardly enemy (whom the Lord had so oft routed and witnessed against in the field) ... as to ride with their drawn swords through the city of London to Whitehall; intimating thereby their resolution to maintain that by force and violence which they had gained the possession of by the height of treachery. And as Charles Stuart passed through the street, multitudes being gathered together ... his looks were very ghastly at the best, yet it was observed that for the most part they were full of revenge, as if he would have the citizens to see that he retained in his memory the injuries which his father and he hath received from them.

(Edmund Ludlow, *A Voice from the Watch Tower*, mid-1660s)

1   What aspects of the Restoration are the authors of sources A and B rejoicing over?
2   How does Ludlow (source C) regard the Restoration?
3   How useful do you consider these sources to be, to a historian trying to gauge public opinion over the Restoration?

Charles II: background

Charles II came to the throne at the age of thirty, having been in exile for most of the previous fourteen years. Following his father's death in 1649, he came to terms with the Scots, demonstrating his cynicism at an early age by swearing to uphold the Covenant and agreeing to the death of his most prominent Scottish supporter, the Earl of Montrose. He landed in Scotland in 1650 and, recovering from defeat by Cromwell at Dunbar, invaded England in 1651. His forces were decisively defeated at the Battle of Worcester, and he only narrowly avoided capture himself, first by hiding in an oak tree ('The Royal Oak' of pub sign fame) and then in a priest hole, belonging to a local Catholic gentry family.

The next nine years were spent on the Continent, his court being forced to move from country to country as the foreign policy of the English Republic dictated. These years of exile were to have a profound effect upon the future King's political development. He learnt the arts of political manoeuvre and intrigue, as he was forced to deal with both a succession of foreign governments and the factions within his own court. More than anything, Charles emerged from these years with a profound mistrust of both his friends and his enemies, an almost limitless capacity for intrigue, and a strong sense of political survival. These were to be important character traits in his rule as king.

On his restoration, Charles inherited an enormous store of goodwill from his subjects. This goodwill was complemented by his striking physical appearance (according to the 'wanted' notices posted by Parliament after the Battle of Worcester, he was 'over two yards long'!) and his personality. Some idea of this can be gained from Sir Sam Tuke's description of the new king, written in 1660:

> He is somewhat taller than the middle stature of Englishmen; so exactly formed that the most curious eye cannot find any error in his shape. His face is rather grave than severe, which is very much softened whensoever he speaks; his complexion is somewhat dark, but much enlightened by his eyes, which are quick and sparkling. His hair, which he hath in great plenty is of a shining black, not frizzled, but so naturally curling into great rings that it is a very comely ornament. His motions are so easy and graceful that they do very much recommend his person when he either walks, dances, plays at tennis, or rides the great horse, which are his usual exercises. To the gracefulness of his deportment may be joined his easiness of access, his patience in attention, and the gentleness both in the tune and the style of his speech; so that those whom either the veneration for his dignity or the majesty of his presence have put into an awful respect, are reassured as soon as he enters into a conversation.

Figure 10.1 Charles II

The political settlement, 1660

The responsibility for producing an acceptable settlement fell to the Convention Parliament, who by December 1660 had managed to pass legislation that dealt with the following areas:

1 *Amnesty*: in line with the Declaration of Breda, a general pardon was issued, with the exception of 51 regicides (i.e. those who had signed Charles I's death warrant) and 29 others. Of these only 13 were actually executed, including Vane who was not actually a regicide, and others such as Lambert and Haselrig were imprisoned. Although several of the regicides were now dead, the grave did not necessarily provide them with sanctuary. Cromwell, Ireton, and Bradshaw (who had presided over Charles I's trial) were dug up, publicly 'hung', decapitated and finally had their heads displayed on pikes on Westminster Bridge.

2 *The army*: provision was made for the demobilisation of the army and the payment of its arrears, although in the event two regiments, the Coldstream Guards and the Life Guards, were retained on an ongoing basis. These troops were to be under the control of the King.

3 *Royalist lands*: contrary to the expectations of many Royalists, little effort was made by Charles to ensure the recovery of their lands. All lands that had been confiscated were returned, but other lands sold by Royalists to pay taxes such as the decimation, were treated as voluntary sales and not compensated. Charles realised that he could afford to take his traditional supporters for granted. As the Earl of Ailesbury bitterly commented, he rewarded 'his enemies to sweeten them, for that his friends were so by a settled principle, and that their loyalty could not be shaken'.

4 *Finance*: the level of ordinary revenue that the Crown was estimated to need was £1,200,000, of which two-thirds was to be provided by Crown lands and customs duties. The remainder was to be made up by the granting of excise (sales tax) on selected goods, replacing old feudal dues, such as wardships and purveyance. Thus the King, in theory, should be endowed with sufficient funds to meet his ordinary expenditure. In practice, the combination of Charles's extravagance, and a miscalculation on the revenue brought in by the excise, saw a short-fall in the Crown's needs of £300,000 by the end of 1660.

5 *Religion*: the issue of religion was more problematic. Despite the obvious political advantages of insisting on conformity to a State Church, Charles seems to have been sincere in his desire to allow religious toleration, or as he had termed it in the Declaration of Breda, 'liberty to tender consciences'. Charles signalled his intentions by taking the Presbyterian, Richard Baxter, as one of his chaplains, and encouraging discussions between the new Anglican bishops and Presbyterian Councils over the future shape of any religious settlement. A conference was promised for the next year to finalise these issues.

However, the policy advocated by Charles was not one that found much favour with the local élites, amongst whom there was little enthusiasm for religious toleration. Freedom of religion was strongly associated with political rebellion and social breakdown, and as such was not acceptable to a political nation, busily embracing the return of traditional, conservative values. They may have found Laud's policies in the 1630s unpalatable, but they were preferable to the alternatives of the 1640s and 1650s. Such considerations prompted the removal of almost 700 ministers appointed by the Long Parliament by the end of 1660, and the reintroduction of traditional Anglican forms of worship in many areas without any directions from central government. This reversion to Anglicanism was to be confirmed by the Savoy Conference in 1661, and a series of statutes between 1661 and 1665, known as the 'Clarendon Code'.

6   *Other areas*: perhaps the strangest aspect of the settlement was that it skirted round the issue of the royal prerogative, and did not explicitly tackle where the dividing line actually was between the powers of the monarchy and the rights of Parliament. Instead, the settlement upheld all legislation pre-September 1641, thereby implying that any statutes after this date were illegal. This meant that the Crown had lost the right to use prerogative courts and prerogative taxation, and was still bound by the Triennial Act (although this was altered by a new act in 1664 that, though it repeated the requirement that Parliament should meet every three years, removed its right to automatic assembly if this requirement was not met). However, it also meant that the Crown's right to control the Church, the army and the militia; to veto legislation; and to choose its ministers remained. Domestic, religious and foreign policy were still the responsibility of the monarch.

1   Why do you think that no real attempt was made to define the extent of the royal prerogative?

2   How good a deal to you consider this to have been for Charles II? Are there any aspects of it with which he might have been disappointed?

3   How workable do you consider this settlement to have been? How far did it address all the areas that it needed to?

The religious settlement, 1661–5

As we have already seen, Charles's religious policy was somewhat out of step with that of most of the political nation, a fact that was emphasised when the Cavalier Parliament met in May 1661 and voted that all MPs had to be communicating members (i.e. regularly taking communion) of the Church of England. Although the exact nature of that Church of England was still not certain, it was further evidence of the link in MPs' minds between religious and political orthodoxy.

The Savoy Conference was held between April and July 1661, and saw the victory of those who supported the restoration of the Anglican church in its traditional form. The Presbyterians and other non-conformists at the conference were marginalised and had little impact on its decisions. The new Prayer Book that was produced was very similar to the old one, and government of the Church by bishops was confirmed. The new forms of service were put into statute form with the Uniformity Act of 1662.

The Uniformity Act formed an important part of a series of acts aimed at non-conformists, known as the Clarendon Code. This label is rather misleading, since although the Earl of Clarendon (formerly Sir Edward Hyde) was more supportive of restricting toleration than Charles II, he was not necessarily in favour of all of the measures put in place by Parliament. The first restriction on religious freedom was introduced in the Corporation Act of 1661. This appointed agents to evict all those holding public office in cities and towns from their posts, if they could not swear an oath of allegiance to the Crown, an oath against the Solemn League and Covenant, or did not take the Anglican Sacraments. The Uniformity Act extended similar restrictions to all post-holders in churches, schools and universities. As a result, somewhere between one and two thousand clergy were deprived of their positions. Charles's attempts to remind his Parliament of his undertaking at Breda to provide toleration had little effect, and the Commons refused to even discuss a bill put forward to allow the King to excuse certain individuals from the effects of these measures. In 1664, Parliament passed the Conventicle Act, which prohibited all religious assemblies that were not held in accordance with the Prayer Book; and, in 1665, it introduced the Five Mile Act, which prevented teachers or clergy who had been victims of the 1661–2 legislation from coming within five miles of any town or city.

Two aspects of the religious settlement are particularly interesting. One is that non-conformism now occupied the position that Catholicism had done for the first half of the century. The events of the last two decades had linked it with political sedition, in a way that had previously been unthinkable. Although the fear of Catholicism still had the potential to cause enormous concern, at this stage it was Puritan dissent that was seen as the main threat to political stability. The other is the stance taken by Charles II. He cannot have been blind to the political advantages of tight State control over religion, nor to those of aligning himself with the religious prejudices of his parliaments, and yet he continued to push for toleration. The most obvious answer is that religious toleration was a matter of principle for him. However, unlike his father, Charles II was not a man known for his attachment to any particular ideals, either personal, political or religious. He was not, to use a twentieth-century term, a conviction politician. Alternatively, it has been suggested that Charles was distrustful of the Anglican establishment, and was reluctant to allow any one group to wield too much power over the Church. He was therefore trying to develop a counter-weight to the established Church. Whatever the reasoning behind Charles's support for toleration, it was to be the source of a great deal of tension during his reign.

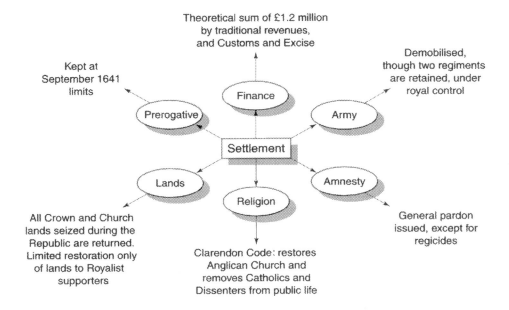

Figure 10.2 The Restoration Settlement, 1660–5

Historians' views on the Restoration Settlement

Historians are divided over the significance of the restoration of the monarchy in 1660, and how far the political settlement marked out a significant constitutional change from that prior to 1641. How good a deal was it for Charles II, and whose victory, if anyone's, did it represent?

A   The Restoration was by no means a restoration of the old regime. It is evidence, not of the weakness of the bourgeoisie and gentry, but of their strength ... Charles II came back ... but he was not restored to his father's old position. The prerogative courts were not restored ... the gentry dominated local government as Justices of the Peace. The King had no power of taxation independent of Parliament ... Charles was called King by the grace of God, but he was really King by the grace of merchants and squires. ... The bishops also came home with the King, but the Church did not regain its old power. ... The Church of England ceased even to pretend to be all-embracing and aimed at holding Nonconformists in subjection rather than at reabsorbing them. ... No longer a powerful organ of government, the Church of England sank to be merely the richest of many rival religious organisations. ... The King became dependent on a Parliamentary civil list, a salaried official. ... He could no longer 'live of his own' on his private income from his estates and feudal dues, and so he could never be independent again.

(Christopher Hill, *The English Revolution*, 1940)

B   It is often claimed that the 'English revolution' permanently altered England, that it brought about (or completed) a seismic [*earth-shattering*] change in the structure of society and unleashed new ideas which, with the King's execution, irreversibly weakened the monarchy ... a premise which at best is not proven. ... The new radical ideas of the mid-century found little support after 1660 and probably served only to strengthen the conservatism of the ruling elite. ... Most had not wanted civil war, the abolition of monarchy or religious confusion. ... The Restoration gave a welcome opportunity to return to normal.

   Historians have looked hard for ways in which the events of 1640–60 could have weakened the monarchy, but have shown less interest in ways in which they might have strengthened it. The most striking improvement was in taxation. The legislation of 1641 had swept away the archaic, random assortment of feudal and property rights which the crown had accumulated over the centuries and which (as a means of raising money) had often proved inefficient. ... In place of these revenues it [Parliament] established the monthly assessment ... and the excise ... Charles II inherited a fiscal system far more rational and efficient than his father's, as well as a population becoming accustomed to substantial, regular taxation.

(John Miller, *Restoration England: The Reign of Charles II*, 1997)

C   Whose victory did the Restoration Settlement represent? Who had effectively won in 1662? The reply most often given in recent years is that the King did. ... The legal issue which had provoked the great Civil War, the question of who controlled the militia, had been decided as Charles I had wished. None of the constitutional checks which the parliamentarians had sought to impose upon the monarchy from 1642 till 1660 had taken hold, and now the very notion of resisting the crown was made the grounds for loss of office. ... There is much truth in this ... yet qualifications are needed. ... It may be doubted if Charles II felt much like a victor in September 1662. ... He had become the first English monarch since the Middle Ages to be successfully defied by his leading churchmen. ... His direct power over the community was truncated [*limited*] by the permanent abolition of the prerogative courts, and his ability to wage war ... depended upon the goodwill of Parliaments. ...

An ironic case could be made for the Restoration Settlement as a confirmation of the victory of John Pym and the original parliamentarian party. Most of the reforms of 1640–1 had been confirmed, and England now had a King who ruled as Pym's set had wished. ... Above all, the monarch was still bound by the Triennial Act to summon regular Parliaments.

(Ronald Hutton, *The Restoration, 1658–1667*, 1985)

D The Convention was dissolved late in December 1660. Its members departed thinking they had achieved a framework for a settlement. Much had been done which gave them confidence: with Charles II, were restored the institution of monarchy, two Houses of Parliament, the Church of England, much of the country's legal system, and its traditional ruling elite of greater gentry and richer merchants. ... It was doubtful though if it would prove a lasting settlement. Impossibly high expectations (of the Savoy Conference, for instance), too many critical unanswered questions (the executive–legislative balance of power), too many decisions based on faulty information (Charles' income for example) – all pointed to an unstable future. ... There was some progress made, but there were unanswered question-marks, the long-standing residue of the 1640 Crisis.

(Barry Williams, *Elusive Settlement*, 1984)

1 In what ways do Hill and Miller disagree over the significance for the monarchy of the Restoration Settlement?
2 How far does Hutton accept the view that the Settlement was a victory for the monarchy?
3 What reservations over the nature of the Settlement does Williams highlight?
4 In your view, how good a deal was the Settlement for Charles II?

The Second Dutch War and the fall of Clarendon

As with the war of 1652–4, the outbreak of hostilities with the Dutch in 1665 was largely the result of conflicting commercial interests. Although Cromwell had cultivated a Dutch alliance, and Charles had himself concluded a treaty with Holland in 1662, the underlying tension between the countries over trade had never gone away. A new Navigation Act in 1660 had required all goods imported to England from Asia, America or Africa to be carried in English ships, and all imports from Europe to be carried either in English vessels, or in those that belonged to the country who had produced the goods. Such a measure struck directly at Dutch interests, as their economy was built upon carrying other nations' trade. The Staple Act of 1663 tried to extend this approach to the colonial trade, by requiring English colonists to import goods only from England and only in English ships. The tensions that such measures created were fanned by the English trading community, amongst whom there was strong support for war, with the East India Company and Royal Africa Company both looking to expand their trading interests as a result.

It seems, at least initially, that this enthusiasm for war was widespread. Charles himself claimed that he had never seen 'so great an appetite to a war as is in both town and country, especially in the parliament men'. Perhaps both Charles and his Parliament were relying upon a repeat of the success of the 1652–4 war, when the seizure of Dutch shipping had almost doubled the tonnage of the English fleet. This would seem to be reflected in Parliament's willingness to provide adequate supplies for war, voting £2,500,000 in February 1665, and a further £1,250,000 in the autumn. A further grant of £1,800,000 in January 1667 saw the total amount voted by Parliament for the war rise to well over £5 million, an unprecedented sum.

The public enthusiasm for the war was initially fed by the naval victory off Lowestoft in June 1665, which was claimed by the diarist, Samuel Pepys, as 'a greater victory never known in the world'. However, early hopes began to wane with French intervention in January 1666 on the Dutch side, and the defeat of Charles's only ally, the Bishop of Münster in April. Further heavy and inconclusive naval fighting took place in the Channel over the summer, and by the autumn Charles was forced to recall Parliament to seek further financial assistance. Although Parliament did vote more money, their dissatisfaction over the conduct of the war was demonstrated by their attacks on various Government officials, and their insistence that a commission be set up to examine how the supplies they had granted had actually been spent.

Deciding that a continuation of the war was unlikely to be productive, Charles started negotiations for peace in January 1667, and began to demobilise the fleet accordingly. As a result, the English forces were unprepared for the attack in June, in which the Dutch fleet breached coastal defences, sailed up the Medway and attacked the naval base at Chatham. Although peace was subsequently concluded with the Treaty of Breda, the Medway disaster had important domestic consequences. The Dutch War had achieved very little, beyond the confirmation of English control over some North American colonies, which were seen at the time as scant reward for the huge amount of financial resources that had been put into it. The humiliation of defeat soured relations between the Crown and Parliament still further. Clarendon, as Charles's chief minister, was targeted as a scapegoat and in October 1667 articles of impeachment were brought against him by the Commons.

Clarendon's fall from office was indicative of Charles's attitudes towards his servants. If he considered them to have become a political liability, they would be sacrificed to protect his own position. Clarendon had been Charles's main adviser during his years of exile, and had played an important role in the negotiations for his restoration to the throne, helping to draft the Declaration of Breda. He had been instrumental in producing such a favourable Restoration Settlement, and had been a loyal and effective servant of the Crown since 1660. Yet, he did not share Charles's views on religious toleration and seems to have annoyed the King by his criticisms of his personal life. Such factors may have eased his dismissal, particularly as he had many enemies within court who saw him as a block to their own advancement. However, the main reason for his fall was Parliament's hostility. As Charles remarked, Clarendon's continuation in office made it 'impossible to do those things with the Parliament that must be done'. Lacking the King's support and facing possible proceedings for treason, Clarendon fled to France where he died in exile in 1674.

Documents: Charles II's style of rule

Charles II was a very different character to his father and grandfather, and his style of rule was markedly different from theirs. In many ways his character was contradictory: approachable but secretive; amiable but deeply distrustful; idle but constantly intriguing. His intentions for much of the reign are difficult to discern, as is his exact relationship with his ministers. Below are three accounts that deal with the way in which Charles governed, or was governed, depending on the writer's view:

A He is very affable not only in public but in private, only he talks too much and runs out too long and too far; he has a very ill opinion both of men and women, and so is infinitely distrustful; he thinks the world is governed wholly by interest, and indeed he has known so much of the baseness [*lowliness*] of mankind that no wonder he has hard thoughts of them. ... He has often kept up differences amongst his ministers and has balanced his favours pretty equally amongst them. ... He loves his ease so much that the great secret of all his ministers is to find out his temper exactly and to be easy to him. He has many odd opinions about religion and morality; and he thinks an implicitness [*moderation*] in religion is necessary for the safety of government and he looks upon all inquisitiveness into these things as mischievous to the state; he thinks all appetites are free and that God will never damn a man for allowing himself a little pleasure.

(Gilbert Burnet, *c*.1683)

B He lived with his ministers as he did with his mistresses; he used them, but he was not in love with them. He showed his judgement in this, that he cannot properly be said ever to have had a favourite, though some might look so at a distance. ... That some of his ministers seemed to have a superiority did not spring from his resignation to them, but to his ease. He chose rather to be eclipsed than to be troubled. ... I do not believe that he ever trusted any man or any set of men so entirely as not to have some secrets in which they had no share; as this might make him less well served, so in some degree it might make him less imposed upon. ... In general, he was upon pretty even terms with his ministers, and could as easily bear them to be hanged as some of them could his being abused.

(The Marquis of Halifax, *c*.1690)

C The council consists of ministers with a mortal hatred of one another, who seek only to be avenged upon each other ... this means that there is great uncertainty in the resolutions which are taken ... [so] that one can never be sure of anything. ... The courtiers are normally attached to Parliament and following the movements of that great body, allow themselves to be drawn along, against the interest of their master, for they know by experience that the most sure way to gain advancement is to make a great deal of noise, which obliges them always to urge the King to satisfy the Parliament, hoping that that assembly will give money, of which they are sure to have the largest share.

(A letter from the French ambassador in London to Louis XIV, 1674/5)

1   How does source A portray Charles's approach to kingship?
2   According to source B, what was the nature of Charles's relationship with his ministers?
3   In the view of the French ambassador in source C, what problems arose from Charles's lack of direction of his ministers?
4   What problems would a historian face in using these documents to draw firm conclusions about Charles's style of rule?

1667–73: the Cabal?

These years have often been referred to as those of the 'Cabal', during which a group of ministers (**C**lifford, **A**rlington, **B**uckingham, **A**shley (Cooper) and **L**auderdale = CABAL) dominated Government. Such an interpretation has now been widely discredited, as it is apparent that not only were other servants of the Crown important during this period, but also that the 'Cabal' were deeply divided amongst themselves, with figures such as Buckingham and Arlington in continual conflict with each other. Most important, however, is the fact that it was Charles, not his ministers, who directed royal policy during this period, a 'pro-Catholic' policy of alliance with France, and renewed attempts at introducing religious toleration.

The Triple Alliance

There was little sign of such policies, however, immediately after Clarendon's fall from office. In January 1668, Charles signed a treaty with the United Provinces and Sweden, thus forming the Triple Alliance, which was aimed against the French. The French had been able to take advantage of the Anglo-Dutch War to launch an invasion of the Spanish Netherlands (modern day Belgium), and now posed a threat to the Dutch Republic itself. For Charles to align England with other Protestant countries against the Continent's now foremost Catholic power was a popular move domestically, and had the effect of forcing the French to surrender some of their gains in the Netherlands and conclude peace with Spain. However, it seems likely that the Triple Alliance was no more than a temporary stopgap as far as Charles was concerned, a means of pressurising the French into seeking an English alliance. If this was the case it was a very successful ploy, as the French sent an ambassador to England, in August 1668, to discuss the possibility of an alliance against the Dutch. Such an alliance had attractions for both parties. For France under Louis XIV, it would provide a chance to recover her losses in the Spanish Netherlands. For England, it would also allow revenge for the humiliation of the Battle of the Medway, and the chance finally to eclipse the Dutch as her major commercial competitor.

The Treaty of Dover

An alliance with France was finally concluded at Dover in May 1670. It committed England to make war with France against the Dutch, and promised that Louis XIV would pay Charles £225,000 a year for the duration of the war. In addition, a secret clause committed Charles to convert to Roman Catholicism 'as soon as the welfare of his kingdom will permit', and Louis to pay him £150,000 and provide 6,000 troops to help overcome any domestic resistance that Charles might face as a result.

The possible advantages of making war on the Dutch have already been discussed, although it could be argued that Charles's strategic vision was poor, as victory over the Dutch could have strengthened France to an unacceptable degree. Even so, Charles's motivations in this are more easily discernible than in his promise to convert to Catholicism. The fact that he was to convert on his deathbed, some fifteen years later, has led some historians to conclude that Charles was sincere. His mother was a Catholic, and his brother, James, Duke of York, was shortly to make his own conversion public, and his ministers, Clifford and Arlington were also crypto-Catholics. It is possible that Charles was influenced by the religious convictions of those around him, and was at least initially sincere in his undertaking. It was only later, when it had become apparent how much it would undermine his authority with his Protestant subjects, that he was forced to shelve the idea. Others have argued that such religious idealism was quite out of character for Charles, whose deathbed conversion owed more to 'fire insurance' than conviction. According to this interpretation, Charles was motivated by a desire to win Louis's trust and admiration, and increase the level of French financial assistance for war against the Dutch. The promise of conversion was therefore nothing more than a bargaining counter, and not one that Charles ever seriously considered implementing. Whichever was the case, Charles's judgement in making such an undertaking in writing must be called into question. By doing so, he had given Louis a potential blackmail tool, which would make it virtually impossible for him to abandon the French alliance in future, if necessary.

The Declaration of Indulgence

The alliance with France and the secrecy surrounding the treaty negotiations at Dover had already aroused some suspicion amongst Charles's subjects, and this was heightened dramatically by the King's 'Declaration of Indulgence' in March 1672. Issued two days before declaring war on the Dutch, it suspended parts of the Uniformity Act, allowing Catholics to worship in private, and dissenting Protestants to apply for licences to worship in public. Charles's motives in issuing the Declaration are unclear. It may have been intended as a signal to Louis that Charles was beginning to implement his under-taking at Dover; or possibly a measure to unite Catholics and Dissenters into a counterbalance to the power of the Anglican Church.

If the Declaration was, as Arlington claimed, designed to 'keep all quiet at home while we are busy abroad', then it failed to achieve its aim. Many people feared that the war against the Dutch was only the first stage of a plan to destroy Protestantism, whose second stage would be the introduction of Catholicism and absolutism in England. Not only did the Declaration's content offend the majority of Charles's subjects, but it also involved a controversial use of the royal prerogative. The House of Commons attacked the Declaration, asserting that 'penal statutes cannot be suspended but by act of

Parliament', and, in the face of concerted opposition, Charles was forced to withdraw it in March 1673 and reconfirm the main provisions of the Clarendon Code in a Test Act.

His position was further weakened by the failure of the Dutch War. Initial successes by Louis's armies had not been mirrored by the English fleet, who were defeated by the Dutch off Southwold in June 1672. A further naval defeat followed in 1673 off the Dutch coast at Texel, and, allied with Spain and Austria, the Dutch were able to drive Louis's armies out of the Netherlands. Faced with huge debts arising from the war and parliamentary hostility to providing financial assistance, Charles had little option but to make peace with the Dutch, which he did in February 1674.

The withdrawal of the Declaration of Indulgence and the failure of the Dutch War did much to damage Charles, but his policies were further compromised, in 1673, by the public conversion to Catholicism of Charles's brother, James, Duke of York. Although Charles had fathered numerous bastards, his marriage with Catherine of Braganza had remained childless, leaving his brother, James, as heir to the throne. The prospect of a Catholic succession, added to the suspicions already current about Charles's commitment to the Protestant cause, threatened seriously to undermine the King's position.

One contemporary, Sir Edward Dering, listed the reasons as to why 'the nation began to think the court inclined to favour Popery and France':

i)   The declaration coming out about this time for laying aside all the penal laws in matters of religion.
ii) The second war made with the Dutch in conjunction with France, there being no sufficient visible cause to provoke it.
iii) The departing from the Triple League. …
iv) The connivance at the Jesuits and priests, who did abundantly swarm in the kingdom and even about the court.
v)   The conference … at Dover, the cause of meeting and the matter there debated and resolved on being kept very secret.
vi) The employing of several known or suspected Papists in great places of trust, especially Lord Clifford, made High Treasurer.
vii) Lastly to these, and much more than all these together, was the Duke of York's being the first suspected and afterwards universally believed to be a Papist, which gave no unreasonable foundation to the fear that, the King having no children, when the Duke should come to the crown the Protestant religion would be at least oppressed, if not extirpated [*destroyed completely*].

1   Summarise the reasons Dering gives for suspecting a Catholic, court conspiracy.
2   The outbreak of war against the Protestant Dutch in 1652–4 and 1665–7 met with popular approval, and an alliance with Catholic France against Spain during the Protectorate caused little concern. Why do you think that the French alliance against the Dutch on this occasion prompted such opposition?

Table 10.1 Main events of Charles II's reign, 1660–73

1660	Convention Parliament
	Restoration of Charles II
	Restoration Settlement
1661	Cavalier Parliament
1661–5	The Clarendon Code
1665–7	Second Anglo–Dutch War
1667	Clarendon falls from office
1668	Triple Alliance
1670	Treaty of Dover
1672–4	Third Anglo–Dutch War
1673	Declaration of Indulgence
	Conversion of James, Duke of York, to Catholicism

11 Charles II, 1673–85

Danby, 1674–8

In the aftermath of James's conversion, the Cabal, such as it was, split apart. Ashley Cooper (now the Earl of Shaftesbury) and Buckingham became critics of the Government. Clifford resigned his post as Treasurer after refusing to take the oath of office demanded under the Test Act, thereby also signalling his conversion to Catholicism. Arlington, also accused by the Commons of being 'popishly affected', saw his influence wane and resigned his post as Secretary of State in 1674. And although Lauderdale continued in office, his influenced was almost exclusively limited to Scottish affairs. It was this political vacuum that Charles's new chief minister, Thomas Osborne, Earl of Danby, filled.

Finance

When he became Lord Treasurer in 1673, Danby inherited a difficult financial situation. As a result of the Dutch War, the Crown had been forced to issue a 'Stop on the Exchequer', suspending the repayment of its debts to creditors. In addition, although Parliament had voted some supplies for the war after Charles had withdrawn the Declaration of Indulgence and agreed to a renewal of the Test Act, they fell almost £450,000 short of the Crown's expenditure. However, these immediate problems obscured the fact that in the longer term the outlook for the royal finances was more promising. This was largely due to the continued expansion of trade, with its proportionate expansion of customs revenues. Although this increase in trade had been going on for a long period, the Crown was now in a position to take full advantage of it. Traditionally, the collection of customs had been the task of 'customs farmers', who paid the Crown a fixed amount per year in return for the right to collect customs duties at a particular port. In 1671, the customs farms were abolished and the collection of customs taken over directly by the Crown, which was thereby able to benefit fully from the increased volume of trade. Similar reforms were also put into place to maximise the collection of revenues from the excise and hearth tax.

Danby's successes in increasing revenue were undermined however by a growth in royal expenditure, and during his time at the Treasury (1673–9) he presided over an increase in the royal debt of around £750,000. Like his grandfather, James I, Charles found it very difficult to control his spending and any attempts to improve the royal finances had to be carried out against a backdrop of his continued extravagance. Danby introduced schemes to cut spending in 1675 and 1677, with the approval of the Privy

Council and the King himself, but Charles was unable to keep to his promises to curb his expenditure. In such circumstances, the only option was to look to Parliament to make up the short-fall.

Danby's analysis of the financial situation led him to press Charles to pursue policies that would make Parliament more likely to vote him the money he needed. His analysis of the situation is set out in a note from him to the King in December 1673:

- State of the present condition of the crown, which cannot be amended but by force or compliance.
- If by compliance then it must be by a Parliament or infinite reducement of expense.
- If by Parliament, by this or a new one.
- If by this [Parliament], they must be gratified by executing the laws both against Popery and nonconformity and withdrawing apparently from the French interest.
- If by a new one [Parliament], they will ... desire ... toleration of all religions but Popery, and as to France the inclinations will be the same, only the new one will in all likelihood press the crown to it with less respect.
- And, as to money, it is probably to be feared that neither the one nor the other will give anything proportionable to the wants of the crown till satisfied in their fears as to France.

Relations with Parliament

In order to gain greater financial assistance from Parliament, Danby needed to overcome its distrust of Charles and his intentions. To accomplish this Danby adopted two main strategies: one was to improve the Crown's management of Parliament, and the other was to persuade the King to adopt more 'Protestant' policies, to counteract the impression that the Government was leaning towards Catholicism. Danby set about building up a Court party within Parliament that owed its allegiance primarily to the Crown. He did this primarily by distributing patronage, such as pensions drawn from excise and customs revenues, and by offering potential supporters Government posts. His letters and papers reveal the amount of energy that he put into this, and into canvassing MPs directly for their opinions and support. An additional weapon in his arsenal was the threat of dissolution followed by new elections, something that many MPs, elected back in 1661, did not welcome. According to Bishop Burnet, this was a very effective tactic as:

> the dissolution of the Parliament was a thing that terrified many of the House of Commons, who were ruined in their fortunes, and lived upon their privileges and pensions ... they had but small hopes of coming into Parliament again [if] it should be dissolved.

The success of Danby's tactics was compromised by accusations that he was trying to manipulate Parliament. They reinforced the suspicion among the Crown's critics that he was trying to manage Parliament to such an extent that it would no longer oppose 'Catholic' policies. Despite the fact that Danby was trying to pursue 'Protestant' policies, he found it difficult to win Parliament's trust. His position was further undermined by

Charles, who never gave his full support to his minister, and continued to intrigue and pursue alternatives behind Danby's back.

Danby's attempts to reach agreement with Parliament over supply in 1675 were not particularly successful, and even saw an attempt by some MPs to have him impeached. The main obstacle to co-operation was Charles's refusal to recall English troops fighting alongside the French, which was seen as continued evidence of the Government's support for pro-French, Catholic policies. These suspicions would have been compounded had Parliament known of the secret negotiations going on between Charles and Louis XIV, by which Charles's support was ensured through payments amounting to around £110,000. In the autumn, Danby did eventually manage to extract some supply from Parliament – £300,000 for the navy – and in November Charles adjourned Parliament for fifteen months.

When Parliament met again in February 1677, Danby had far more success. It voted £600,000 and approved the renewal of additional excise duties, originally granted in 1670. In return, Danby promised Government support for a proposal to limit the powers of any Catholic successor to Charles, something that critics had been demanding since 1673, when James's conversion to Catholicism had been made public. However, this new found harmony was almost immediately soured by divisions over foreign affairs. During the spring and summer of 1677, the French army invaded the Spanish Netherlands once more, and the Commons demanded that Charles ally himself with the Dutch against Louis XIV, before they would vote him any further supplies. The King responded by adjourning Parliament until January 1678. For Danby, the King's actions were deeply frustrating. His strenuous attempts to win Parliament's support on the back of Protestant policies had been jeopardised by Charles's inability to accept the importance of gaining Parliament's trust. As Danby complained after the adjournment, until Charles could 'fall into the humour of the people, he can never be great or rich'.

Charles indicated that he may have grasped the necessity of doing this, when in October 1677 he agreed to the marriage of the Dutch prince, William of Orange, and James's eldest daughter, Mary, who were both Protestants. This was followed by negotiations with the Dutch which proposed an alliance against the French, if they did not withdraw their forces from the Netherlands. It is extremely unlikely that Charles really anticipated going to war with Louis, but rather that he was trying to accommodate the prejudices of his subjects, while hoping to pressure the French king into making peace. Certainly his apparent change of policy did little to calm the suspicions of Parliament, who, when they reassembled in January 1678, were reluctant to provide the King with the money he needed to raise an army of 30,000 men. Many feared that any such army would be used not against the French but against them, and to usher in absolutism and Catholicism.

By the summer, feelings within Parliament were still running high. Parliament had only supplied Charles with around £300,000 of the estimated £2,500,000 required, but an army was still assembled, and kept in being throughout the summer. Ignoring Parliament's requests to disband the army, following an armistice between the Dutch and France in June, Charles adjourned Parliament once more in July 1678, amid widespread fears of a Catholic conspiracy. This was a fear that was brought up to fever pitch in the autumn, with the alleged discovery of the 'Popish Plot'.

The Popish Plot

> Upon the evidence that has already appeared to this House, that this House is of the opinion that there hath been and still is a damnable and hellish plot contrived and carried on by the popish recusants for the assassinating and murdering of the King, and for subverting the government, and rooting out and destroying the Protestant religion.

> (Resolution of the House of Commons, 21 October 1678)

News of a Popish Plot was first presented to Charles II and his council in August 1678 by two very questionable individuals, named Titus Oates and Israel Tonge. Historians are generally agreed that Oates and Tonge fabricated the plot, but its contents were well pitched to fit the popular mood of the country. The plot involved the murder of the King, followed by Catholic uprisings in England and Ireland, that would be supported by armed force from abroad, probably France. Despite discrepancies, their story was given some credibility by two important coincidences. Firstly their 'evidence' had implicated James, Duke of York's former secretary, Edward Coleman, who was duly arrested. His papers were seized and found to include correspondence with Jesuits and French agents, discussing possible ways to promote Catholicism in England. This in turn implicated James himself, who was already suspect in the eyes of some, as the obvious beneficiary of any such plot. The second was the mysterious death of Sir Edmund Berry Godfrey, a JP with whom Oates had deposited his original allegations, who was found in a ditch, strangled and run through with his own sword. Many were convinced that he had been killed by Catholics, who were trying to prevent him from sharing the damaging evidence that he held.

The parliamentary resolution (above) reflects a general acceptance of the truth of the Popish Plot, and bearing in mind the general climate of fear and suspicion during this period, it is perhaps understandable as to why Oates and Tonge were so easily believed. By the end of the year, Coleman and three others had been executed for their part in the conspiracy, and five Catholic Lords named by Oates were facing impeachment. By the next summer, seventeen more Catholics had been tried and executed for their alleged involvement in the plot.

Documents

Much of the written material generated during the Popish Plot is of a rather hysterical and fervently anti-Catholic nature. Perhaps more critical and detached analyses are provided by the diarist, John Evelyn, and the poet and wit, John Dryden, below:

A   *October 1, 1678*: I went with my wife to London: The Parliament being now alarmed with the whole nation, about a conspiracy of some eminent papists, for the destruction of the King and introducing popery. Discovered by one Oates and Dr. Tonge [who] I knew … I went to see and converse with him, now being at Whitehall, with Mr. Oates. … He seemed to be a bold man, and in my thoughts furiously indiscreet; but everybody believed what he said; and it quite changed the genius [*thoughts*] and motions of the Parliament. ... This discovery turned them all as one man against it, and nothing was done. ... to finding out the depth of this.

October 21: The barbarous murder of Sir Edmund Godfrey, found strangled about this time, by the Papists, put the whole nation in a new fermentation against them.

November. Oates ... grew so presumptuous as to accuse the Queen for intending to poison the King; which certainly that pious and virtuous Lady abhorred the thought of, and Oates and his circumstances made it utterly unlikely in my opinion. 'Tis likely he thought to gratify some, who would have been glad his Majesty should have married a more fruitful lady: but the King was too kind a husband to let any of these make impression upon him. However, divers [*various*] of the Popish Peers sent to the Tower, as accused by Oates, [and] all the Roman Catholic Lords were by a new Act, for ever excluded [from] the Parliament.

July 18, 1679: I went early to the Old Bailey ... to the famous trial of Sir Geoffrey Wakeman and 3 Benedictine Monks ... the first for intending to poison the King, the others as accomplices to carry on the plot, to subvert the Government, and introduce Popery. ... After a long and tedious trial of 9 hours, the Jury brought them in 'Not Guilty' ... not without sufficient disadvantage and reflection on the witnesses, especially Oates. ... For my part, I do look on Oates as a vain, insolent man, puffed up with the favour of the Commons, for having discovered something really true, [i.e.] detecting the dangerous intrigue of Coleman, proved out of his own letters ... but that he was trusted with those secrets, he pretended, [nor] had he any solid ground for what he accused divers noble men of. ... The Commons had so exalted him that they took for gospel all that he said, and ruined all whom he named to be conspirators, nor did he spare whomsoever came in his way.

(Extracts from the diary of John Evelyn, 1678/9)

B   From hence began that Plot, the nation's curse,
     Bad in itself, but represented worse,
     Raised in extremes, and in extremes decried,
     With oaths affirmed, with dying vows denied,
     Not weighed or winnowed by the multitude,
     But swallowed in the mass, unchewed and crude.
     Some truth there was, but dashed and brewed with lies
     To please the fools and puzzle all the wise.
     Succeeding times did equal folly call
     Believing nothing or believing all.

(John Dryden, 'Absolom and Achitophel', 1681)

1   How does Evelyn's view of Oates develop during his diary entries?
2   How much truth do Evelyn and Dryden seem to think was in the allegations of a Popish Plot?

It was against this backdrop of anti-Catholic hysteria that Danby's enemies saw their opportunity to attack the King's chief minister. Letters written by Danby were presented to the Commons that indicated his part in negotiating secret subsidies from Louis XIV. Within days, articles of impeachment were drawn up against Danby, alleging his involvement in secret treaties with foreign powers, plotting to create a standing army, and of trying to conceal the allegations made in the Popish Plot. Charles reacted by dissolving Parliament in January 1679, but when further attempts were made by the next Parliament to convict Danby of treason, the King bowed to pressure, removing him from his post as Lord Treasurer and placing him in the Tower.

The Exclusion Crisis, 1679–81

If Charles had hoped that the dissolution of the Cavalier Parliament, which had been in existence since 1661, might produce a more pliable successor, then he was mistaken. When the new Parliament met in March 1679, it continued to press for three things: the impeachment of Danby; the disbanding of the army; and placing limits on a Catholic successor to the throne. However, many MPs felt that restricting the powers of a Catholic monarch was not a sufficient guarantee against the threat of absolutism, which in the popular mind was an inevitable consequence of Catholic government. How far could they be sure that James would observe any statutory limits that they would put on him? An alternative would be actually to exclude James from the succession, a 'violent and bloody' man determined 'to introduce a military and arbitrary government', according to one of the Government's most vocal critics, the Earl of Shaftesbury. In May, an Exclusion Bill was put before the Commons proposing that on Charles's death the Crown should pass not to James, but to the next in succession after him. It was approved by 207 to 128 votes. Nevertheless, Charles's opposition to Exclusion was absolute, and he responded by dissolving Parliament.

Over the next two years, the issue of Exclusion was to dominate politics and split the political nation down the middle. It also saw the emergence of two distinct parties, the Whigs and the Tories:

> *The Whigs*: led by the Earl of Shaftesbury, the Whigs were in favour of Exclusion, fearing that a Catholic monarch would forcibly impose Catholicism and absolutism. The only means of ensuring the preservation of Protestantism and the liberties and rights of Parliament was to exclude James from the succession. In the elections for the parliaments of 1680 and 1681 the Whigs won clear majorities in the House of Commons. Nonconformists, in particular, gave them support, hoping to win religious toleration for themselves in return. They also enjoyed the backing of much of the urban electorate, including London, who saw them as guarantors of the liberties and privileges they enjoyed under their town and city charters.

> *The Tories*: the Tories opposed Exclusion. They drew most of their support from the alliance of the Anglican Church and rural, conservative gentry, who saw the Crown as the defender of their own positions. They viewed the Whigs' attempts to alter the line of succession as extremely dangerous, striking at the ancient principle of hereditary right that applied not only to the Crown, but also to their own positions in society. Their election slogan in 1681, 'Forty-one is here again!' (i.e. 1641),

illustrates their conviction that the Exclusion campaign had the potential to plunge the country into civil war once more.

Despite holding elections in August–September 1679, Charles did not actually summon his new Parliament to Westminster until October 1680, hoping that in the interim their enthusiasm for Exclusion might have cooled. His hopes of receiving supplies were soon dashed, however, as the Commons proceeded to discuss Exclusion instead. Within nine days, they had approved a bill for Exclusion by an overwhelming majority. The bill then passed to the Lords, where Lord Halifax led the opposition to it. Summoning up images of civil war, he argued that Exclusion would inevitably lead to military struggle, and repeated Charles's offer to provide limitations on James's power instead. The King attended the debate in person, standing framed against the fireplace, and moving around the chamber canvassing peers individually. The combination of Halifax's eloquence and Charles's presence was effective and the bill was defeated by 63 votes to 30.

In January 1681, Charles dissolved Parliament and summoned another to meet at Oxford in March. Calculating that his opponents would be weakened away from London and the potential support of the mob, Charles hoped to benefit from the Royalist associations of the city, and steer Parliament away from the issue of Exclusion. In his opening speech, he repeated his opposition to Exclusion and his willingness to consider limitations instead. However, Shaftesbury ignored his offer and the Commons continued to press for James's Exclusion from the throne. Charles's response was to call the Lords and Commons together and after only one week to dissolve the Oxford Parliament. He did so without any warning, and only after having stationed 600 troops outside the building. The Whigs, despite some talk of resistance, dispersed without any trouble, intimidated by the presence of the army and deprived of the support they would have expected in the City of London. Charles returned to the capital and did not call Parliament again. The Exclusion Crisis was over.

The failure of Exclusion

Exclusion failed, but given the popular support for it, and the overwhelming backing of the House of Commons, why should it have done? The parallels between 1679–81 and 1640–1 are marked: fear of Catholicism; distrust of the monarch; attacks on his ministers; and an attempt to use Parliament to force the King to agree to fundamental constitutional changes. Why did Exclusion not succeed? Or if it was to fail, why did it not lead, as some Whigs threatened it would, to armed conflict?

The first reason is that, for many people, Exclusion threatened the traditional laws and order of society as a whole. If Parliament could alter the succession, what other aspects of the law might be tampered with? How sacred would other hereditary rights, such as the inheritance of property, be if such a law was put in place? There was also the fear that altering the succession might lead to civil war, the spectre of which was even more alarming to most than absolutist Government. Although few relished the thought of James's succession, to some he was the better of two evils; as Lord Ailesbury commented in the Exclusion debate in November 1680, 'If the right heir should be thrown out, may we not be subject to invasions abroad or wars at home? More insecurity from wars than to suffer him to reign.'

The memory of civil war and the instability of the republic years still weighed heavily in the minds of the political nation, and there were few who, even if they supported Exclusion, were prepared to fight over it if it failed. Shaftesbury and his supporters went to great lengths to mobilise popular support through petitioning and party organisation, and provided a formidable bloc of opinion within Parliament. However, they were unable, or unwilling, to fall back on armed force. The release of the demons of social and political chaos was not a price many were willing to pay.

Charles's own role in defeating Exclusion was an important one. He made good use of delaying tactics, leaving periods of time, for instance over a year between elections and summoning Parliament in 1679–80, to try and take some of the heat out of the debate. While refusing to move on the hereditary principle, he tried to signal his flexibility in offering limitations on a Catholic successor. He also made a great deal of capital out of the fact that the Church was squarely behind him, and worked hard to foster his image as a Protestant ruler, working faithfully within the traditional framework of Government. His own intervention in the Lords debate of November 1680, and at the Oxford Parliament, were also examples of his political skill and his sense of timing, both qualities sadly lacking in his father.

Another factor that undermined the Exclusion campaign was the lack of unity among the Whigs over who *should* succeed Charles II. Some, including Shaftesbury, favoured Charles's illegitimate son, the Duke of Monmouth, and others preferred Mary, the eldest, Protestant daughter of James. However, both candidates had serious drawbacks. Monmouth's illegitimacy was unacceptable to many and the fact that Mary was married to a foreign prince, William of Orange, raised the possibility of England's interests being subjugated to those of another nation.

Perhaps the most fundamental flaw in Shaftesbury's strategy was that it was dependent on the King's need of parliamentary revenues. Supply would be given, but only in return for Exclusion. Yet, by 1681, Charles's financial situation was improving as he continued to benefit from the customs reforms of ten years earlier, which allowed him to enjoy the full revenues from the continuing growth of trade, and for the first time his ordinary revenues actually came to the £1,200,000 envisaged in the Restoration Settlement. In addition, Charles was still in secret negotiations with Louis XIV, who had promised him a subsidy of £125,000 a year in return for dissolving Parliament. Therefore, when Charles dismissed the Oxford Parliament and did not recall it, he was able to do so because he was no longer financially dependent on it. Unlike his father, he had no rebellions in Ireland or Scotland to deal with, and provided he continued to avoid war there was no reason to call Parliament again. It was this factor, more than any other, which enabled Charles to defeat Exclusion.

The Royalist reaction, 1681–5

Following the dissolution of the Oxford Parliament, Charles went on the offensive. He issued a declaration explaining his actions, which he ordered to be read from the pulpits of all churches. The declaration smeared his Whig opponents as republicans aiming to overthrow monarchy, religion and property, and to introduce anarchy in their place, with the Exclusion campaign having its origins in 'the restless malice of ill men who are labouring to poison our people'. Shaftesbury was arrested in July 1681 on a charge of treason, although he was subsequently acquitted because the jury for the trial had been selected by two Whig sheriffs. He fled abroad, where he died in 1683, the same year as a number of Whig leaders were arrested for their alleged involvement in the Rye House Plot. Lord Russell, the Earl of Essex and Algernon Sidney were accused (probably falsely) of planning to assassinate Charles; Essex committed suicide after his arrest and the others were duly tried and executed.

However, Charles went much further than simply attacking the Whig leadership; he also purged local government of Whig supporters. Whig sympathisers lost their militia appointments, and Whig JPs and sheriffs were replaced with Tory loyalists, giving control over the legal process in the localities. Urban areas were also brought to heel, by the use of 'Quo Warranto' writs that required town charters to be surrendered for inspection. Most were medieval in origin and could be declared invalid on technicalities, and then replaced by new, more restrictive, documents. The case against the City of London was drawn out and took two years before it was resolved in the Crown's favour, after which the resistance of the other towns crumbled. The new charters required royal consent for appointments such as mayors or sheriffs, which again put them effectively under Tory control. In total, Charles issued fifty-one new charters during the last four years of his reign, giving him a significant degree of influence over municipal affairs.

In addition to the above, Charles drew great strength from his financial position and his alliance with the Church. His finances continued to improve during this period, as trade expanded, and, by 1684–5, his ordinary revenues had almost reached £1,400,000. As for the Church, Charles belatedly took the advice of Clarendon and Danby, and opted for the political advantages that went with allying with the Anglican establishment. He abandoned any attempts at introducing toleration, and, with his encouragement, Tory JPs enthusiastically implemented the penal legislation against both Catholics and Dissenters. Recusancy fines were levied and the terms of the Corporation Act applied.

By the time of his death, Charles had not only defeated Exclusion and the Whigs, but had also increased the authority of the Crown enormously. What John Miller has described as 'perhaps the most authoritarian royal regime of the century' had been erected on the back of financial strength, and an alliance with the conservative body of Tory opinion. How far this could hope to survive under a new, Catholic King remained to be seen.

Table 11.1 Main events of Charles II's reign, 1674–85

1674	Peace with the Dutch
	Emergence of Earl of Danby as chief minister
1677	Marriage of Charles II's niece, Mary, to William of Orange
1678	Popish Plot
1679	Fall of Danby
1679–81	Exclusion Crisis
1681–5	Personal Rule of Charles II
	Purge of Whig opponents
	Rye House Plot
1685	Charles II dies

Verdicts on Charles II

In the final analysis, how able a king was Charles II? His vices and pleasures were thoroughly chronicled by contemporaries, and certainly the 'Merry Monarch' tag is one that has survived to this day, but did his morals have any effect on his ability to govern? Should his reign be seen as one of lost opportunities, or of skilful manoeuvre amid difficult situations? A range of opinion is provided by contemporaries and historians below.

Documents

A   Thus died King Charles II. ... He was a prince of many virtues, and many great imperfections; debonair [*dashing*], easy of access, not bloody or cruel; his countenance fierce, his voice great, proper of person, every motion became him. He loved planting and building, and brought in a politer way of living, which passed to luxury and intolerable expense. He would doubtless have been an excellent prince had he been less addicted to women. ... Certainly never had king more glorious opportunities to have made himself, his people and all Europe happy, and prevented numerable mischiefs, had not his all too easy nature resigned him to be managed by crafty men.

(The diary of John Evelyn, 1685)

B   Thus reigned and died King Charles the Second, a prince endowed with all the qualities that might justly have rendered him ... one of the greatest geniuses that ever sat upon a throne, if he had not sullied those excellent parts with the soft pleasures of ease, and had not entertained a fatal friendship that was incompatible with the interest of England. ... He loved not business and sought every occasion to avoid it, which was one reason he passed so much time with his mistresses; yet when necessity called him none of his Council could reason more closely upon matters of state, and he would often outdo his ministers in application and diligence. ... If he had any one fixed maxim of government, it was to play one party against another, to be thereby the more master of both.

(James Welwood, *Memoirs*, late seventeenth century)

1   How far would sources A and B suggest that Charles was not a success as King?

Historians

C   Fond of novelty, lazy and intolerant of routine, he succeeded in combining kingship with comfort and even amusement. ... As a man and a Stuart, he was a remarkable exception ... he had a sense of humour, and he knew when to yield; as a man, he had the gift then known as second sight, and after thirty years he had nothing more to learn. His jests served to disarm his associates, as his intuition enabled him to read their minds; where others excelled in cleverness, industry, or virtue, he concealed instinct, determination, and a sound political sense. Such were his assets; his most serious liability was his brother James.

(D. Ogg, *England in the Reign of Charles II*, 1934)

D   Although it is difficult to take seriously the case for Charles as a great king, his detractors have sometimes criticized him for the wrong reasons, judging him on highminded moral grounds rather than in the light of whether or not he was an effective ruler. His extra-marital adventures are fascinating for the scope and catholicity of the king's sexual appetite which they reveal ... [but] it is possible to place too much emphasis on them in accounts of the political history of the period. Mistresses and effective monarchical rule, as Louis XIV's activities illustrate, were not incompatible in the seventeenth century. ... Moreover, criticisms of Charles' undoubted cynicism and unprincipled behaviour are often also moral rather than political judgements. His cynical treatment of his friends and enemies alike, his double-dealing, and resort to short-term political expediency were just the amoral qualities required by Machiavelli [a fifteenth-century Italian political thinker] in a successful ruler. ... Yet, it cannot be denied that many of Charles' activities and his lifestyle were detrimental to the efficient running of the king's government and to good relations with the parliamentary classes. He did prefer the racecourse and associated pleasures of Newmarket and the brothels of Covent Garden to the day-to-day tedium of government. Royal government suffered in consequence. ... Not even Clarendon in the early 1660s had enough of the king's confidence to take his place. Similarly ... Danby was rarely taken into the king's secret counsels.

(Barry Coward, *The Stuart Age*, 1994)

E   It can be argued that ultimately Charles realised that the survival of the monarchy and the preservation of the legitimate succession were about all he could hope to achieve. When he had recovered his right, Charles was already a realist; the bitter years of exile and the humiliations he had suffered left him a young man without illusions. ... When he wished to do so, Charles could behave in a cold or even cruel manner, and his habitual amiability was often assumed in order to put men and women off their guard. As the portraits of his last years show, he developed into a formidable, even intimidating monarch. The reality was far removed from the myth of the 'Merry Monarch'.

(J.R. Jones, 'Introduction', in *The Restored Monarchy (1660–1688)*, 1979)

F   If Charles survived to live out his last years in peace, this owed as much to luck and the monarchy's inherent strength – especially in terms of popular strength – as to his own skills as king. For all his cleverness, perhaps over-cleverness, in diplomacy and intrigue, he seems never to have understood or trusted the men who made up the political nation or sat in Parliament. His distrust, frivolity and (despite his cynicism) openness to suggestion led him to embrace unwise and provocative policies. ... Despite his folly and irresponsibility, Charles survived. This owed much to his sense of self-preservation and to the fact that 'he was not striving, nor ambitious, but easy, loved pleasures and seemed chiefly to desire quiet and security for his own time'. In that respect, Charles was well suited to the politically conservative age in which he lived. His brother, who tried to bring about major changes, lost his throne.

(John Miller, *Restoration England: The Reign of Charles II*, 1997)

2   In source C, what qualities does Ogg identify in Charles's style of kingship?
3   On what grounds, according to source D, should we judge Charles?
4   How do sources E and F disagree over Charles's abilities and success as King of England?
5   Bearing in mind sources A–F, and the other material you have read, how able a monarch do you think Charles II was? Do you think his personality was a help or hindrance to him?

12 James II, 1685–8

The situation in 1685

Given the fact that James was deposed after only three years on the throne, it is tempting to assume that his failure as King was, in some sense, inevitable. Yet, if one considers James's position on his accession, it is hard to substantiate such a view. The Exclusion campaign had been defeated, and James had come to the throne as undisputed successor to Charles II. He had the unqualified support of the Anglican Church; the Whigs had been crushed in Charles's final years; and the Tories, supportive of the hereditary rights of the King, were in firm control of local government. The Crown had dispensed with Parliament for the last four years of Charles's reign, in contravention of the Triennial Act, and had sufficient revenues to continue to govern without parliamentary aid if necessary.

When James explained his intentions to his Privy Council at the beginning of the reign, he did so in terms that his Tory supporters would have found reassuring:

> I shall make it my endeavour to preserve this government, both in Church and State, as it is by law established; and as I shall never depart from the rights and prerogatives of the Crown, so shall I never invade any man's property.

It seems as though much of the political nation saw every possibility of harmonious relations between James and themselves, as the Tory peer, the Earl of Peterborough, commented on James's accession:

> Everything is very happy here. Never a king was proclaimed with more applause than he that reigns under the name of James the Second. He is courted by all men, and all orders pay him ready duty and obedience. I doubt not but to see a happy reign.

Any concern that *was* felt by the Tories over the King's Catholicism was lessened by his promises to preserve the Church, and by the fact that his marriage to Mary Modena had failed to produce an heir, thereby leaving the succession to his Protestant daughter by his first marriage, Mary. Yet despite the promising situation that James inherited, by the autumn of 1688 he had succeeded in uniting most of the political nation against him, and was unable to prevent his own overthrow. How could such a dramatic reversal of fortunes have come about?

Character of James II

At least part of the answer to this question is to be found in the character of James himself. Below we have two contemporary accounts of the new King:

A He was very brave in his youth ... that till his marriage lessened him, he really clouded the King [Charles II], and passed for the superior genius. He was naturally candid and sincere, and a firm friend, till affairs and his religion wore out all his first principles and inclinations. ... He had no true judgement, and was soon determined by those whom he trusted; but he was obstinate against all other advices. He was bred with high notions of kingly authority, and laid it down for a maxim, that all who opposed the King were rebels in their hearts. ... [Even so] if it had not been for his popery he would have been, if not a great, yet a good prince.

(Bishop Burnet, 1690s)

B King James was certainly a far better man than his brother, although of a far inferior understanding. His designs were in general of a public nature; most pernicious [*harmful*] indeed to this country, but the restoration of popery here was a great object in the eyes of most of his own faith everywhere, and was a great and meritorious attempt with them. He fell a sacrifice to it and was undoubtedly very conscientious in it. Whereas King Charles, in *his* government, had himself neither conscience, religion, honour nor justice; and does not seem to have had even the feelings of them ... all he meant ... was to enjoy a lazy, thoughtless ease, in the constant debauchery of amours and in the pleasures of wit and laughter with the most worthless, vicious and abandoned set of men that even that age afforded.

(Arthur Onslow, late seventeenth century)

1 What strengths and weaknesses in James's character are identified by source A?
2 How far is this judgement backed up by source B?
3 How far do you accept the grounds that Onslow uses for judging James and comparing him to his brother?

Political harmony

The elections of spring 1685 confirmed the strength of James's position, and the effectiveness of the purges of local government started by his brother and continued by him in the early months of his reign. When Parliament assembled in May, it was dominated by Tories with perhaps as few as forty Whig members. There were only nine Whigs elected out of the 195 MPs who were returned from boroughs that had had their charters amended. Parliament's support for James was illustrated by the confirmation of the revenues that had been granted to Charles for life, as well as additional customs duties for eight years to pay off debts left by him. Although the same Parliament also passed resolutions in defence of the Anglican Church and in favour of implementation of the penal laws, there was little sign that MPs saw the Church as being under threat. If this had been the case, then such resolutions would surely have been linked to the financial grants that Parliament had made. In the event they were unconditional.

The strength of James's position was further underlined by the failure of two rebellions during the summer of 1685. The first, led by the Earl of Argyle, was in Scotland and was put down with relative ease. The second, led by Charles II's illegitimate son, the Duke of Monmouth, was more serious. He succeeded in attracting support from Dissenters in the south-west, but his followers were largely artisans and tradesmen, rather than the gentry or nobility. Despite raising an army of around 13,000 men, Monmouth was defeated by royal forces at Sedgemoor on 5 July. His execution was followed by the brutal suppression of his followers by Lord Chief Justice Jeffries, in what became known as the 'Bloody Assizes'. Some 250 people were convicted of treason and hung, drawn and quartered, and had their dismembered corpses distributed around the south-west for public display. The failure of Monmouth's rebellion, and its lack of support from the higher social classes, revealed that the political nation was still behind James and viewed the possibility of rebellion with horror. Their opposition to the rebels is illustrated by the declaration of the House of Commons that Jeffries's actions were 'punishments rejoiced at by all good men'.

James's aims

What James was actually trying to achieve during his reign, especially in his religious policy, has been the subject of much discussion amongst historians. Traditionally, James has been portrayed as wanting to establish Catholicism as the sole religion of the country, by force if necessary, together with a programme of religious persecution. This religious policy would be accompanied by the introduction of a continental style absolutism. Most historians writing currently see James as having far more limited ambitions. They would argue that he had no plans to rule without Parliament, and simply wanted to give Catholics equal status to their Protestant counterparts, both in terms of freedom of worship and in holding State office. He was convinced of Catholicism's superiority, and believed that the only reason that Protestantism had enjoyed such success in England was due to political factors. Given a level playing field, Catholicism would soon eclipse Protestantism without the need for coercion. Hence, James's rejection of the more extreme counsels of some of his advisers, such as the legitimisation of his bastard son, the Duke of Berwick, to ensure a Catholic succession, or to request French aid to facilitate the imposition of Catholicism. Indeed, James spoke on several occasions of being opposed to religious persecution on principle, as he told his brother in 1680, he considered 'it unlawful to force any man, much less a kingdom to embrace' any religion.

Although James's aims may have been relatively modest, it does not mean that they were necessarily very realistic. His hopes of promoting Catholic involvement in State affairs were limited by the small numbers of Catholics in England, probably no more than 20,000, and their relatively low social status. Few Catholics had any political or governmental experience, and, even at Louis XIV's court, James had to use Protestant diplomats. His hopes were also unrealistic in the sense that they underestimated the depth of hostility of his subjects to Catholicism. It was inextricably identified with persecution and tyranny in the minds of most Englishmen, who had been brought up on Foxe's *Book of Martyrs* and tales of Catholic atrocities in Ireland and on the

Continent. It is difficult to see how any programme of promoting Catholic interests, no matter how limited, could have failed to provoke enormous popular opposition.

Political division

What perhaps James did not realise was that the support he received on his accession was not unconditional. Although the Tories were enthusiastic supporters of the principle of hereditary right and the maintenance of the royal prerogative, they also had strong loyalties to the Church of England, and expected James's policies to reflect this. Hence, James's announcement in November 1685 that he wanted Parliament to repeal the Test and Corporation Acts upset many Tory MPs, who saw religious toleration as a threat to the Anglican Church and therefore deeply undesirable. James further strained their loyalty by announcing that he was not going to disband the army raised to put down Monmouth's rebellion, and that he had already overridden the Test Act by appointing Catholic officers to the army. There was immediate opposition to these developments in Parliament, led by some of the King's own privy councillors, such as the Earl of Nottingham, and by the Bishop of London, Henry Compton. James's reaction was to suspend Parliament.

The next year saw the deepening of these divisions between James and his natural supporters. In June 1686 a case (Godden vs Hales) was brought to test the legality of the King's 'dispensing power', i.e. his right to dispense with parliamentary laws in certain cases. The judges found for the King by a margin of eleven to one, asserting that the dispensing power was 'an inseparable prerogative of the Kings of England' and that the 'King himself is the sole judge' of when such dispensations should be granted. Not only did this have implications as far as appointments of Catholics to the army were concerned, but it opened the way for James to override any or all of the penal laws as he saw fit. The King further expanded his powers through the establishment of the Court of Ecclesiastical Commission in July, which gave him sweeping powers over Church matters. This was demonstrated the following month, when James suspended the Bishop of London for refusing to take action against an anti-Catholic preacher in his diocese. James was also determined to open up Oxford and Cambridge to Catholics. The vice-chancellor at Cambridge University was removed for refusing to award Catholics degrees, and, at Magdalen College in Oxford, the fellows were deprived of their positions for refusing to accept a Catholic as their president.

The international backdrop against which these actions were taken made them seem more worrying than they might otherwise have been. James may have been aiming at establishing legal equality for Catholics, but in light of developments in France it seemed to many that his intentions were far more sinister. In October 1685, Louis XIV had revoked the Edict of Nantes, as a result of which French Protestants lost the religious and political freedoms that they had enjoyed for the previous eighty-seven years. The revocation prompted a flood of Huguenot refugees into England, bringing with them stories of Catholic persecution. Not only did this reinforce popular hostility to Catholicism, but it strengthened the perception that James's attempt to introduce religious toleration might actually be only the first stage of the forcible conversion of the whole nation to Catholicism. Such a suspicion was fed by the general belief that Catholicism and Protestantism could not coexist side by side. As the House of Commons had asserted back in 1621, Catholicism 'will press for a toleration: if that should be obtained, they must have an equality: from thence they will aspire to superiority, and will never rest till they get a subversion of the true religion'. For many, any concessions to Catholicism were profoundly dangerous.

By the end of 1686, James had succeeded in putting the alliance between the Crown and the Tories, which his brother had so effectively built up in his final years, under serious strain. He had managed to reawaken the fear of Catholic absolutism, with many regarding its implementation by the 14,000-strong army, stationed just outside London on Hounslow Heath, as a very real possibility. James seemed either unaware or unconcerned that his actions were undermining the support of many of those who had welcomed his accession less than two years earlier.

The search for alternative support

Although James had been successful in promoting Catholic interests to some extent, he had only been able to do so by using his prerogative. To ensure that Catholics had religious and political equality on a more secure basis, he needed to persuade Parliament to repeal the penal legislation directed against them. It was obvious that the Tories would oppose any such moves and that if James were to succeed, he would have to win support from another source. James therefore turned his back on the Tories and appealed instead to the Dissenters, in the hope that they, together with the Catholics, could provide sufficient support for such a programme of legislation.

Documents

The first evidence of this policy was in April 1687, when James issued his first Declaration of Indulgence, suspending the penal laws. Below are extracts from the Declaration and from an open letter from Halifax, now one of James's most prominent opponents:

A   There is nothing now that we so earnestly desire as to establish our government on such a foundation as may make our subjects happy, and unite them to us by inclination as well as duty. Which we think can be done by no means so effectively as by granting them the free exercise of their religion for the time to come, and add to that the perfect enjoyment of their property, which has never in any case been invaded by us since our coming to the crown. ... We cannot but heartily wish, as it will be easily believed, that all people of our dominions were members of the Catholic Church, yet we humbly thank Almighty God it is and hath of a long time been our constant sense and opinion, that conscience ought not to be restrained, nor people forced in matters of mere religion. It has ever been directly contrary to our inclination, as we think it is to the interest of government, which it destroys by spoiling trade, depopulating countries and discouraging strangers; and finally, that it never obtained that end for which it was employed. ... We have thought fit further to declare, that we will maintain [our subjects] in all their properties and possessions, as well of church and abbey lands as in any other lands and properties whatsoever.

(Declaration of Indulgence, April 1687)

B   Consider that notwithstanding the smooth language which is put on to engage you, these new friends [Catholics] did not make you their choice but their refuge. They have ever made their courtship to the Church of England, and when they were rejected they made their application to you. … This alliance between liberty and infallibility is bringing together the two most contrary things that are in the world. The Church of Rome doth not only dislike the allowing of liberty, but by its principles it cannot do it. … The Church of England, with all her faults, will not allow herself to be rescued by such unjustifiable means, but chooseth to bear the weight of [royal] power rather than to lie under the burden of being criminal.

(Halifax's 'Letter to a dissenter', 1687)

1   What reasons does James give for wanting to introduce toleration?
2   What assurances does James give in the Declaration, and why do you think he felt it necessary to make such undertakings?
3   According to source B, what considerations lay behind the Declaration?
4   How well judged would you consider the Declaration to have been?

Although most Dissenters were willing to take advantage of the Indulgence to allow them freedom of worship, they were distrustful of James's motives. They were just as hostile to Catholicism as their conforming Protestant counterparts, and were aware of the possibility that James might only want their support in the short-term. What guarantee was there that once James had established toleration with their help, that he would not then move on to impose Catholicism by force? These doubts were voiced by the Marquis of Halifax, who had resigned from the privy council in protest at James's Catholic policies. In his 'Letter to a Dissenter' (see above) he warned that their likely fate was 'to be hugged now, only that you may be better squeezed at another time'. It was a fear that many shared, and at best all James received was qualified Dissenting support.

James realised that even with the support of the Dissenters, any attempts to repeal the penal laws in Parliament would still face considerable opposition. The other key part of his strategy therefore was aimed at creating a Parliament that would be more pliable to the royal will. This campaign began with the replacement of eleven out of the fifty Lords Lieutenant in the summer of 1687 and was followed, in October, with all JPs being asked for their reaction to the proposed repeal of the penal laws and the establishment of toleration. On the basis of the answers given, a large number of JPs were ejected from their posts and replaced, largely with Dissenters. In the borough seats, a similar purge took place, with unsupportive officials being removed, and more charters withdrawn and amended.

How successful this attempt at packing Parliament would have been is open to speculation, as James did not have the opportunity to summon it. Supportive local officials could have done much to assist the return of MPs sympathetic to James's goals, but whether they could have produced a majority within the Commons is another matter. By 1688, less than one-quarter of JPs were Catholics and James was still heavily dependent on the support of the Dissenters, whose attitudes towards toleration were unclear. Even if James could ensure their support, it is uncertain whether their influence over the election process, especially in the rural, county seats would have been sufficient to overcome the hostility of the local élites to James's proposals.

Perhaps the most important consequence of these purges was that they completed the breakdown of trust between the Tories and the Crown. Not only was the Anglican Church under threat, but now the Tories' influence and standing in the localities was being undermined. They resented the interference of central government and saw their monopoly over local government under attack, as Anglican landed gentry were being replaced by Dissenters or even Catholics, often of a lower social standing than themselves. James's actions had alienated his traditional supporters, those people who had resisted attempts to exclude him from the throne and had welcomed his accession so enthusiastically.

1688

By the spring of 1688, James felt that his policies still stood a good chance of success. Purges of local government were continuing, and hopes were high of producing a Parliament later in the year that was in favour of toleration. In addition, his wife was pregnant, and, although she had had problems with miscarriages previously, there was a chance that she might produce an heir to secure the Catholic succession.

In April, the King issued a second Declaration of Indulgence, in a continuing attempt to secure the support of the Dissenters. It was no different in content to the previous Declaration, except in that the King demanded that it should be read from the pulpit of every church in the country, for two weeks running. This was a serious tactical error, as it gave the Anglican clergy a platform to express their opposition to James's policies. Many refused to read the petition, and seven bishops led by the Archbishop of Canterbury, William Sancroft, published a petition against the declaration on the grounds that it was 'founded upon such a dispensing power as hath often been declared illegal in Parliament'. In addition, they offered the prospect of toleration for Dissenters, with whom they claimed they were 'willing to come to such a temper as shall be thought fit'.

James responded to the bishops' defiance by arresting them on charges of seditious libel and having them placed in the Tower. Again the King's decision back-fired, as their arrest merely served to illustrate to many the dangers of Catholicism and further evidence of James's absolutist tendencies. The trial of the Seven Bishops was a crucial turning point, which prompted the emergence of an alliance of Anglicans and Dissenters against the King. James's position was further damaged by the bishops' acquittal on 30 June, and their subsequent release amid scenes of great rejoicing on the streets of London. The political temperature was raised still more by the news that, shortly before the bishops' acquittal, James's wife had finally born him the son and heir on which a Catholic succession depended. James's announcement that he wanted the Pope to be his son's godfather was yet further evidence of his insensitivity to the fears and prejudices of his subjects.

Documents: how justified were his subjects' fears of James's intentions?

It is clear that many of James's subjects were deeply concerned about his motivations. Not only Anglicans, but also many Dissenters, suspected that his policy of toleration was a cloak under which he wished to restore Catholicism and remove toleration for anyone else. But with what justification did they harbour such suspicions? Was James II really working towards establishing a Catholic absolutism?

A   We think we may very well declare the opinion of the court to be that the King may dispense in this case; and the judges go upon these grounds:

-   That the Kings of England are sovereign princes
-   That the laws of England are the King's laws
-   That therefore 'tis an inseparable prerogative of the Kings of England to dispense with penal laws in particular cases and upon particular necessary reasons
-   That of those reasons and necessities the King himself is the sole judge

(The judgement from the Godden vs Hales case, 1686)

B   Gentlemen, we must consider what they [the Seven Bishops] say is illegal in it. They say … the declaration is illegal because it is founded upon a dispensing power that the King claims, to dispense with the laws concerning ecclesiastical affairs. Gentlemen, I do not remember any case in our law … that there is any such power in the King. … I can see no difference, nor know of one in law, between the King's power to dispense with laws ecclesiastical and his powers to dispense with any other laws whatsoever. If this once be allowed of, there will need no Parliament; all the legislature will be in the King, and I leave the issue to God and your consciences.

(Justice Powell, from the trial of the Seven Bishops, 1688)

C   As far as I can see, the King is sincerely concerned to leave [his Catholic subjects] in security after his death, because the ardour with which he seeks the repeal of the penal laws is more for their sake than his own, and … it is also a question of the security of the Catholics, whose lives and safety will be at the mercy of his successor and of Parliament if these laws are still in being on the day of his death.

(Letter of the French ambassador to Louis XIV, July 1687)

1   From the evidence of sources A and B, what concerns were there about the constitutional implications of toleration?
2   How far are these supported by the observations of the French ambassador in source C?
3   Judging by these sources, and from the other material in this chapter, how far would you accept that James's approach to religious policy was underpinned by absolutist tendencies?

By the end of June 1688, James's regime had become extremely unpopular. His policies had succeeded in driving together both the Whigs and Tories, and Dissenters and Anglicans, in opposition to his Catholic policies. He had done much to confirm their fears that Catholicism inevitably led to persecution and absolutism. And yet, despite his unpopularity, there is little reason to suggest that James was on the verge of being deposed. He was financially strong, and had no need to call Parliament if he did not want to. He also had a large standing army at his disposal, and the memory of Monmouth's rebellion to discourage those who might have been tempted to take up arms. In addition, as was demonstrated by the Exclusion Crisis, there were relatively few who wanted to plunge the country into civil war, and risk the social and political upheaval that would follow. James was widely disliked, but without foreign intervention there was little prospect of his overthrow. This intervention was to come in the shape of William of Orange.

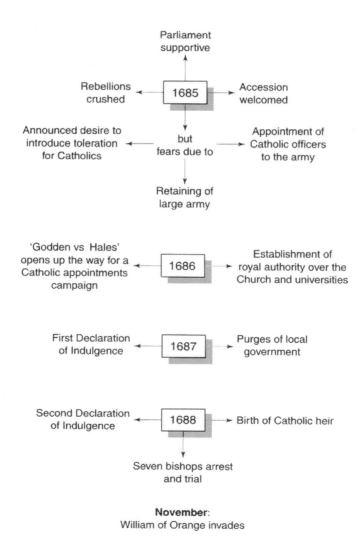

Figure 12.1 Summary of the reign of James II, 1685–8

The invasion of William of Orange

On the same day that the Seven Bishops were acquitted, seven other leading Protestants met and wrote a letter to William of Orange, inviting him to intervene in English affairs. Representing both Whig and Tory opinion, they included figures such as Bishop Compton, and the Earls of Danby and Shrewsbury, who assured William of their own support, and that of 'nineteen parts out of twenty of the people throughout the kingdom' if he were to intervene.

William's decision to invade England has been widely debated by historians. When he landed in Devon in November 1688, he asserted that it was to maintain 'the liberties of England and the Protestant religion'. Whig historians have represented him as the champion of Protestantism and parliamentary government, and yet it is unlikely that William's invasion was prompted by such high minded, disinterested motives. The birth of James's son in June had been greeted with widespread suspicion and claims that the child had been smuggled into the Queen's bedchamber in order to ensure a Catholic succession. William's position had suffered as a result, as his wife, Mary, had been next in line to the throne. Whether William was looking to seize the throne for himself, or merely safeguard his wife's claim is a matter for conjecture, but it is likely that dynastic issues played a part in his decision. At the very least, William was motivated by strategic considerations. Since Louis XIV's invasion of the Netherlands in 1672, he had been committed to resisting the expansion of French power in Europe and to constructing a European coalition to this end. The prospect of an alliance between a Catholic England and France was deeply concerning, as it seriously threatened Dutch security, and William was determined to try and prevent any such development. If his invasion was successful, not only might he neutralise this threat but he might also be able to bring England into an anti-French coalition, and harness her resources in the struggle against Louis XIV.

With Louis occupied in an invasion of the Palatinate, William took advantage of strong easterly winds, which enabled him to sail along the Channel but kept James's fleet helplessly in port. His army of 12,000 men landed in Torbay on 5 November 1688. William was encouraged by the support of the local gentry and by the declaration of a number of towns, such as Nottingham and York, in his favour. James, on the other hand, who had marched his 40,000-strong army as far as Salisbury to block William's advance, seems to have lost his nerve, for instead of advancing to meet the invasion force, he ordered his forces to retreat back to London. This prompted the defections of the King's daughter, Anne, and his army commander, John Churchill, to his opponents. As William advanced slowly and circuitously on London, so James's position worsened and on 10 December he fled the capital for France. Despite being captured and returned to London, he escaped again on 22 December, this time successfully.

William's success was by no means inevitable. His invasion involved huge risks. It has been estimated that his expedition would have cost around £1.5 million, and there was no guarantee that the campaign would be over as quickly as it was. It was quite possible that William could have found himself embroiled in a long, drawn out civil war, which would have left his homeland exposed to French invasion. Equally, it is by no means certain that William's forces would have been victorious if brought to battle soon after landing. William's intervention could have ended in humiliating defeat.

The one thing that stands out is how greatly William's position was strengthened by James's actions. There was a good chance that if James had been more decisive and brought William to battle, his army's numerical superiority would have resulted in victory. Even after James's retreat from Salisbury, William was in a delicate position. He wanted to avoid armed conflict if possible, as his position depended on being able to pose as a Protestant liberator, rather than a Dutch invader. His advance on London was deliberately drawn out so as to lessen the likelihood of battle and to avoid forcing James into a corner where he had to fight. Although this strategy was very successful, William's position would still have been difficult had James not fled abroad. William may have had the support of many Tories as well as Whigs, but the former did not necessarily want to see James overthrown. Still bound by their loyalty to the monarchy, the Tories had supported William as a means of restraining James and forcing him to abandon his Catholic policies. They were less enthusiastic about the idea of William taking the throne. By abandoning England, James left the Tories without a figurehead around which to rally.

Documents: how much popular support was there for William's invasion?

The degree of popular support enjoyed by William of Orange is an important issue. William emphasised that he had come in response to an invitation to secure England's religion and liberties, and determinedly presented himself as the nation's saviour. Certainly his invasion did receive a great deal of support, but how far it extended to his removal of James from the throne is altogether less clear:

A   The people are so generally dissatisfied with the present conduct of the government in relation to their religion, liberties and properties (all of which have been greatly invaded), and they are in such expectation of the prospects being daily worse, that your Highness may be assured there are nineteen parts out of twenty of the people throughout the kingdom who are desirous of a change, and who, we believe, would willingly contribute to it; and there is no doubt but that some of the most consider-able of them would venture themselves with your Highness at your first landing.

(The letter of invitation to William of Orange from seven leading Protestants, June 1688)

B   *(early November 1688)* We are very glad to hear you are well, though I will suppose you are in the same uneasy circumstance of fear as everyone is. That the Prince of Orange is landed with 50,000 men is certain, some have affirmed in Scotland or northern parts. Yesterday, it is said, in Sussex and Hampshire; this morning, it is said, in three places of Devonshire. All the forces are drawn out of this county [Essex]…[and] marched yesterday in the afternoon to London, but found Aldgate shut against them by the City, and absolute denial of coming in. News was carried of it to the King, who commanded fires to [be] made for them in the streets and churchyards without the gates, and they lodged in their tents after a cold, wet, long, march. … The King has not slept for some nights. It is said that the Prince's Declaration hints at an invitation he has had from the lords temporal and spiritual, upon which the King has urged the latter to sign a paper with [a denial] of such design, but they have excused themselves, how, I know not.

(mid-December 1688) Yesterday morning, the King left Whitehall so privately that no one knows the way he took, but certainly not with the intent of returning; for

we are informed by an eye-witness that all the hangings and goods were taken down. ... The Archbishop of Canterbury went to the Guildhall and summoned the Lord Mayor and Aldermen. After a council held, they sent a summons to the Lieutenant of the Tower to deliver it up to them, who sent word that he was ready to receive them. Accordingly they went together, entered the Tower ... and placed in it a sufficient number of the trained bands of the City to keep it. ... We were all alarmed that London was on fire ... [but] the flames we saw was of bonfires made, by the gentlemen of the mob, of the mass-houses and other popish houses, which they pulled down and, carrying the materials to Lincoln's Inn, piled them up and burnt them there. All the [City] are on their guard, disarming the Papists and expecting the Prince of Orange, who makes up all the haste that the ways and weather will permit.

(Letters of Anne Mildmay, to her brother, Dacre Barret)

C *5th November*. I went to London; heard the news of the prince having landed at Torbay, coming with a fleet of 700 sail. ... These are the beginnings of sorrow, unless God in His mercy prevent it by some happy reconciliation of all dissensions among us. This, in all likelihood, nothing can effect except a free Parliament; but this we can not hope to see, whilst there are any forces on either side. I pray God to protect and direct the King for the best and truest interest of his people!

2nd December. Plymouth declared for the Prince. Bath, York, Hull, Bristol, and all the eminent persons of quality through England declare for the Protestant religion and laws, and go to meet the Prince, who every day sets forth new declarations against the Papists. ... Expectations of the Prince coming to Oxford.

7th. My son went towards Oxford. I returned home.

9th....The rabble demolished all Popish chapels, and several Papist Lords' and gentlemen's houses, especially that of the Spanish Ambassador, which they pillaged, and burnt his library.

13th. The King flies ... is rudely treated by the people; comes back to Whitehall ... goes to mass, and dines in public, a Jesuit saying grace (I was present).

18th. I saw the King take barge to Gravesend at twelve o'clock – a sad sight! The Prince comes to St. James's, and fills Whitehall with Dutch guards. ... All the world go to see the Prince at St. James's, where there is a great Court. There I saw him, and several of my acquaintance who came over with him. He is very stately, serious, and reserved. The English soldiers sent out of town to disband, not well pleased.

(Extracts from the diary of John Evelyn)

D Good People, come buy
The Fruit that I cry
That now is in season, tho' winter be nigh;
It will do you all Good

And sweeten the Blood
And I'm sure it will please you, when you've understood
'Tis an Orange.
Its cordial Juice
Does such Vigour infuse
I may well recommend it to every one's Use;
Tho' some it quite chills,
And with Fear almost kills:
Yet it's certain each healthy man benefit feels
By an Orange.

(Anonymous ballad, autumn 1688)

1   What problems are there with using source A to gauge the level of support for William's intervention?
2   Look at sources B and C. How far do they indicate a lack of support for James II?
3   How far would you say that sources B–D demonstrate that people wanted William of Orange to overthrow James II?
4   What limitations are there for a historian using sources B–D as an evidence base for popular support for William's invasion?

Why did William invade?

A   We come to preserve your religion, and to restore and establish your liberties and properties; and therefore we cannot suffer ourselves to doubt but that all true Englishmen will come and concur with us in our designs to secure these nations from popery and slavery. You must all plainly see that you are only used as instruments to enslave the nation and ruin the Protestant religion; and when that is done, you may judge what you yourselves ought to expect. ... We hope, that you will not suffer yourselves to be abused by a false notion of honour, but that you will in the first place consider what you owe to Almighty God and your religion, your country, to yourselves, and to your posterity. ... We do, therefore, expect that you will now consider the honour that is now set before you, of being instruments of serving your country and securing your religion; and we will ever remember the service that you shall do us on this occasion.

(An open letter from William of Orange to the officers of James II's army, September 1688)

B   His actions were not dictated by base [*low*] motives; undoubtedly he was not merely taking candy from a babe. He intervened, not for himself or for his wife but for his faith and for the protection of his native land, the United Provinces [Holland]. In that cause he had lost his principality of Orange, his estates in Franche-Comté and Luxembourg – roughly half his income. In that cause he was prepared to risk the English inheritance which was by far the greatest asset he had left. It was a real risk, a real sacrifice. He might well have decided not to make it if he had a son. Since he did not have one he was free to act in the public interest. The fact that the Prince's gamble succeeded is irrelevant. It was a great gamble, and only a man of the highest devotion to duty would have ever consented to make it.

(S. Baxter, *William III*, 1966)

C   [William] saw in the ambitions of Louis XIV the greatest threat to Dutch independence and to stability in Europe. He had been Louis' implacable enemy since the French invasion of the United Provinces in 1672. His marriage to James' daughter, Mary, in 1677 had been for political reasons … [and] since that date he had manoeuvred in vain to get English support against Louis. 1688 afforded a fresh opportunity. … He seemed to have no desire to reign in England, and as late as 24 December he spoke publicly of the kingship, 'which I have no ambition for'. Yet sometime in the autumn of 1688 he accepted in his mind that reluctantly he would have to intervene to take the crown of England in order to secure his objectives. … William came to the conclusion that only a revolutionary reversal of England's role – from being variably an ally or benevolent neutral with France to active military participation against France – could save Europe.

(Barry Williams, *Elusive Settlement*, 1984)

D   England was invaded by a large and well-trained foreign army, initially 12,000 men but later increased, that was brought here in November 1688 on 500 ships – an armada four times larger than the Spanish armada of 1588. … The invasion was planned and organised long before a tiny group of unrepresentative, and not particularly important English dissidents sent their so-called 'invitation' to the Prince of Orange. And although William led the invasion, he had very limited powers in the Dutch Republic. The armada and army were sent, and paid for, by the Dutch States General … who ran the Dutch state. … When the Prince of Orange marched in triumph into London, in December 1688, he did so after ordering all the remaining English troops in the capital to withdraw a minimum of 20 miles from the city. The bulk of the Dutch army was brought into, or placed around, London … and London remained under Dutch military occupation for 18 months … James II … was 'escorted' to Rochester and encouraged to leave for France. In effect, the King of England was deported, by the Prince of Orange and a foreign army, from his own land. The States General … clearly calculated on being able to topple James II quickly and turn England, with her resources, ships and troops against France, thereby putting an end to Louis XIV's threatened dominance of continental Europe in general and the Low Countries in particular. For the Dutch, that was the whole point of the exercise.

(Jonathon Israel, 'History in the making', the *Independent*, 1992)

1   What reasons does William himself put forward for invading England?
2   How does source B seek to explain William's actions?
3   How might sources C and D be used to challenge the claim that William invaded to 'preserve' Protestantism and to 'restore and establish' liberty and property?

13 Glorious Revolution?, 1688–1701

The accession of William and Mary

Although William was in control of London by December 1688, it was still uncertain what form any future settlement should take. Elections were held for a Parliament to consider the options. There were a number of possibilities: James could be invited back, providing he accepted limitations on his powers; William might rule as Regent for James in his absence; James could be deposed and replaced by Mary, or by Mary and William as joint monarchs. Any option which involved the removal of James from the throne was unappealing for the Tories, for whom the issue of hereditary right was fundamental. Yet political realities dictated otherwise. William declared that he was not willing to rule as a Regent, nor as a Prince Consort to his wife, but only as a joint monarch. If Parliament were to decide otherwise, according to Bishop Burnet, William declared that 'he would not oppose them in it, but he would go back to Holland and meddle no more in their affairs'. Without William, England would again be plunged into crisis and possibly even civil war. In this situation, Parliament could not afford to call William's bluff and opted instead for stability and public order. They declared that James had left the throne vacant by fleeing abroad, thereby forfeiting his hereditary rights. His place was to be taken by William and Mary as joint monarchs.

The Glorious Revolution Settlement

What has become known as the Glorious Revolution Settlement was not arrived at as consciously as its title might suggest. Comprising initially of a Bill of Rights, the settlement evolved over the reign in response to the needs of the Crown and the political agenda of some Parliamentarians. How far it was a 'Glorious Revolution' designed to impose nineteenth century Whig ideals of parliamentary government and religious freedom is questionable.

Parliament's immediate concern after William and Mary's accession was to draw up the basis for a future settlement, which would, unlike that of 1660–5, provide clear guidelines for Government and the division of powers between Crown and Parliament. In the event, the Declaration of Rights that was produced was a more limited document, due to the length of time a more comprehensive body of legislation would have taken to produce and agree. The Declaration was made into the Bill of Rights later in 1689, and provided the first part of the Glorious Revolution Settlement. It stated that:

Figure 13.1 William III

- The pretended power of suspending of laws or the execution of laws by regal authority without the consent of Parliament is illegal
- The late Court of Commissioners for ecclesiastical causes and all other commissions and Courts of like nature are illegal and pernicious
- Levying money for the use of the crown by pretence of prerogative without the consent of Parliament is illegal
- The raising or keeping of a standing Army within the kingdom in the time of peace unless it be with the consent of Parliament is against law
- The elections of members of Parliament ought to be free
- For redress of all grievances and for the amending, strengthening and preserving of the laws, Parliaments ought to be held frequently
- All who shall profess the popish religion or marry a papist shall be forever incapable to inherit, possess or enjoy the Crown or Government of this realm.

1   Which of the above were actually new restrictions on the monarch?
2   What key issues were not mentioned in the Bill of Rights?
3   In your view, how substantial were the limits placed on the prerogative by the Bill of Rights?

In 1689, a Mutiny Act was also passed, which dealt with control of the army in more detail. It repeated the provision of the Bill of Rights, that standing armies in peacetime were illegal without parliamentary approval, and stated the King's right to appoint senior officers to the army and to hold court-martials. However, the Act also stated that it required annual renewal by Parliament.

William was less than enthusiastic about legislation for regular Parliaments, and he not only opposed the idea of a Triennial Act, but actually vetoed a bill for one in 1693. However, in 1694, William eventually agreed to a Triennial Act that asserted the need for 'frequent Parliaments' and laid down that 'Parliament shall be holden once in three years at least ... and no Parliament whatsoever ... shall have any continuance longer than for three years at the farthest'. It did not, however, specify what should happen in the event of these conditions not being met. Like the Act of 1664, the potential existed for a monarch with sufficient financial means to ignore such legislation.

Religion was to prove a divisive issue. Non-conformists' hopes had been raised by the Anglican hierarchy during James's reign, who had suggested that they would agree to religious toleration for Protestant Dissenters. However, once the immediate threat of popery had receded, the Protestant unity of 1688 crumbled away. With James removed, the Tories were less enthusiastic over proposals for religious freedom for all Protestants, which they saw once again as an attack on the Church of England. Their worries were compounded by the fact that William was a Calvinist, and had already indicated that he was willing to open up State office to 'all Protestants that are willing and able to serve'. These fears led to the Toleration Act of 1689, which established only a limited measure of toleration for Dissenters. It allowed them freedom of worship, but only providing they were meeting in premises licensed for the purpose by the local Anglican bishop and did so with open doors. Moreover, the Test and Corporation Acts, which restricted the ability of non-conformists to hold office, were not repealed.

Finance and foreign policy

One area which could not be settled so easily was that of finance. William clearly expected to receive a similar settlement to that enjoyed by Charles II and James II, but both Whig and Tory MPs were aware of the dangers to their own position of being too generous. One Tory, Sir Thomas Clarges, noted: 'We ought to be cautious of the Revenue, which is the life of the government, and consider the last two reigns.' Another, Sir Edward Seymour, warned his colleagues that they should 'support the crown' but 'not carry it to excess. We may date our misery from our bounty here. If King Charles II had not had that bounty from you, he had never attempted what he had done.' A monarch that was financially independent of Parliament would also be politically independent. As a result the Commons suggested in March 1689 that the King's revenues should be limited to £1,200,000 (the same sum as in the 1660 settlement). William's financial position was further eroded in the following year when Parliament agreed to grant him excise for life, but increased his dependence on them by only voting him customs duties for four years. Even with these revenues, war with France hit customs and William's ordinary income struggled ever to exceed £1,000,000.

To an extent it was no longer realistic to differentiate between the King's ordinary and extraordinary needs, as much of William's reign was taken up with war against France, and his finances were dominated by the demands of that war. Long before he had taken the English throne, William had been committed to curbing the ambitions of Louis XIV, and probably his main reason for intervening in English affairs in the first place was to further this commitment. In 1689, he took England into a Grand Alliance with Holland, Spain, the Emperor Leopold of Austria and many of the German states against France, sparking off the Nine Years War. His energies were diverted by James II's arrival in Ireland in the same year, and the need to allocate troops and resources to deal with him. After some initial successes, James was decisively defeated at the Battle of the Boyne in July 1690, and by 1691 the revolt was finally extinguished.

This left William free to concentrate on the war against Louis XIV, which consisted mainly of naval battles in the Channel and long, drawn out siege warfare in the Spanish Netherlands. The fortunes of war were mixed, with the French initially winning a resounding victory over the Anglo-Dutch fleet off Beachy Head, but in turn suffering defeat in the Bay of La Hogue two years later. The land war saw no decisive battles in open field, but did result in the capture of several border cities by the French, such as Mons, Namur, Huy and Charleroi, between 1691 and 1694. The only major success for William's forces was the recapture of Namur in 1695. The fighting became bogged down in interminable sieges, with neither side able to win a clear advantage. This, together with the financial exhaustion brought about by such a lengthy and large-scale conflict, led eventually to the Treaty of Ryswick in 1697. In it, William finally won recognition as King of England and a promise from Louis not to aid his enemies in future. In addition, the French promised to abandon their recent gains in the Spanish Netherlands. Although these terms were on the whole favourable to William, they fell far short of his professed aim of destroying French power. Moreover, they did not deal at all with the issue of the succession to the Spanish throne, which Louis claimed for his eldest son. The Treaty was more of a reprieve from hostilities than a solution to them. Conflict was to erupt again in 1701, with the death of Charles II of Spain, and the outbreak of the War of the Spanish Succession. This epic conflict was to outlive William, continuing after his death in 1702, well into the reign of his successor, Anne.

The financial demands made by such a high level of military activity could only be met through Parliament. The Nine Years War cost around £50 million alone. Although many MPs did not share William's enthusiasm for war, it was something that they had to accept as the price of securing a Protestant succession. The power of Catholic France, and its continued harbouring of James II, meant that a French-backed invasion and restoration of a Catholic monarchy was regarded as an ever-present threat. Parliament was willing to vote large sums of money, but in return wanted more control over its use, and over public finance as a whole. For instance, in 1690, William received two parliamentary grants worth around £4,600,000, but also had to accept the setting up of a committee of public accounts, which scrutinised the Government's wartime spending. By 1697, William's financial independence had been further curtailed, with his acceptance of the principle of a 'Civil List'. This consisted of parliamentary grants of £700,000 a year, that were designed to meet the costs of running the King's household, and domestic Government. All other costs of Government were to be met by parliamentary grant. By this mechanism, Parliament took on direct responsibility for funding much of the Government's activity, particularly war, and by doing so increased its say in how that money should be spent. It also took on responsibility for Government borrowing, which was channelled through the recently established Bank of England. The Crown Debt thereby became the National Debt, as the Bank's borrowings were underwritten by Parliament on the security of future taxation.

Concern over the King's financial demands can be seen throughout the 1690s, with calls by MPs to oversee Government spending, attempts to limit royal patronage through a succession of Place bills, and attacks on Government ministers – Danby, once again in royal service was only saved from impeachment proceedings (for the third time!) by William dissolving Parliament in 1695. William's own position was weakened by the death of Queen Mary in 1694, which left him more open to the attack of those MPs, mainly Tories, who had never really been able to reconcile themselves to the new regime. Furthermore, William found himself weakened by the respite from hostilities after 1697. While it enabled him to reduce his demands for taxation, it also made him seem less necessary to those who questioned his right to sit on the throne. As Bishop Burnet commentated with relation to the events of 1690–1, 'The French fleet, by lying so on our coast ... and the King's behaviour in Ireland, as well as King James' meanness, has made so wonderful change in all men's minds with relation to them both.' William had been needed to guarantee political stability and protection from a French-backed restoration of James II. With the Treaty of Ryswick, those threats had receded and the compromises that they had helped some to make became, as a result, less palatable.

It is important to realise, therefore, that the financial aspects of the Glorious Revolution Settlement came about only after prolonged wrangling, and were the subject of bitter conflict. William was against the limitations imposed by a Civil List, and had rejected earlier suggestions in 1689 that his revenues be designated for particular purposes. Yet it was the price that had to be paid for access to sufficient funds for his foreign wars. Some MPs were opposed to the Civil List on the grounds that it gave the King too much money, which could be distributed in patronage and used to 'buy' the votes of other members. There was also considerable concern amongst Tories from country constituencies over levels of taxation and the activities of the Bank of England. The Bank had been set up by merchants and financiers of Whig sympathies, who were making large profits out of its activities. And yet its borrowing was undertaken on the security of parliamentary taxation, which was largely made up of the Land Tax, the major burden of which was borne by Tory landowners in country areas.

Documents: contemporary criticisms of William

Although there was widespread support for William's intervention in English affairs in 1688, this was soon qualified once James had been removed and the new King began to make serious financial demands on his subjects. Some sense of the disaffection with William III that surfaced during the 1690s can be gauged from the documents below:

A   I see no certainty of the number of men in England, Scotland and Ireland. I think the account that has been transferred to you comes from the muster-master and the King is abused. I would go on regularly to the state of the war, what the King thinks fitting and they to bring in where the men are. ... I think it fitter to apply to the fleet and retrench the land men. England knows no need of them. I believe the money is not all spent. I think it may be embezzled. I never saw a worse account. ... I would have accounts brought here by somebody. ... Let the money be rightly applied and I will go with the highest and I desire the King to give us the state of the war.

(William Garroway, MP, 1689)

B   We have provided for the navy, we have provided for the army, and now at the latter end here is a new reckoning brought us; we must provide likewise for the civil list. Truly, Mr. Speaker, it is a sad reflection that some men should wallow in wealth and places, whilst others pay away taxes the fourth part of their yearly revenues for the support of the same government. ... The king is pleased to lay his needs before us, and I am confident expects our advice before it. We ought therefore to tell him what pensions are too great, what places may be extinguished. ... When the people of England see that all is saved that can be saved, that there are no exorbitant pensions or unnecessary salaries, that all is applied to the use for which it is given, we shall give and they shall cheerfully pay whatever his Majesty can want to secure the Protestant religion, to keep out the King of France, aye, and King James too.

(Speech of Sir Charles Sedley, MP, in response to proposals for a civil list, 1691)

C   Hail, happy William, thou art wonderous great,
What is the cause, thy virtues or thy fate?
For thee, the child his parents hearts doth sting;
For thee favourite will desert his King;
For thee, the patriot will subvert the laws;
For thee, the judge will still decide the cause;
... The loyal slaves love thy oppression more
Than all their wealth and liberty before.
For thee and tyranny they all declare,
And beg the blessing of eternal war.
And that the wonder might more wondrous seem,
Thou never yet didst one kind thing for them.

Rebels, like witches, having signed the rolls,
Must serve their Master, thou they damn their souls.

(Anonymous pamphlet, 1696)

1   What concerns does Garroway express over the conduct of William's foreign policy?
2   How supportive is Sedley of William's Government, on the evidence of source B?
3   According to source C, why are the people of England unable to resist the 'tyranny' of William III?

Perhaps the most significant aspect of Parliament's increased financial role was that it led to more regular sessions. William's reluctance to agree to a Triennial Act, and the lack of any provision for automatic assembly in the Act of 1694, became irrelevant as Parliament's sessions became annual by necessity. This in turn led to increased rivalries between MPs and the development of 'the rage of parties'. With annual sessions of Parliament, often lasting five months or more and elections every three years, party organisation and hostility grew as both Whigs and Tories fought for access to the rewards that office brought with it. And yet, despite the horror with which many contemporaries regarded these developments, they did have certain advantages. As Barry Williams notes:

> Party division had one supreme virtue: it replaced the violence of civil war, actual or feared, by the stylised conflict of party warfare waged in words across the divide of the House of Commons. The confrontation of Stuart politics was replaced in the eighteenth century by Hanoverian manoeuvre.

(Barry Williams, *Elusive Settlement, 1637–1701*, 1984)

The Act of Settlement 1701

The last component of the Glorious Revolution Settlement was the Act of Settlement 1701. It was required to clarify the succession, as William and Mary had been childless, and their heir, Mary's sister, Anne, had also failed to produce children. However, it also dealt with other constitutional issues, in a manner which suggests that the division of powers between Crown and Parliament was still a very 'live' issue.

It established that the succession should pass to the House of Hanover (descended from James I's daughter, Elizabeth), as next in succession 'in the Protestant line'. It also required that all future monarchs not only had to be Protestants, but also needed to be communicating members of the Church of England. Restrictions were placed on the monarch's movements, requiring parliamentary consent for absences from the British Isles, a response to William's long periods abroad in the Netherlands and to the concern that a Hanoverian monarch might be tempted to act in a similar fashion. Demands were also made for 'open' government, in which business would be discussed by the privy council, and not among small, secretive groups of favourites. The Crown's influence was further curtailed by losing its ability to remove members of the judiciary, pardon any ministers impeached by the Commons, or to distribute patronage to MPs in the Commons.

The act was only to be implemented upon the death of Anne, which did not come about until 1714. In the event, many of its clauses were ignored or repealed, as they were impossible to enforce, but, even so, they indicate an important point. William's accession to the English throne and the emergence of a workable settlement during the 1690s had not, in itself, eliminated the potential for conflict and tension between the Crown and Parliament. The Glorious Revolution was an important stepping stone, a turning point even, in the constitutional development of England, but it did not automatically herald a smooth transition to parliamentary government.

Why did the Glorious Revolution Settlement emerge in the form it did?

For many historians, the Glorious Revolution has been seen as a pivotal point in the constitutional history of the English nation. It was the point at which parliamentary Government finally triumphed over monarchical rule, and the country was set upon the road to liberal democracy. This Whig view has been challenged by Revisionists, who have tended to question the extent to which the Glorious Revolution was a conscious attempt to do this. Others have gone even further, suggesting that there was little revolutionary about the Glorious Revolution, and that English Government was to continue to be dominated after 1688 by monarchy, rather than Parliament:

A   By the Bill of Rights the tenure of the Crown was made strictly conditional. ... By this beneficent Revolution, the liberty of the subject and the power of Parliament were finally secured against the power of the Crown. The tradition of the ages was snapped. In the eyes of no section of his subjects did William succeed to the majesty that had hedged the ancient Kings of England. While few felt affection for

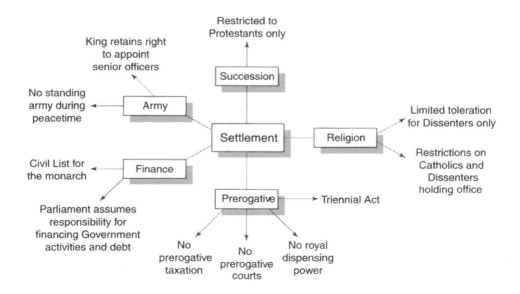

Figure 13.2 The Glorious Revolution Settlement

his person, none felt reverence for his office. Tories and Whigs agreed to think of him as a temporary caretaker for the English people. Loyalty to him was binding as a patriotic duty, not as an inalienable allegiance. ... The rule of England by the contests of the two parties now began in earnest, no longer complicated by a struggle for supremacy between Parliament and the King. ... Party spirit was the spirit of the age. Its coarse, free, vigorous breath kept the nation heartily alive. It pervaded the worlds of high society, commerce, and even scholarship; it inspired literature, religion, finance; it guided diplomacy and war. It was the motive power of our great achievements.

(G. Trevelyan, *England Under the Stuarts*, 1904)

B   Compared with many other revolutions, the English revolution of 1689 appears a very tame affair. There was no execution of the King, no reign of terror, and no confiscation ... though great changes were made in the law, they were so made as to appear as little radical as may be. ... It must be remembered that William and most of his supporters in 1688–9 professed to desire, not a revolution, but a restoration. The manifesto issued by William on the eve of his expedition laid great stress on the illegalities, real and alleged, committed by James II. ... James had striven to exercise arbitrary power; William and Mary were to respect the law. The monarchy had not been abolished, but restored to its rightful position. Moreover, the Church, Parliament, and the law had been delivered from a King who had set himself against them. ... For the future, attempts alike by the King and by Parliament to go beyond what were thought to be their due bounds aroused strong opposition. ... The constitution thus came to be envisaged as a system of checks and balances designed to secure the observance of rights.

(Mark Thomson, *Constitutional History of England, Volume IV*, 1938)

C   Why, after failing so often and so dismally before, did Parliament finally triumph in the 1690s? ... Two things seem to stand out. One of these is the war with France. This conflict was fought on a scale hitherto unknown in England. King William's war cost three times as much every year as the Second Dutch War of 1665–67. ... It was, more than anything, this colossal war expenditure which led Parliament in the course of the 1690s to rethink the whole problem of government finance, and to evolve a new monetary system which, as we have seen, did so much to enhance the standing of the legislature. The second factor which helps to explain the revolutionary character of the 1690s is the attitude taken by the King himself. ... Although William was, to quote Bishop Burnet 'inclined to be arbitrary', he was, paradoxically, far less tenacious of the crown's prerogatives than any of his predecessors had been. William's real interest was in the war against France, not in the English constitution. In consequence, during the course of the 1690s, he cheerfully signed away the royal position in order to get the necessary war supplies. ... He was ... the betrayer of English absolutism.

(Angus McInnes, 'When was the English Revolution?', in *History*, October 1982)

D   The eventual effect of the Revolution was to create a new balance between Crown and Parliament. But this was not because it was 'glorious', but because the King lacked all legitimacy and because William's concern all along had been to exploit English resources to fight France, not to maximise his power in Britain. During the 1690s he spent much of his time campaigning in the Low Countries, content to let Parliament assume control of the administration and taxation in England so long as it provided him with money, troops, ships and supplies.

(Jonathon Israel, 'History in the making', in the *Independent*, 1992)

E   The rebellion of 1688 was not a bid for a weak monarchy, but for a Protestant monarchy. Consequently ... [the Settlement] which followed had much to do with religion, but little to do with placing limits on the monarch's prerogative in other spheres. ... We can at least say what 1688 was *not* about, it was *not* a conflict between the institutions of monarchy and Parliament, let alone between King and Commons. ... In the early-Hanoverian as in the early-Stuart period, Parliament and government were not synonymous; monarchy, not democracy, generated society's dominant ideology.

(Jonathan Clark, *Revolution and Rebellion*, 1986)

1   In what terms does source A seek to explain the Glorious Revolution? Why do you think Trevelyan holds this view?
2   How does source B disagree with source A in its interpretation of the Glorious Revolution?
3   In the view of sources C and D, how significant was William's role in formulating the settlement of the 1690s?
4   How far do you accept Clark's interpretation of the Glorious Revolution?

Conclusion

Seventeenth-century England was characterised to a large extent by internal turmoil and conflict. Although the reign of James I was relatively stable, his successor's was to see the outbreak of civil war and rebellion in Ireland and Scotland. Three civil wars and fighting across the British Isles were to follow, Charles I was executed and the monarchy abolished. A republic was set up, and experimented with various constitutional forms, before it too fell and the monarchy was restored. A period of domestic peace followed, before Charles II had to face the upheavals of the 1670s and the Exclusion Crisis. The reign of James II was to witness foreign invasion and the overthrow of another monarch. The 1690s were marked by long and bitter wrangling over the constitution of the country. Even by the death of William III, it was clear that the Glorious Revolution had not brought an end to political instability and conflict.

Perhaps the largest single factor in creating instability in Stuart England was religion. The Reformation had shattered the religious unity of Christian Europe in the previous century, and when James I came to the English throne, he was faced by serious religious divisions across his three kingdoms. The existence of different religious groups presented a problem to governments at a time when religious difference was associated with political disobedience and rebellion. The relatively enlightened approach adopted by James I in his religious policy helped to minimise the potential for conflict, but his son was to find the issue of religion far more troublesome. Charles I's attempts at imposing religious uniformity on Scotland were to lead to war with the subjects of his northern kingdom, and to force the recall of the English Parliament. The implementation of Thorough in Ireland was also to provoke rebellion among the Catholic population, and further heighten a sense of political crisis back in London. The outbreak of the Civil War itself was due in no small part to fears over religion. Arminianism was not easily distinguished in the minds of many from Catholicism, and the fear that the King was being driven by sinister, popish forces led many to take up arms for Parliament.

It is difficult for the modern-day observer to appreciate fully the strength of anti-Catholicism during this period. It was a powerful motivating force that extended throughout society, from the members of the London mob to the members of the Houses of Parliament. If a monarch failed to associate themselves clearly enough with the Protestant cause, it would invariably lead to political problems. James I soon found that he had to temper his enlightened views towards his Catholic subjects, if he was to gain the co-operation of his Parliaments. Later in his reign, his failure to align himself squarely with the Protestant cause in Europe was to create great confusion and concern among his subjects. Charles I's marriage to a Catholic, and the toleration of Catholics and Catholic sympathisers in his Court, did much to undermine his position, and to compromise his support of Arminian reforms. Charles II's alliance with Louis XIV of France, and his attempts at introducing religious toleration disturbed many, doing much to create a climate in which an Exclusion Crisis was able to develop. The brevity of James II's reign is in itself a testimony to the depth of anti-Catholic sentiment among his subjects, as is their acceptance of his replacement on the throne by a Dutch prince, William of Orange.

The structural problems inherited by the Stuart kings were also to be of great significance. The inadequacies of the financial system left behind by Elizabeth were to cause problems for both James I and Charles I, and it was not until the end of the reign of Charles II that the monarch's ordinary revenues were really sufficient for Government to operate as it wished. Experiments such as the Personal Rule of Charles I demonstrated that it was possible for a monarch to survive without recourse to Parliament, as long as they could avoid war. Charles II's final years gave an even more powerful indication of the strength of the monarch who had no need to call Parliament.

It was war, however, more than anything, that forced a monarch back on to Parliament. This in turn gave MPs the opportunity to raise other issues of concern. While matters such as the exercise of the royal prerogative, or religious change, may have been of concern throughout the period, it was only during the sitting of Parliament that they could be properly aired. The need for parliamentary finance forced a monarch to bargain and compromise, if they were to gain access to the funds that they needed. James I dissolved Parliament in 1621 for encroaching on his royal prerogative, but had to recall it, and strike certain compromises with it to obtain tax revenues for war against Spain. Charles I was forced to recall Parliament in 1640 because of the Scots Wars, thereby opening up the possibility of renewed conflict with them, as he attempted to gain their financial backing. More than any other time, Parliament's power during a time of war was demonstrated in the reign of William and Mary, where the Crown was forced to bargain away large areas of its prerogative powers in return for supply.

As we noted in the Introduction to this book, interpretations of the seventeenth century have varied widely. Descriptions such as the 'Century of Revolution' have been championed and criticised, as historians have sought to understand the underlying nature of the events which they have described. The exact nature and location of the 'English Revolution' has been debated at length, with some going so far as to deny its existence altogether. It is hard to deny the title 'revolution' to the events of December 1648 to January 1649, and equally hard to argue that the Commonwealth was to maintain this revolutionary flavour. Despite the growth of radical opinion in society, and even briefly in Government with the Parliament of Saints, it was the conservatism of the traditional élites that was the dominant feature of the 1650s, as they sought to retreat from revolution. The Restoration in 1660 was to confirm most of the ancient rights of the Crown, and gave Charles II the potential to wield significantly more power than his father.

The events of 1688 have been traditionally described as the 'Glorious Revolution', but it is debatable how applicable this label is in reality. The overthrow of James II and the introduction of the Bill of Rights settled little. Rather it was the emergence of a settlement during the 1690s, hesitantly and through much conflict, both *within* Parliament, as well as between it and the Crown, that was to define the nature of future Government. The royal prerogative was limited in a number of key areas, and the role and powers of Parliament were increased. And yet, it is clear that by 1701, with the Act of Settlement, MPs still feared that the concessions they had wrung out of William III were not enforceable. If there had been a fundamental shift in power from the monarch to their Parliaments, it was not a shift that all necessarily recognised or favoured.

In looking at the seventeenth century, we can draw attention to rebellion, war and turmoil, and to the changes in Government, religion and thought that took place during it. However, it is also worth remembering that no matter what changes did occur, it was a century that both started and ended as the preserve of the élites. While much changed, even more remained unchanged. The last word should perhaps go to Christopher Hill. In his seminal work, *Century of Revolution*, he reminds us of the limited nature of any revolution that may have taken place:

The struggle for freedom, then, in the seventeenth century, was more of a complex story than the books sometimes suggest. The men of property won freedom – freedom from arbitrary taxation and arbitrary arrest, freedom from religious persecution, freedom to control the destinies of their country through their elected representatives, freedom to buy and sell. ... The smaller men failed in all spheres to get their freedom recognized, failed to win either the vote or economic security. ... Freedom is not something abstract. It is the right of certain men to do certain things. Wildman had hoped that the Agreement of the People would 'lay down the foundations of freedom for all manner of people'; but ... the efforts of the Levellers, Diggers, and others failed. ... Only very slowly and late have men come to understand that unless freedom is universal it is only extended privilege.

Appendix

Notes on authors of documents

Below are explanatory notes on some of the main seventeenth-century authors that you have encountered. The information should help you to develop a greater awareness of their standpoints and prejudices, and thereby to use their accounts more critically.

Edward Hyde, The Earl of Clarendon: initially a supporter of Pym in the Long Parliament, Clarendon was an opponent of the policies pursued by Charles I during the Personal Rule, and a supporter of the execution of the Earl of Strafford. However, he abandoned Pym in the autumn of 1641, as his proposals became more radical, and offered his services to the King instead. Throughout the Civil War he remained a moderate, supporting Charles but working for a negotiated settlement, rather than for one by conquest. He went into exile in 1646, becoming chief adviser to Charles II five years later. A central figure in the negotiations which led to the Restoration, he became Charles's chief minister until 1667, when he was sacrificed by the King to appease Parliament over the failure of the Second Dutch War. He went into exile in France to avoid impeachment proceedings, where he died in 1674. His *History of the Rebellion* is a major historical source for the Civil War period, managing to maintain a surprising level of objectivity for much of its duration, and reflecting a great deal of the political moderation that he displayed during his years in public life.

Lucy Hutchinson: wife of Parliamentarian, Colonel Hutchinson, and author of his *Memoirs*. The Hutchinsons were devout Puritans, and Colonel Hutchinson fought against the King during the Civil War. He became an MP for Nottinghamshire in 1646 and was one of the signatories of Charles I's death warrant in 1649. He remained active in the Rump and opposed its dissolution by Cromwell in 1653. He was pardoned as a regicide by Charles II, but was arrested in 1663 on suspicion of treason and died in prison the following year.

Richard Baxter: served as a Presbyterian chaplain to the parliamentary army during the Civil War. Appointed as a royal chaplain to Charles II, and played a leading part in the Savoy Conference, in trying to establish toleration for Presbyterians. He refused Charles's offer of a bishopric, and retired from public life with the introduction of the Uniformity Act in 1662. From this point onwards, he devoted his time to writing, until his death in 1691.

Edmund Ludlow: a Parliamentarian in the Civil War. He took a seat in Parliament in 1646 and supported both Pride's Purge and the King's execution, for which he signed the death warrant. He served in Ireland with Cromwell, and as Lieutenant-General from 1651–5 completed its pacification. He opposed Cromwell's actions in setting up a Protectorate, and helped to remove his son, Richard, from the post in 1659. He fled England in 1660 to avoid execution as a regicide, and lived in exile until his death in 1692, still an unrepentant republican.

John Evelyn: famous for his diary, which he kept for sixty-six years. He was a Royalist during the Civil War and Anglican in his religious loyalties. He retained good political contacts throughout the Restoration and beyond, and his diary is a good source of information about the political scene during this period.

Bishop Burnet: departed his native Scotland in 1672 to become a royal chaplain to Charles II. Willing to take the King to task over his private life, Burnet also incurred royal displeasure by becoming increasingly associated with the Whig leaders accused of treason in the Rye House Plot of 1683. The following year he went abroad, returning in 1688 with William of Orange, who was subsequently to make him Bishop of Salisbury. His *History of My Own Time* was rewritten extensively, and only published after his death.

Glossary

Absolutism system of rule where the monarchy has absolute, or complete, authority

Anglican belonging to the Church of England

Arminianism form of Protestantism that rejected the doctrine of predestination and emphasised the role of ceremony in the Church

Arrears back pay

Bourgeoisie emerging middle classes, particularly associated with trade and enterprise

Calvinism religious beliefs based on the teachings of the Protestant reformer John Calvin

Catholicism beliefs of the Roman Catholic Church, presided over by the Pope

Cavalier Royalist supporters

Clubmen neutrals who used force to protect their communities from the Civil War

Commonwealth official title of the English Republic, 1649–60

Conservative someone who is reluctant to support social and political change

Constitution the collection of laws that laid down the framework of how the country should be governed. The English Constitution was based on a mixture of parliamentary law, common law and tradition

Counter-Reformation Catholic reaction against the Protestant Reformation

County committees set up by Parliament to supervise tax collection during the Civil War

Covenant agreement drawn up by the Scots rebels in 1639 to resist Charles I's religious policies and restore Presbyterianism instead

Decimation 10 per cent tax on lands of Royalist supporters

Dissenter term used to describe Protestants who refused to conform to the Church of England (previously called 'Puritans')

Divine Right constitutional theory that asserted that the King ruled as God's representative, and, as such, was answerable to God alone

Dynastic related to the status of a particular royal family

Ecclesiastical relating to Church matters

Episcopacy institution of bishops

Excise sales tax

Exclusion the attempt to bar James II from the succession, on the grounds of his Catholicism

Extra-parliamentary something done without Parliament's agreement

Faction group of individuals, usually within Government, who are struggling to increase their influence

Feudal   traditional ties, whereby tenants have certain duties towards their landlords

Franchise   right to vote

Godly   term used by Puritans to describe themselves, or their ideas

Grandees   army leaders in the late 1640s

Habsburg   royal family whose members ruled both Spain and the Holy Roman Empire during this period

Impeachment   proceeding taken by Parliament against a King's minister for failing to carry out his duties properly

Impositions   additional taxes imposed on imported goods, without parliamentary consent

Independents   supporters of religious freedom; a label used for those who opposed the introduction of Presbyterianism after the Civil War

Kirk   assembly in Scotland that oversaw Church matters

Levellers   radical group who wanted to 'level' society by extending the right to vote and by reforming the law

Lutheranism   religious beliefs based on the teachings of the Protestant reformer Martin Luther

Militia   unpaid, emergency defence force made up of all local, able-bodied males

Millenarianism   belief in the imminent return of Christ, to begin a 1,000-year rule on earth

Ordinance   parliamentary decree, issued without royal authority

Orthodox   traditional

Papist   Catholic

Patronage   material rewards (titles, offices, lands, pensions, etc.) given to ensure loyalty to the Crown

Political nation   people in society who had political influence or standing

Popery   Catholicism

Popish   Catholic

Predestination   belief that God decides the eternal fate (i.e. whether they go to heaven or hell) of everyone, before they are even born

Prelate   Bishop

Prerogative   rights; usually used in reference to the rights of the Crown

Prerogative courts   courts to uphold the rights of the Crown

Prerogative taxation   taxes collected by the Crown, without parliamentary consent

Presbyterianism   Calvinist form of Church government, which does not accept the need for bishops or royal control over the Church

Protector   figure who wields kingly powers, but without taking the Crown itself

Protestant   Christians who had broken away from the Catholic Church; this would include Lutherans, Calvinists, Anglicans, Arminians and Puritans

Providence   belief that everything that happens is part of God's overall plan

Puritans   hardline Protestants, who wanted to see further reform of the Church of England

Radical   someone who wants to see extensive change

Recusants   those who failed to attend Anglican services and thereby became liable for recusancy fines. A term usually reserved for Catholic non-attenders

Regicide   killing the monarch

Roundhead   parliamentary supporters in the Civil War

Rump   purged Parliament, which sat from December 1648 to April 1653

Separatists   those who believed that each church congregation should be free to govern their own affairs

Ship Money   form of tax, levied traditionally on coastal counties, to help defend the country against seaborne threats

'Structural' problems   difficulties originating from the way that the Government was traditionally structured and expected to operate

Tithes   Church lands, whose rental income was supposed to support the local clergyman

Tonnage and poundage   taxes, or duties, on certain imported goods

Tories   those who emerged as supporters of monarchical power, hereditary right and the Anglican Church

Transubstantiation   belief that the bread and wine used in the communion service turns into the actual body and blood of Christ, through it being consecrated by the priest

Vestments   ceremonial robes worn by priests during church services

Wardship   the right of the Crown to assume control of estates left to minors, until they reached the age of twenty-one

Whigs   those who opposed the succession of a Catholic monarch, and tended to oppose the extension of the royal prerogative

Guide to further reading

The purpose of this book is to provide an introduction to the issues and questions of the seventeenth century. The student will find that they need to develop their ideas and knowledge base by reading other texts on the period, for which a guide is included below.

Documents

There is a wide range of sources from this period available in print, including many individual diaries, memoirs and histories by figures such as Hutchinson, Clarendon, Evelyn, Pepys and Burnet. Perhaps more useful for students initially, however, are the following collections of documents:

For material that ranges *across the period* see: J.P. Kenyon, *The Stuart Constitution* (CUP 1966); A. Hughes, *Seventeenth Century England, A Changing Culture 1: Primary Sources* (Ward Lock 1980); and J. Wroughton, *Seventeenth Century Documents* (Macmillan 1980).

Sources on the reigns of *James I and Charles I* are provided by: R. Ashton, *James I by his Contemporaries* (Hutchinson 1969); and C. Daniels and J. Morrill, *Charles I* (CUP 1988).

For the *Civil War and Commonwealth* period see: B. Coward and C. Durston, *The English Revolution* (John Murray 1997); K. Lindley, *English Civil War and Revolution* (Routledge 1998); H. Tomlinson and D. Gregg, *Politics, Religion and Society in Revolutionary England, 1640–60* (Macmillan 1989); and D. Smith, *Oliver Cromwell* (CUP 1991).

For the reign of *Charles II*: J. Thirsk, *The Restoration* (Longman 1976); and D. Lunn, *Charles II* (Blackie & Sons 1976).

And for the *latter part of the century*: A. Browning, *English Historical Documents Vol. VIII* (Eyre & Spottiswood 1953).

It is also worth looking in the Longman Seminar Studies series, all of which contain a selection of relevant documents. Of particular use are J. Miller's works on Restoration England and the Glorious Revolution (see below).

Secondary works

General texts

For examples of the *Whig* approach: T. Macaulay, *The History of England* (1848); G. Trevelyan, *England under the Stuarts* (Methuen & Co. 1904).

For a *Marxist* interpretation: C. Hill, *The Century of Revolution, 1603–1714* (Thomas Nelson 1961).

Of more recent, *Revisionist* works, B. Coward, *The Stuart Age* (Longman 1994) is the only text that covers the whole of the period, and is the best general work currently available. For texts up to the Restoration, look at both A.G.R. Smith, *Emergence of a Nation State, 1529–1660* (Longman 1997) and D. Hirst, *Authority and Conflict: England 1603–58* (Edward Arnold 1986). C. Russell, *Crisis of Parliaments, 1509–1660* (OUP 1971) is quite dated in some respects, but is still very readable and informative, and well worth consulting. B. Williams, *Elusive Settlement, 1637–1701* (Nelson 1984) provides a general text for the later part of the period, tracing the development of key areas of conflict between the end of the Personal Rule and the Glorious Revolution.

Pre-Civil War

Good outlines on the pre-Civil War period are provided by K. Brice, *The Early Stuarts, 1603–42* (Hodder & Stoughton 1994) and R. Lockyer, *The Early Stuarts* (Longman 1989).

For shorter treatments of the reigns of the first two Stuart kings, together with a discussion of other historians' work, see C. Durston, *James I* (Routledge 1993) and C. Durston, *Charles I* (Routledge 1998).

C. Carlton, *Archbishop William Laud* (Routledge 1987) is not only a fascinating biography, but also provides some interesting insights into the ecclesiastical politics of the period, and into government during the Personal Rule.

On the Personal Rule itself, the essay by Kevin Sharpe on 'The Personal Rule of Charles I' from Howard Tomlinson (ed.) *Before the English Civil War* (Macmillan 1983) is important. The views he puts forward here are the foundation for his later, though much longer work, *The Personal Rule of Charles I* (Yale University Press 1992). The reaction of the localities to Personal Rule and Civil War is dealt with in J. Morrill, *Revolt of the Provinces* (Longman 1976), which also contains some useful documents on this area.

For influential *post-Revisionist* work on this period see C. Russell, *Causes of the English Civil War* (Clarendon Press 1990), in which is explored the idea of the English Civil War being only one part of a much larger 'three kingdom' phenomenon. A. Hughes, *Causes of the English Civil War* (Macmillan 1991) is also important, challenging Revisionist interpretations that play down the existence of longer-term socio-economic or constitutional issues.

Civil War and Commonwealth

The best text available on the war itself is J.P. Kenyon, *The English Civil War* (Weidenfeld & Nicholson 1988), although C. Carlton, *Going to the Wars* (Routledge 1992) also provides some valuable insights into the motivations and experiences of the combatants. For a wider perspective, see P. Gaunt, *The British Wars, 1637–51* (Routledge 1997), which gives a brief overview of the wars in England, Ireland and Scotland, and of the historiographical debate over the 'three kingdoms' interpretation of these conflicts.

A stimulating analysis of the period 1640–60 as a whole is provided in G. Aylmer *Rebellion or Revolution?* (OUP 1984). On the Commonwealth years specifically, relatively brief and accessible accounts are provided in T. Barnard, *The English Republic* (Longman 1997) and M Lynch, *The Interregnum, 1649–60* (Hodder & Stoughton 1994).

Probably the most useful biography currently available on Cromwell is B. Coward, *Oliver Cromwell* (Longman 1991), although the collection of essays provided in J. Morrill (ed.) *Oliver Cromwell and the English Revolution* (Longman 1990) gives a range of perspectives by leading scholars.

The Cambridge History Project 'People, Power and Politics' series on 'Was there a mid-seventeenth century English Revolution?' also contains a great deal of interesting material. In particular see Modules 1 and 2 (R. Ellis) for the political aspects, and 3 and 4 (A. Anderson) for an analysis of radical movements.

Restoration and Glorious Revolution

A useful overview of this period is provided in J.R. Jones, *Country and Court, England 1658–1714* (Edward Arnold 1979). Ronald Hutton, *The Restoration, 1658–1667* (OUP 1985) contains a detailed analysis of the Restoration years, and P. Seaward, *The Restoration* (Macmillan 1991) is also worth consulting.

For the reign of Charles II itself, a concise yet very helpful account is provided in J. Miller, *Restoration England: The Reign of Charles II* (Longman 1997). For a much fuller examination of Charles himself, see Miller's biography, *Charles II* (Weidenfeld & Nicholson 1991).

J.R. Jones (ed.) *The Restored Monarchy, 1660–1688* (Macmillan 1979) is a collection of essays dealing with key themes from the reigns of Charles II and James II. On the Glorious Revolution, again the Seminar Studies' offering *The Glorious Revolution* by J. Miller (Longman 1983) gives a concise and very useful basis for further study.

Reference

An invaluable reference source for the personalities of the period is to be found in C.P. Hill, *Who's Who in Stuart Britain* (Shepheard-Walwyn 1988).

And finally, an excellent guide to the historiographical maze is to be found in R.C. Richardson, *The Debate on the English Revolution Revisited* (Routledge 1988).

Subject index

Name index